The Enterprise Culture

The Enterprise Culture

Peter Sedgwick

First published in Great Britain 1992
SPCK, Holy Trinity Church, Marylebone Road, London NW1 4DU

© Peter Sedgwick 1992

All rights reserved. No part of this book may be reproduced
or transmitted in any form or by any means, electronic or
mechanical, including photocopying, recording, or by any
information storage and retrieval system, without permission
in writing from the publisher.

British Library Cataloguing in Publication Data
A catalogue record for this book is available from the British Library

ISBN 0 – 281 – 04576 – 3

Typeset by Action Typesetting Ltd, Gloucester
Printed in Great Britain by The Longdunn Press Ltd, Bristol.

Contents

Acknowledgements   vii

Introduction   1

1   Enterprise and Enterprise Culture   8

The rise of enterprise   8
Entrepreneurial behaviour   9
The motivation for enterprise   16
Enterprise education   19
Enterprise and society: attitudes to enterprise culture   23
Enterprise and theology   27
   a) An enterprise culture redefined   27
   b) Theology, institutions and enterprise   28
Conclusion   34

2   Small firms   37

Government policy 1979 – 91   37
Small businesses   40
   a) Industrial relations and motivation   40
   b) Innovation   42
   c) Training and cultural change   44
   d) Difficulties   46
   e) Values and aspirations   47
Theology and values   50

3   Enterprise Beyond Industry   60

The influence of culture   60
Community enterprise   61
Theology and society   63
Enterprise and education   65

4	Ethnic Enterprise	70
	Ethnic communities in business	70
	Ethnic community enterprise	73
	Theology and ethnic enterprise	76
5	Self-employment and Attitudes to Work	82
	Introduction	82
	Openness and change in human beings	82
	The attitudes of the self-employed	90
	Women's attitudes	93
	Young people's attitudes	98
	Successful entrepreneurs: different aspirations?	101
	Theology and social attitudes	103
6	The Ethics of Enterprise	126
	Responsibility and ethics	126
	Social ethics	131
	Business ethics	139
7	A Theology of Enterprise	143
	Christianity and wealth-creation	145
	a) The story of purity	150
	b) The story of wealth	152
	c) The story of poverty	154
	d) The story of vocation	156
	e) Enterprise and wealth-creation	158
	A theology of creation	159
	Conclusion	173
	The story of this project	173
	Enterprise and wealth	174
	Theology, enterprise and wealth	176
	Bibliography	181
	Index	193

Acknowledgements

I owe a particular debt of thanks to SPCK for making this book possible. In 1988 I was appointed Lady Elizabeth Hastings Fellow by the Society, to work on the theology of wealth-creation. Since then their advisory panel, chaired by Patrick Gilbert, the General Secretary of SPCK, has been a source of encouragement and support. I am especially sorry that Mrs Beatrice Shearer, a member of that panel, did not live to read this book. Her wit and penetrating comments on theology were very helpful. Judith Longman, SPCK Editorial Director, guided the manuscript to completion, and I am grateful to her for much advice and great patience!

The grant from SPCK enabled me to convene a small group who met three or four times a year to discuss what wealth-creation might mean. It is this group I have learnt most from. John Atherton, Gillian Ashmore, Chris Beales, Ian Christie, Kate Mortimer, Ian Smith and Trevor MacDonald have continually challenged my thinking with insights from government, industry and the Churches. The book would not have been possible without them.

The book was completed at the Center of Theological Inquiry, Princeton, New Jersey. I would like to thank it for the opportunity to reflect upon the project. The inspiration provided by its Director, Dan Hardy, will be evident in the book. I would also like to thank the Fulbright Trust for financial support.

SPCK's fellowship also enabled me to travel around England interviewing some twenty-five business people, and another twenty from the civil service, community groups, academics and other organizations. They are too many to thank individually, but I enjoyed much hospitality and good conversation. A large number of people gave generously of their time and attention to answer my questions. The Industrial and Economic Affairs Committee of the Church of England, to which I belong, also provided support and an invaluable forum to discuss this project.

My typist, Gill Fincham, spent many hours transcribing interviews and deciphering rough notes. I am grateful to her for all her work. Lastly, I must thank my wife Helena, and our three children. I spent much time away from them on motorways and trains, carrying out interviews and listening to conferences. It must have been very frustrating for them. Their warmth and interest has meant a great deal. I felt again and again as I studied the 'enterprise culture' that this was the world that our children – Hugo, Verity and Sophia – would inherit. I hope it is a world that can offer them some hope and encouragement. The purpose of this book was to discover that sense of value in the confusing world of Britain in the 1980s.

Introduction

In 1982 my family and I left Birmingham to return to the north-east of England, and lived in Durham. I worked as Theological Consultant to the North-East Churches from 1982 to 1988. Three developments emerged from that work. First, I became aware of Industrial Mission's work in Britain since the 1940s. In 1985 I joined the Church of England's Industrial and Economic Affairs Committee (IEAC) of the Board for Social Responsibility. I remain a member of that committee, and it is an immensely valuable and rewarding committee to work with. Secondly, the theology that I worked at from 1982 to 1988 was a collaborative theology. It represented work with clergy and laypeople; Christians and non-Christians; academics and those with little formal education. It was overseen by a group of Christians who were themselves diverse: ordained and lay, some teaching theology, and some with experience of industry. It showed me how theology could be done in contemporary society. Thirdly, it become clear how much the North-East was changing. I have written of this extensively in my earlier book *Mission Impossible? A Theology of the Local Church*,[1] and I will not repeat this analysis here.

The outcome of this experience was that when I moved back to university life in 1988, where I teach an MA course at the University of Hull as well as being Adviser in Industrial Issues to the Archbishop of York, a clear idea for future research presented itself. The SPCK grant made it possible, and this book is the result. As our society has come to change in ever more rapid ways in recent decades, the question of a theology of work has come to the fore in the Churches.

Initially the 1980s saw the debate on theology of work as revolving around the meaninglessness of the old division between paid employment and work. This was for two reasons. First, mass unemployment had put paid to the idea of full employment for all. Secondly, the experience of women was discovered by the Churches. It became obvious that the distinction between paid work and employment did

not match the reality of people's lives. The book that spoke
most powerfully to this debate was Roger Clarke's *Work in
Crisis*.[2] He had worked for many years as an industrial
chaplain in Dundee. The end of the 'Protestant work ethic'
was written in the unemployment figures of the 1980s. It
was time to reassess what a theology of work might mean,
and to find ways of sharing paid employment. The Industrial
Committee of the Church of England also published reports
on this issue. The question of women's experience was taken
up later by Anne Borrowdale's *A Woman's Work: Changing
Christian Attitudes*,[3] and the Industrial Committee's *And All
That is Unseen* (1986) on the same subject.

Much of this debate was carried forward in the Churches
by Industrial Mission. Ever since its formation in the 1940s
it had sought to find a way of working with those who
seemed most estranged from the Churches themselves –
namely, the working class. Recent studies, such as those
by Erlander and Hewitt,[4] have shown how much issues of
class and class solidarity represent a complete challenge to
the desire of the Churches to evangelize Britain. A similar
analysis, although not from the perspective of Industrial
Mission, has been offered by Kenneth Leech.[5] The debate
in the 1980s on the rise of unemployment took Industrial
Mission even further away from the traditional understanding
of the Churches about their place in society. Not only were
the working classes estranged from the middle-class world of
churches, and the rural/suburban churches at that, they were
now threatened by the disappearance of their livelihood. In
so far as it could be argued that the term 'working class' was
an anachronism, because of the decline in class solidarity, an
appeal could be made to other ways in which people felt
marginalized: as women, as members of ethnic groups, etc.

The debate among industrial chaplains was part of another
debate, which has even older roots in the British Churches,
especially the Church of England. What was the place of
laypeople in the way in which the Church thought out its
theology and expressed its liturgy? A few people, such as
Ian Ramsey and John Habgood, both bishops of Durham, had
worked in the collaborative theological way described above.
Indeed, Ian Ramsey began the Theological Consultancy, and
John Habgood strongly supported its existence when I worked
on its behalf. Nevertheless, this style of theology was until

recently very rare in Britain. Theology tended to be academic, historical and clerical, and not easily related to the daily lives of men and women. There was also the long-standing factor of the anti-industrial bias of the English upper middle class, extensively charted by Weiner and Correlli Barnett. While some of their analysis is controversial, there is no doubt that the Church of England, in spite of Industrial Mission, found it very hard to take the experience of paid work seriously. Other groups, such as the Industrial Christian Fellowship, have for many years published pamphlets and sponsored services that try to unite the world of work and the world of religious faith, but for many people in the Church any real appreciation of their work seemed lacking. Together the commitment of Industrial Mission to a dialogue with the working class (in which the Churches had most to learn, as in the French worker-priest movement at the same period) in the 1940s and 1950s, and the growth of unemployment in the 1970s and 1980s, meant that a theology of work came close to a theology of deprivation, justice and a new social order. It became the British version of liberation theology. In the last decade there were many examples of Industrial Mission setting up work-training schemes, centres for the unemployed, etc. In so far as laypeople were taken seriously, and a great deal of literature (which is not the same thing) was written about this dimension of church life from the 1980s, there came to be a concern about their place in the Church.[6] Adult education schemes, lay training officers, new patterns of worship and new calls to responsibility inside the Churches all developed. Again I have written about this in *Mission Impossible?*, especially in relation to Newcastle upon Tyne. It became obvious that if the Churches were to grow again, laypeople would have to exercise a much more collaborative ministry with clergy.

There were also serious ethical questions that only a collaborative theological method could address. Here the scientific expertise of bishops such as Ramsey and Habgood came into their own, on issues such as *in vitro* fertilization and energy policy. The Church of England's Board for Social Responsibility developed a whole style of bringing together experts in their respective fields, with moral theologians, and has published over the last two decades a series of impressive reports on subjects ranging from divorce reform to medical science.

However, neither the model of theological collaboration with experts, nor the development of lay ministry inside the Churches, could answer the basic question that the Industrial Christian Fellowship and others had long sought to address: what should the Churches say and value concerning the world of paid employment, where so many of their lay members worked? Nor would the development of a non-stipendiary group of clergy who worked in secular professions, but were none the less ordained to ministry, really fill the gap. Valuable though they were, they were too few in number. Many eventually became paid clergy, and anyway their jobs were often confined to certain areas in the world of work – such as teaching.

This survey of the debates inside the Churches since the 1940s thus is left with a serious omission. What is the *significance* of work for those who are in paid employment? Even in society as a whole, the debate in the late 1980s has moved away from the straightforward issue of employment/unemployment. Although much unemployment remains, the new debate has been concerned with the end of organized, industrial life as we have known it this century.

The rapid extension of new technology into all sectors of the economy has meant much greater devolution of responsibility inside organizations. Organizations have become much smaller, and have broken up into many different components. There has been an enormous increase in self-employment, and the possibility of a person having several different careers in their working lifetime. The products that the economy generates are located more in the service sector (especially the information sector) and less within heavy engineering.

All this has raised a number of questions. What is the meaning of vocation and Christian service in this fast-changing world? Can any consistent description be given to a term such as wealth-creation? Is it simply the pursuit of financial greed, as demonstrated in the business scandals of the last decade? From this perspective, some ethical criteria are needed to evaluate these changes. Yet it is not simply a matter of morality. Some of the persistent phrases in this decade have been the 'release of people's energy', or the 'search for freedom', or 'self-realization'. If there is a change in popular culture that is being echoed in people's experience of paid work, then that is very significant.

This book represents three years' study of the 'enterprise culture'. Although it is a term promoted by the Conservative government in the 1980s, I came to realize that the culture has a life of its own. The way in which the book has been written is important. Intensive discussions with my 'support group' convinced me of the value of spending much time away from the academic world, the Churches and the media. Many of the people interviewed, often thanks to contacts from my support group, had little connection with the Churches.

What was common to this group was that they were nearly all self-employed, or running community businesses, or civil servants and businesspeople carrying out such extensive devolution of responsibilities that they had virtually become independent businesses. (The degree of that independence is a matter of keen debate, especially in the civil service.) All of them had been through many changes, often traumatic, as they established their new business. I have spent over a year in dialogue with my support group on the findings that I discovered. Only then did I turn to the extensive academic literature on small businesses, privatization, etc.

Yet this is not a book directly about small businesses. Its central question is what are the values of this new culture, even if it is a culture damaged by the recession? The opening chapter thus looks at what might be meant by enterprise, risk-taking and enterprise education. The next few chapters give examples of enterprise found in my research, concluding with an extensive discussion both of race and the motivation that lies behind starting a business.

Only then do I examine the moral values that are present in this new world, and the theology of enterprise and wealth-creation. Yet this is a theological book through and through. In each chapter there is reference to theology, both in the formal academic sense and in the conversations had with my support group and the interviewees. The only distinctive element about this book is its theology. It is not one more book about the Thatcher era, nor is it about small firms, civil service reforms or modern management. Instead, it seeks to ask what might a theology of work mean in future discussions and conversations with those who are employed in industry, local government, or whatever.

What then of the other debates that I have mentioned? There is a great sense of work incomplete here. I spent a very valuable day in York with twenty-five industrial chaplains in 1991 discussing the research. Part of the SPCK fellowship has also gone to Peter Dodd of Newcastle upon Tyne, who looked at how enterprise might be affected by regional culture, and to Chris Beales who spent part of the summer of 1990 in the United States examining how wealth-creation and enterprise schemes were used in inner-city anti-poverty programmes.[7] Nevertheless, I feel that there are now a series of debates, which this book adds to but does not resolve. One is the Industrial Mission's commitment to work with the unemployed, low-paid and marginalized, as well as the traditional links with factory visiting and the unions. On this analysis paid/unpaid work is a fairly unhelpful distinction. What is needed is a redefinition of work and leisure. Roger Clarke, while at the William Temple Foundation at Manchester extended his strategy across Western Europe in the West European Network (WEN) of small groups working with poverty and unemployment. A second debate inside the Churches is how leadership can be shared between clergy and laypeople. There are certainly theologians who would appear to stress that the distinctive contribution of a lay Christian is his or her time, outside of paid employment, in working for the Church. However this debate is resolved, which clearly carries within itself a discussion on the relationship of Church and world, there is no doubt that more of a layperson's vocation as a Christian is likely to be taken up in Church-related activities.

This research is different. It asks what the nature and purpose of paid employment might be in the future. Does it have a Christian value and, if so, what? How these three debates are brought together remains an unanswered question in the Churches. There has been a suspicion of the market, wealth-creation and enterprise in the Churches for a long time. It is time this balance was redressed. The purpose of this research is to show how in the last two decades these concepts themselves have changed profoundly. So before there can be any resolution of the discussion of the nature of employment and work, or the place of the laity, it is time to look again at how paid employment (especially self-employment) might be seen in the light of the Christian faith. That is the point of this book.

Notes

1. London, Collins, 1990.
2. Edinburgh, St Andrew Press, 1982.
3. London, SPCK, 1989.
4. L. Erlander, *Faith in the World of Work. On the Theology of Work as Lived by the French Worker-priests and British Industrial Mission*, 1991; G. Hewitt (ed.), *Strategist for the Spirit: Leslie Hunter, Bishop of Sheffield, 1939–1962*, 1985.
5. *Struggle in Babylon*, 1988.
6. *All Are Called: Towards a Theology of the Laity*, 1985.
7. P. Dodd, *The Influence of Culture upon Enterprise*, 1990; C. Beales, *Mainstream and Marginal*, 1990.

1

Enterprise and Enterprise Culture

The rise of enterprise

Enterprise came to be of interest in the 1980s for many reasons. The recession affected manufacturing, especially large-scale manufacturing. Many firms sub-contracted; others encouraged management buyouts of 'indirect sectors of their companies. There was a switch from manufacturing to services in employment. A large number of small businesses were started.'[1]

As well as these economic reasons, there were cultural ones. Computer technology encouraged small businesses and devolved administration, as did advances in communications. These technological changes facilitated a desire among a section of the middle class for self-employment.

It is important to mention these economic and cultural changes at the outset. It is often assumed that the 'enterprise culture' is a product of Mrs Thatcher's government of 1979–90, especially connected with Lord Young at the Department of Trade and Industry.[2] However, as is often the case, the government was simply exploiting deep-rooted economic and cultural changes that were already in existence. The changes would have happened anyway, and have many years left to run in the 1990s.

The argument of this book is that these economic, cultural and political changes are of great importance, demanding a reassessment by the Churches of their theological position in many areas. This book is not primarily an exhaustive analysis of small businesses, British social attitudes or the ideology of the Conservative (and now other) political parties. There is reference throughout the text to such matters, but the primary emphasis lies elsewhere.

What I wish to argue is that the cultural changes of the 1980s represent a deep challenge to the contemporary Christian understanding of individualism, freedom, work and wealth-creation. Throughout the decades since 1945 the British Churches have built up a sustained analysis of work and society. They have allied this to a belief in the power of the state, the importance of social change by state intervention, and a general suspicion of capitalism.[3]

This book does not dissent from the overall development of Christian social ethics in Britain since William Temple, Archbishop of Canterbury during the Second World War, and the leading social ethicist in the British Churches this century.[4] In general, the commitment to the poor, the vulnerable and the victims of change is a deeply impressive one. Emphatically this book is not an onslaught from the 'New Right', which saw in the enterprise culture a vehicle for its own ideological aspirations.[5]

Nevertheless, there have been changes in the understanding of work, employment and wealth-creation. It is these issues that this book addresses. The nature of freedom and self-realization in employment is one such topic. So too is the question of the moral framework surrounding wealth-creation. Is regulation by the state the best solution to problems of the environment, the treatment of employees, etc? Where should the line be drawn between regulation and self-regulation? Most difficult of all to answer is the question of how the Churches can affirm wealth-creation, the market economy and competition, while also maintaining a positive stance towards the underprivileged, the poor and disadvantaged.

Entrepreneurial behaviour

A distinction must be made between the entrepreneur and the owner of the small business. A small-business venture is 'any business that is independently owned and operated, not dominant in its field, and does not engage in any new marketing or innovative practices'. An owner of a small business is a person whose business is 'the primary source of income', consuming, 'the majority of one's time and resources. The owner perceives the business as an extension of his or her personality, intricately bound with family needs and desires'. Establishing a business furthers personal goals.[6]

Entrepreneurship is classically defined by Schumpeter in his *Capitalism, Socialism and Democracy*, published in 1943.[7] The principal goals of an entrepreneurial venture are profitability and growth, with innovative strategic practices. An entrepreneur thus is characterized by innovative behaviour.

Schumpeter speaks of capitalism as the process of creative destruction. Capitalism is never stationary, but is always evolving. 'The fundamental impulse that sets and keeps the capitalist engine in motion comes from the new consumers' goods, the new method of production or transportation, the new markets, the new forms of industrial organization that capitalist enterprise creates.'[8]

Therefore capitalism creates and destroys existing structures. In Schumpeter's words, 'Every piece of business strategy acquires its true significance only against the background of . . . the perennial gale of creative destruction.' Competition is thus not simply about prices, quality or marketing, but about competition from 'the new commodity, the new technology, the new source of supply, the new type of organization . . . competition which strikes not at the margins of the profits and the outputs of the existing firms but at their foundations and their very lives'.

Schumpeter's argument was set in a technical discussion of restrictive practices and price structures that is of no concern here. It is, however, interesting that he felt that the entrepreneurial function was becoming obsolescent when he wrote in 1943. He argued that it was the entrepreneur who in the past enabled capitalism to proceed by leaps and bounds, reforming or revolutionizing the economic system. This kind of activity caused the recurrent prosperity that revolutionized the economic system, and the recurrent recessions that resulted from the destructive (or disequilibriating) effects of new practices. It might be new inventions, new outlets, or introducing new management methods. Whatever aspect it involves, the task of the entrepreneur is a difficult one, and constitutes distinct economic functions:

> They lie outside the routine tasks which everybody understands and . . . the environment resists in many ways. . . . To act with confidence beyond the range of familiar beacons and to overcome that resistance requires aptitudes that are present in only a small fraction of the population. . . . This function does not essentially consist in either inventing anything or otherwise creating the conditions which the enterprise exploits. It consists in getting things done.[9]

Schumpeter believed, however, that the day of the entrepreneur was now over. It was still true that capitalism would continue to destroy and rebuild existing institutions, but he believed that innnovation itself was being reduced to routine. The creation of teams of trained specialists would, he argued, take over the task of forwarding technological progress. Environments were now accustomed to economic change, and accepted this as a matter of course. There would always be resistance which came from interests threatened by innovations in production, but consumer and producer resistance in themselves had 'well-nigh vanished already'.

Schumpeter drew the analogy of military welfare. At one time leadership had meant the personal charisma of the person in command, even the actual presence of the general on a horse. However, rationalized office work had now blotted out such a military strategy. Equally, the armoured knights of the Middle Ages practised an art that required lifelong training, and every ounce of personal skill. Once again, social and technological changes had undermined and then destroyed both the function and the position of that social group. Schumpeter continued:

> Now a similar social progress – in the last analysis the same social progress – undermines the role and, along with the role, the social position of the capitalist entrepreneur. His role, though less glamorous than that of medieval warlords, great or small, also is or was just another form of individual leadership acting by virtue of personal force and personal responsibility for success. His position, like that of warrior classes, is threatened as soon as this function in the social process loses its importance.[10]

Schumpeter thus contributed to political economy perhaps the classic statement of the role of the entrepreneur, and then denied him any contemporary relevance. He argued that the very success of capitalism led to 'the perfectly bureaucratized giant industrial unit', where economic innovation and success became automatic. Such firms would swallow up smaller ones, and their specialist departments would render the innovative genius of the entrepreneur redundant.

Schumpeter's arguments for a gradual evolution into the planned, rational socialism of the late twentieth century do not concern us. It was a brilliant study – Denis Healey cited it as one of the great influences on his thinking when he entered politics in 1945. And yet the decline of the entrepreneur did *not* happen, and some twenty-four years later (in 1967) Schumpeter's analysis was taken up by J.K. Galbraith in *The New Industrial State*. Here Galbraith argued that the entrepreneur was being replaced by 'the technosphere'. Galbraith defined the entrepreneur as the person who in the past provided leadership in a business organization: 'the individual who united ownership or control of capital with capacity for organizing the other factors of production and, in most contexts, with a further capacity for innovation'. Unlike Schumpeter, Galbraith argued that it was not bureaucratic management alone that would replace the entrepreneur. 'It embraces all who bring specialized knowledge, talent or experience to group decision-making. This, not management, is the guiding intelligence – the brain – of the enterprise. There is no name for all who participate in group decision-making or the organization which they form. I propose to call this organization the Technostructure.'[11]

Galbraith believed that for a while senior officials of the mature corporation behaved and thought of themselves as entrepreneurs. They saw themselves as self-reliant, competitive, arrogant, individualistic, and with a desire to live dangerously. Galbraith argued that there was an identification of modern American management with the flamboyant entrepreneur. Nevertheless, it was impossible to reconcile this model with the requirements of organizational planning, co-operation and sensitivity required by the 'technosphere'. Furthermore, Galbraith believed that more and more organizations were moulding their executives into a lifelong identification with, and employment within, the corporation. The modern young executive of the 1960s was a corporation person, welcoming the growing security of employment she or he was offered, and the integration of the economic system into the state.

Both Schumpeter and Galbraith held up a moral vision for the passing away of capitalism and the entrepreneur into socialism (Schumpeter) or the technosphere (Galbraith). Schumpeter held that socialism was a new social religion: any defence of capitalism was looked upon 'as an indication of immoral servitude'. He argued that it would be as difficult to be sympathetic to capitalism in the mid-twentieth century as it would have been in AD 300 'to expound the achievements of ancient civilization to a fervent believer in Christianity'.[12] Schumpeter could certainly have cited such prominent Anglican theologians as V.A. Demant, Professor at Oxford, or William Temple, Archbishop of Canterbury, for their belief that socialism was both inevitable and desirable in modern Britain. Galbraith argued that the freedom of the human spirit in this planned technosphere lay in the personal exploration of intellectual and aesthetic interests. He therefore sought to build a new cultural civilization upon the economic success of corporate America.

Nevertheless, socialism did not come about in the industrial West in the manner envisaged by Schumpeter. The reasons for this need not concern us and are very complex. Likewise, the trend towards more secure management in large organizations, and the centralization of decision-making foreseen by Galbraith in the 1960s, did not happen either. One reason for this was that modern management theory began to rediscover the virtues of entrepreneurial behaviour within the large organization – sometimes called 'intrapreneurship'. On the other hand, the growth of larger and larger corporations that took over smaller firms and also moved closer to the state did not happen either. For a variety of reasons, large corporations were broken up. Sub-contracting became the norm, and a revival of small firms began. The trend to larger organizations slowed down in the 1970s in Britain and the United States, and went firmly into reverse in the 1980s.

Thus Joseph Schumpeter provided the classic illustration of the entrepreneur, yet felt that his or her day had gone. Galbraith argued in the same way, but without Schumpeter's commitment to socialism. Instead, he represented the pragmatic liberal closely associated with John F. Kennedy, and displayed the confidence of that era. Common to them both was the belief, on the one hand, that technological planning had destroyed the role and function of the individual, let alone the individual entrepreneur, in the economy and in civic society. On the other hand, both espoused a new moral vision, which would either replace bourgeoisie values with socialism or transcend it with a new aesthetic civilization.

Schumpeter's economics are still of interest today. It is significant, however, that in most economic theory there is almost no reference to the role of the entrepreneur. Partly this is because Schumpeter defined this role very narrowly: the entrepreneur need not own the company, and never bears the risk if he does not own the company. Risk, however, need not simply involve capital: it can involve human beings. Equally Schumpeter saw the entrepreneur as driven only by the joy of creating or the will to conquer. This ignores too much the desire for profit, and higher living standards.[13]

Entrepreneurship is not obsolete, however, in contemporary capitalism. The question is, rather, whether it can flourish outside small-scale production. This raises further questions about whether large-scale firms should be split up into smaller ones, each one run by an entrepreneur. These issues have been much taken up in recent years by economists who are followers of von Hayek. This is because they equate entrepreneurship with unrestrained free enterprise, which in turn is linked with political libertarianism. Personal freedom means, in principle, that entrepreneurs have a free hand. Others, including Hayek himself, argued that the only alternative to free enterprise is centralized, bureaucratic socialism. This extreme argument excluded every economic institution in the middle ground.

A more convincing approach is to ask what are the limits of entrepreneurship. What are the aims of private and public enterprise? If a public corporation has no clearly defined goals, but may include both the pursuit of profit and of social welfare, it is not surprising that public corporations may appear inefficient. What is needed here is a clear recognition of what the aims of the corporation are, and how entrepreneurship may help. This leads into questions of how production is best organized. If one simply opts for maximum profits produced by entrepreneurs who deploy their talents unrestrained by the state, then the answer is simple. All that matters is whether to work for an entrepreneur, or to become one oneself.

Obviously there are serious flaws in this argument. First, there are limits to what one entrepreneur can do in a modern economy, even by delegation. Delegation can work up to a point, but then each leader of a group becomes an entrepreneur in their own right. Economies of scale will force firms to remain at a size where devolution by an entrepreneur becomes inevitable.

The question then becomes one of how these devolved responsibilities are monitored. Once devolved responsibilities are linked to incentive schemes, what in fact happens is that a series of mini-entrepreneurs proliferate. The complexity of the nature of the modern firm becomes evident. Who runs a firm is a very difficult question to answer. Peter Hammond of Stanford University shows how Schumpeter's ideas on entrepreneurship run into the reality of management consultants, accountants, etc. who are hired for a short period. Ownership, shareholders and nominated managers only make the picture more diffuse.

Management theory in particular has changed. The person who has done most to synthesize academic theory on organizations and managerial practice is Charles Handy. His best-selling book *The Age of Unreason* has been reprinted several times since it was first published in 1989. Handy argues that change has accelerated to such a level that it is no longer continuous. It is random, and far-reaching. This is so not only in such areas as technology and the nature of employment, but also in the shift to a very different society and culture. The challenge that this poses to organizations was how they could adapt simply to survive. It was Handy more than any other writer and consultant who realized how much Galbraith's viewpoint was itself, paradoxically, obsolete: the proponent of the obsolescence of the entrepreneur was already becoming dated himself. Handy drew on such books as R.M. Kanter's *The Change Masters: Corporate Entrepreneurs at Work* (1981) and W.E. Deming's *Out of the Crisis* (1984).

Handy argues that the concept of spending one's whole working life in one job is now over. Companies no longer have an exclusively full-time, permanent workforce. Instead, many work full time for a company, stay a few years, and then move on. These comprise the core group, with two hierarchies. One is simply that of expertise, with three levels: the qualified but junior person; the senior executive; and those with ultimate responsibility. The other hierarchy is that of project team, where a person with more seniority may work under a more junior person.

The rest of the company will be either part time or flexible, or sub-contracting. Marks & Spencer, for instance, have branches where part-time staff constitute the majority. A large company will devolve responsibility, with the chief executives of subsidiaries increasingly taking decisions. The company will be inspired by a learning culture, expecting the future to produce a different way of working. The goal is to create innovation.

A number of questions are raised by the renewed interest in enterprise. Could enterprise be related to education, or to the empowerment of small groups? Many community groups in the 1980s realized that 'empowering' people meant creating new patterns of behaviour that were innovative and that challenged decision-making by others on their behalf.

Secondly, was Galbraith's judgement of the attributes of enterprise correct? Did these attributes have to be individualistic, aggressive and self-reliant? Could not people also work together in co-operative ways? Thirdly, was enterprise to be associated with small businesses? Many of them could be profoundly conservative.

A theological interest concerns both wealth-creation and enterprise. Issues of creativity, responsibility and education are all important. The theological appraisal is wider than an evaluation of economic life, for it includes cultural changes as well.

The motivation for enterprise

The attributes of enterprise have been much charted: creativity, initiative taking, persuasiveness, leadership, high autonomy, achievement motivation, imagination, moderate risk-taking, analytical ability and networking. These attributes are found in the entrepreneur. Entrepreneurs, as shown in the section above, behave in an 'innovative fashion', bringing together a series of factors that result in change. Change may be incremental, or a more dramatic major change.[14]

These attributes are usually found in people with high levels of energy and charisma, and those who welcome responsibility. The reason why such people decide to become innovators is difficult to discern. There appears to be a series of events, which lead the person with the characteristics described above to what has been called the 'entrepreneurial decision'. Some have suggested that those who become entrepreneurs are difficult employees. Those who work in large organizations have to alternate between varying patterns of behaviour, depending on whether they are taking decisions and exercising authority, or receiving them and being under authority. For some people the change in behaviour is too great. Used to being in control, they find the only answer is to create their own world where they are always in charge and never need to be submissive. Also, such people may be workaholics who can justify their behaviour by creating a small business that can only survive if they work very long hours. This darker side of enterprise clearly reveals inadequate personality behaviour: when such people are in control they become dominant, sometimes reducing subordinates to infantile patterns of behaviour. This need always to be in control includes a distrust of others, the desire for personal recognition and admiration, and an inability to be receptive. It comes close to what Christian spirituality has called 'the restless search for self-justification'. It can of course lead to someone becoming the personal benefactor in a local community; conversely, it can result in personal destruction.

Such is the darker side of entrepreneurship. There is also a positive side. Bureaucracies frustrate those who wish to take initiatives, and much management theory is now designed to avoid this. The motivation to become an entrepreneur can be a function of adversity. Many minority groups in society have responded to disasters by developing their own innovative behaviour. Malcolm Harper has written:

> The very existence of living in a difficult environment, and of planning, financing and executing a move and then surviving in a new and often hostile environment requires qualities of self-restraint, abstinence, hard work and voluntary postponement of gratification which are normally far more severe than those demanded by the lifestyle of those who remain at home.[15]

Studies of entrepreneurs reveal in particular the extraordinary determination needed to survive, and the sheer physical energy. Equally, there is an enormous drive for personal independence and creativity.[16] The feeling of challenge, personal involvement in decisions, and exploration of new opportunities are all crucial. There may well be considerable confusion at management level, with no clear divisions of responsibility but with organic relationships.[17] Independence, flexibility and control go closely together, in a holistic pattern.

It is also possible to analyse why people **actually** become entrepreneurs. It may be that some individuals with great independence of spirit will never create a new venture –

therefore motivation on its own is not sufficient explanation. Lifetime experiences are as important as genetic influences – as Sue Birley says, entrepreneurs are made, not born.[18]

Cooper defined three crucial factors that might contribute to an entrepreneurial decision. These were:

1. Genetic factors, family influences, educational choices, past career experiences and the effect all this has on motivations, perceptions, skills and knowledge.
2. The organization in which the decision is made, including its skills, workers, and geographic location. There may be contact with possible fellow founders of the enterprise; experience that is relevant to running the enterprise; and motivation to stay with or leave the organization.
3. External environmental factors, such as economic conditions, examples of entrepreneurial action, accessibility of capital, support networks and customers.[19]

Each one of these factors becomes significant in its own right. Many people become entrepreneurs in their thirties, because personal confidence is growing, frustration has developed, and there is a solid base of personal experience. This is also a time of personal crisis: 'Who am I?' or 'What have I achieved?' are common questions. As Chapter 2 shows, the influence of family and friends is all-important. Certainly the organization itself may contribute to the decision to leave or to stay. Many of those interviewed in this study had left large firms such as GEC or ICI some ten years ago, after experiencing much frustration. Since then, there has been a great deal of change within large British companies. Common to much of the change inside organizations is an emphasis on devolution, greater responsibility, an ability to change more rapidly – what has been called 'intrapreneurship'.

Finally, there is the question of the opportunity to get started. Even with great personal motivation, and with a high degree of frustration, there may be no examples of entrepreneurial action to follow. This is not simply an economic matter. It could also refer to whether the possibility of action is realizable, what support networks there are, and how hostile the environment is. The high rate of casualties in small businesses and community enterprises speaks volumes: but so too does the increasing determination not to be put off by failure.

Entrepreneurial motivation is therefore a difficult area to analyse. There is both a dark side and a very positive aspect. Even if the motivation is there, the conditions may not be right for action. There is also the much-discussed question of whether enterprise can be developed or stifled by education.

Enterprise education

Professor Allan Gibb at Durham University Business School has built up a considerable team of researchers on this topic.[20] Does the present education system enable enterprise to be developed? The question goes to the heart of the debate on the nature of education and training which has been a prominent feature of recent years. Should education, especially at higher levels, be concerned with the development of ideas and concepts, which are synthesized into theories? Such an approach will stress detachment and ambiguity, and place an emphasis on written communication and neutrality. Critical analysis of knowledge is at a premium. A different approach is increasingly used in adult learning, and has been taken up by some theologians in Britain and especially the Third World. Here there is an emphasis on the present and future. There is emotional involvement, which is recognized in the self and in others. Information is received through personal communication, which is concerned to anticipate problems, realize opportunities and produce certain outcomes. So learning is achieved through personal experience, and much time is spent on evaluation and the concept of 'owning experience'. Feelings are at a premium here: there is little regard for critical analysis of the past.

Whether it is possible to reconcile these two approaches, and in what way this would be done, is at the centre of much educational discussion. The world of the entrepreneur seems to belong to the second approach. This raises the question of whether entrepreneurship can be taught and, if so, whether it should find a place in higher-education sectors such as schools of business management, universities and polytechnics. The conflict is a real one. Most university disciplines are not at home with action research, multi-disciplinary approaches and intuitive judgements. Yet it is increasingly in higher education that management education, especially the ubiquitous Master of Business Administration (MBA) degree, is located.

Entrepreneurs usually have limited resources of knowledge, time and personnel. They work intuitively, relying on what Gibb calls the 'judgement of trust and competence of those involved'. Whether this information is reliable as a basis for action is probably the most crucial question. The pressure of events always requires there to be an appropriate, or sufficient, solution: often not the best one.

Allan Gibb's model shows clearly the two different approaches to the nature of education. There are a series of options that education can address. These are as follows:

1. learning by doing, including problem-solving in actual situations;
2. multi-disciplinary approaches to understanding an issue;
3. using immediate data, and people thinking for themselves, as well as relying on impersonal, external information;
4. coping with conflict, uncertainty and stress, so that the choices that are made arise from a proper emotional response;
5. building networks and contacts in the outside world as the learning proceeds;
6. learning by overcoming failure, using feelings and attitudes, and relying on successful role models.

Effect of focus on the process and utilization of learning

University/business school?	Entrepreneurial?
Critical judgement after analysis of large amount of information	'Gut feel' decision-making with limited information
Understanding and recalling the information itself	Understanding the values of those who transmit and filter information
Assuming goals away	Recognizing the widely varied goals of others
Seeking (impersonally) to verify absolute truth by study of information	Making decisions on the basis of judgement of trust and competence of people

Understanding basic principles of society in the metaphysical sense	Seeking to apply and adjust in practice to basic principles of society
Seeking the correct answer with time to do it	Developing the most appropriate solution under pressure
Learning in the classroom	Learning through doing
Gleaning information from experts and authoritative sources	Gleaning information personally from anywhere and everywhere and weighing it
Evaluation through written assessments	Evaluation by judgement of people and events through direct feedback
Success in learning measured by knowledge-based exam pass	Success in learning by solving problems and learning from failure

This model reflects many approaches used in contemporary Christian education. Walter Hollenweger describes the integration of prayer, singing, worship and meals into a course on theology for the Centre for Black and White Christian Partnership in Birmingham.[21] He makes the point that black people do not speak about God (doctrine) without speaking to God, and would not debate their position in society (social ethics) without following it with a celebration. In exactly the same way as the issue of what is appropriate to its context, so too the issue of dialogue between black and white goes beyond forms of communication that are simply propositional, philosophical and conceptual. They are not inferior or superior, but different. The connection between mind and body is assumed, so this unity is expressed in educational design.

Walter Hollenweger argues that this not only applies to theology but to 'medicine, psychology, pedagogy and economics', and that 'the model of interaction is not a luxury in which we may indulge when we have nothing else to do, but it is part of the very essence of theological education'. There needs to be a move away from the authoritarian teaching of certain practices to people, without resulting in a situation so open-ended that there can only be reactions and exploration of what might be the case.

One example known to me brings the examples of entrepreneurial education and Christian education together. Students on the Aston Training Scheme in the Church of England were trained on part-time courses to discern where their vocation lay: were they called to be ordained clergy in the Church?[22] What was striking was that many of them were late developers who had been unsuccessful at school but had advanced a long way in their own job by virtue of personality, and by skills that they had picked up along the way. In some cases this included entrepreneurial or other vocational training as described above, in others there had been none offered. What was significant was that these 'students' found that formal education was difficult to get back into, as they began to study theology. In ways that used much role play, learning by experience and group work, the course participants found that they could begin to approach Christian theology and what their own vocation might be without denying their past experience of intuitive learning. There was one example of the son of a docker who had become a senior executive in a European company without any formal qualifications: he worked as an entrepreneur within his company, selling and exploiting gaps in the market. Despite his new-found Christian faith that led him to consider ordination, he was quite unprepared for formal academic study and he began to doubt his vocation. It was only on a course like that at Aston that his heart and head began to come together. There were other examples of people who had not been economically successful, but had taken a leading role in their local community. Similarly, they found that community experience, or training, resonated with experiential learning at Aston.

What is interesting is that the educational model that fits entrepreneurship is similar to models developed by the Churches, and other groups, in promoting experiential education. In other words, there is a whole movement away from formalized academic study to one that is in tension with that. It is important to realize that academic study is not decried as such: it is much more a question of what is appropriate to its context.

Enterprise and society: attitudes to enterprise culture

There are many attitudes to this newly discovered culture.[23] Many small businesses are seen as exemplifying the attributes of enterprise. They are therefore practitioners, although their degree of growth varies. Indeed, it has been suggested that some businesses are more interested in survival, even if this appears as a contradiction in terms with regard to the attributes of enterprise. While growth itself can be defined as necessary for survival, the suggestion that small firms are predominantly interested only in survival seems unduly negative. This may be true during the 1989–91 recession, but it can hardly be the case over all.

The second group to examine is that fast-growing sector of advice-giving bodies. They urge further growth of small businesses, both in the numbers of small firms and the expansion of their turnover. Advice-giving agencies are neither part of government, nor practitioners themselves. Often their staff are seconded from much more traditional large organizations, such as British Rail, and their funds and accountability are not ultimately related to their clients. How far such bodies will persist into the 1990s is now much debated. There have been great successes, but others have been much more critical of the 'enterprise industry'.

The third group takes us inevitably into the realm of the party-political. This book is not one with a political message. It seeks to read a cultural change, and make theological comments about it. However, it would be foolish to deny that the enterprise culture has not been deeply political throughout the last decade. Many political commentators, such as Hugo Young and Peter Jenkins, have repeatedly emphasized that the Thatcher administration did not come to power in 1979 with a fully worked-out philosophy. However, it is the case that by the mid-1980s there was a firm belief in 'enterprise', even if it was not fully integrated with other beliefs (such as 'the caring citizen', the 'social market', or 'national sovereignty'). Belief in enterprise was especially associated with Lord Young, a government minister who was Secretary of State for Employment, and then for Trade and Industry. Characteristically he renamed the latter Department the 'Department for Enterprise', although it still retained its original title as well. He argued that it was the task of government to 'release enterprise' (again the title of one of his Department's White Papers). He argued that small businesses could drive the British economy on and create new jobs. Britain in recent decades had, like other West European countries, neglected their potential. Much of Lord Young's vision was inspired by the United States, and he worked tirelessly to convert others to his viewpoint. He was distinguished from many government ministers not only by his non-political background (he had been a successful businessman, and returned to this area by the end of the decade), but by the tenacity and conviction of his beliefs. Yet there were many others who became committed to this cause. Their language was consistent: terms such as 'new', 'dynamic', 'individual', 'change' and 'enterprising' were portrayed via the mass media with punchy messages, advertising slogans and graphic illustrations. Furthermore, there was a belief that small businesses enshrined certain qualities or characteristics which, if fostered, could promote a better society. They were seen as democratic, social, liberating institutions. Thus phrases such as 'the spirit of enterprise' or medical metaphors (where the 'patient' returned to the 'health' of late-Victorian capitalism) were increasingly part of political discourse.

The next category to look at is the effect of the mass media. As the decade unfolded and the enterprise culture became a reality, it became important that institutions should be seen to relate to this new phenomenon. It was not a matter of giving advice, as in the intermediary bodies that stood between government and small firms, nor was it a question of preaching a revivalist message. It was instead part of the manufacture of new images and popular cultural presentation. Advertising agencies showed banks as friendly to the growth of small businesses. Major companies began to promote new images of themselves as dynamic, devolved, flexible organizations. Educational establishments used the term as well. It is important to distinguish two facets of this change. One is simply the manufacture of images. Newspapers, in particular, took up the theme. Ritchie suggests several common headlines: 'local boy (or girl) makes good'; 'kids break in'; 'surprising new idea'; 'make it in business'; 'young entrepreneur of the year'. There was a predictable pattern of 'problem overcome/good news for the region'. Increasingly, though, others (as we will see) chimed in with their disagreements: 'problems remain/more bad news for the region'. It became a battleground of images.

The second aspect of this change goes beyond the world of mass persuasion. There was in fact a dramatic change in the involvement and attitude of banks with small firms, and changes within large companies, education, and many other institutions. How much of this was due to government is something that must be explored further, but the reality of change is undeniable. Nor was it simply related to small firms. As the decade wore on, it became clear that attributes and qualities found in small firms were, as we have seen above, part of any organization that sought to be flexible.

The next group would include this research project itself. A growing number of academics sought to understand enterprise and analyse it. Research began in the academic world in the late 1960s with the Bolton Committee of Inquiry into Small Firms, which published its report in 1971. At the same time, the Institute of Economic Affairs under Lord Harris was promoting the cause of enterprise in a series of publications.

The United States Birch report in 1979 undertook further research on the role of small firms in job generation. In Britain, the Department of Employment commissioned more research throughout the 1980s, despite the considerable debate on its findings. In 1989 the Economic and Social Research Council committed £1 million on research on four themes: the role of small firms; their creation, survival and growth; local labour markets; and organizational issues inside small firms.

There are two further groups that must be mentioned in this survey. First, many have become deeply hostile to enterprise culture or, at the very least, profoundly sceptical. There are a number of reasons for this. Some point to perceived mismanagement, low pay, insecure employment and exploitation. In brief, enterprise culture is a synonym for sweatshops. Others look at the growth of large firms who have sub-contracted to smaller ones, and argue that there is very little growth in true self-employment. It is a sleight of hand, where capitalism changes its appearance. They say that the real power still lies with large corporations. Furthermore, sub-contracting is a device that enables large corporations to avoid paying those levels of wages, benefits and conditions of service that they would have to pay if they employed people directly and on a full-time basis. Yet others examine the reality of the long-term unemployed, and doubt whether these policies offer anything to those on the margins of British society. Other sceptics doubt that the deep-seated problems of both the British economy and society will be changed by the romantic vision of entrepreneurs flourishing in every sphere of life. Finally, there were several critical studies from social and philosophical psychology on the cult of the consuming or enterprising self in modern Britain.

The final group is one of the most interesting of all in this spectrum of possibilities. I have found many community groups who are becoming interested in the enterprise culture. Sometimes they will substitute the language of need, involvement and accountability for the language of profit, method and performance. This is the alternative culture of co-operation, 'as if people mattered', to quote the title of one study. Others, however, believe that community groups themselves can use the methods of small businesses, while ensuring that there is a community benefit and not just an individual one; that the success of a community business should therefore lead its participants on to wider forms of community action, which may include political campaigns on behalf of the area and its inhabitants.

There are therefore a whole range of reactions that the enterprise culture has engendered in people. When one reflects that the growth of this culture coincided with the collapse of communist regimes in Eastern Europe, it becomes clear that the cultural implications are very far-reaching indeed. Many Eastern European governments sought advice on the promotion of small businesses, privatization and the creation of popular capitalism. Above all, however, they sought to change people's attitudes to wealth-creation: they wished to replace decades of communist rule with creation of an enterprise culture. The relationship between the enterprise culture and 'living in the truth' has been examined by Vaclav Havel, President of Czechoslovakia.[24]

The first part of this chapter looked at the terms enterprise, entrepreneur, small business and wealth-creation. This second part has now moved on to place these concepts in the cultural life of Britain in the last decade. What is needed now is an . explanation of how enterprise as a concept, and enterprise culture, relates to Christian theology, and to the theology of wealth-creation or enterprise. Why should theology be concerned with such issues at all?

Enterprise and theology

a) An enterprise culture redefined

An enterprise culture arises when a series of circumstances come into being.[25] The key to an enterprise culture probably lies in the early years of a person's life. If the period of childhood and adolescence is such that young people have the relevant attributes brought out and reinforced in these formative years, an enterprise culture can emerge. Traditionally, sub- or counter-cultures allowed minority groups to behave with a freedom denied to them in the wider society. For example, much of the history of Judaism in Britain this century, especially in areas like the East End of London, has reflected both a religious conservatism and a benevolent attitude to economic and social innovation.[26]

Also necessary are abundant positive role images of successful enterprise. Small businesses, community development and new initiatives within an organization generate further enterprise by providing role models (the first missionary to a country; the first small business; the first initiative by a group of women), a social status that is attractive and desirable, and ways of repeating the initiative. The myths of being unattainable or impossible (because of tradition or custom) are broken. It is possible for ordinary people to follow. Indeed, precisely because they may have no status by birth or education, it may be more attractive for ordinary people, and they will be less hampered by social tradition.

Then there should be a network of contacts, either through friendship or families. These 'informal' social contacts enable individuals and groups to subvert the barriers of tradition, substitute for the lack of formal education or opportunity, and resource one another. The links between the creation of an integrated culture, however loosely bound together, and an enterprise culture are very close. Finally, either this network or the existence of more formal structures should provide knowledge and insight into the processes of running organizations, taking initiatives, creating a small business or a community venture.

However, to be precise, it is not clear whether there is any such thing as 'an enterprise culture'. Rather, there are a series of cultures – youth, ethnic, regional, male and female, young and middle-aged – where entrepreneurial attributes are more or less admired. These cultures interact with the political process, and the social and economic opportunities that are offered to them. However, there are some cultures that do achieve a critical degree of solidarity and cohesion to allow the individual or group within them the opportunity to practise real innovation. Real innovation and change will occur when a culture is sufficiently coherent to hold up certain role models of independence, innovation and entrepreneurship as practicable and desirable.

b) *Theology, institutions and enterprise*

Therefore enterprise is closely related to the culture we live in. Theology will also be part of that culture, for good or ill. Peter Dodd's research, on the relationship of culture to enterprise, shows how much the influence of a region can affect the existence of enterprise. How then should theology seek to respond to the phenomenon of an enterprise culture? What is opposed to the enterprise culture may well be called the bureaucratic culture, but the two are not completely separate. Business usually embodies the enterprise culture, while institutions embody the bureaucratic culture. There can be an interplay between the two, for businesses can become institutionalized.

The Church of England, like many religious bodies, has become in its secular manifestation a bureaucratic institution in the twentieth century: it has structures, hierarchies, committees and formalized consultative processes. Not only is the Church of England (and other mainstream denominations) an institution, but those who work within it tend to imbibe its ethos. This process is all too familiar to sociologists of religion: there is the formal theological training, and then the assimilation of that person into the mores and ethos of the organization. This assimilation means that the values and beliefs of one generation, often hardly articulated, are passed on to another generation – usually implicitly and without it being realized.

How does an institution move towards change? Most leaders of major organizations effect change within their structures from time to time.[27] This reduces the risk of becoming entirely institutionalized, and those involved in it operating it for their own ends. It is, though, extremely difficult for such an organization, and those integral to its inner workings, to have any appreciation of the growth of an enterprise culture. However, as that culture develops, emphasizing risk, innovation and self-reliance, institutions will be forced to change. With regard to the Church, it was not without good reasons that Charles Handy began his book *The Age of Unreason* with a quote from a debate in the Church of England's General Synod. The speaker concerned made the following point: 'In this matter, as in so much else in our great country, why cannot the status quo be the way forward?'

Enterprise does not just happen; it thrives upon and requires the maximum devolution of real responsibility. However, there are ways in which such responsibility can be retained by the central organization. There can be centralization on a leader, such as the traditionally autocratic Roman Catholic diocesan structure, and much of the international organization of the Roman Catholic Church. Alternatively, an organization can so follow the past practices of the institution that no change is allowed.

At this point we clearly move into a discussion of tradition and innovation. There are two separate issues here. One is what the attitude of the Churches as institutions should be to their organizational structure, given that much of their thinking will be circumscribed by that ethos. The ideological nature of Church thinking is important here. The other point, though related, is a separate one. How should Christians think about innovation and risk at all? A useful and pertinent collection of essays is the volume edited by Richard Holloway, Bishop of Edinburgh, entitled *The Divine Risk*. These essays were originally given as lectures in Edinburgh in 1989. Both issues concern tradition, hierarchy and the management of change.

It was a concern of Protestant, especially German, theologians in the 1950s that the story of the New Testament was one of a deterioration into institutionalization. Such writers as Ernst Kasemann, in his *Jesus Means Freedom*, saw the early Christian message as gradually becoming bound up with the growth of hierarchy, formal procedures and tradition. The Christian gospel was for him, and other theologians concerned with the inner meaning of faith, a fundamental challenge to a person's own security, values and self-assessment. Everything turned on the one-to-one confrontation with the person of Jesus, whether in Palestine or risen and glorified. Any congregation that resulted from this meeting with the Lord was in essence a collection of individuals, who put little weight on past tradition and external practices. The Church was open to the Spirit, and there was an acceptance of the necessity of change.

Nevertheless, Kasemann was to be much criticized by theologians far more aware of the sophisticated analysis offered by the sociology of religion than he was. It became clear that all religions move through periods of great change and flexibility. The foundation of Christianity was no exception to this. When religious practices are challenged by a particular individual, the traditional justification for beliefs and values within the framework may dissolve in the enthusiasm generated by a new leader. Such a 'charismatic' person is seen to be of extraordinary power, integrity or conviction. A movement forms around this person, and a new set of beliefs and values come into being.

However, there remains the necessity sociologically of creating structures that will allow the continuation of the message: what in Christian terms is called the true (or authentic) preaching of the gospel. It is a normal pattern of any social movement that it will create procedures and structures which allow the charisma generated to be handed on from one generation to another. In this sense, Kasemann was quite naïve: there cannot be a pure, spiritual reality open to the breath of the Spirit without structures. Yet there are enormous costs in all of this. The struggle between Paul, a charismatic figure if ever there was one, and the Jerusalem church is all about the compromises he resisted in the name of the true gospel. (There is a fascinating account of the process in Holmberg's *Paul and Power*.)

Therefore we are left with the necessity of institutional structures, yet aware that the institutions may become closed to their own charismatic origins. Stephen Sykes points to the paradoxes of the Church. The Church stands for unity and reconciliation, yet the abolition of frontiers creates new divisions between those who accept the abolition (or struggle for it) and the rest. As Sykes recognizes, there can be no permanent liberation of the Church from 'the world'. Human society is able to be laid open to the possibility of a new order of love, peace and equality, yet the world has its price to exact. In time the Church becomes deeply corrupted by the world, and the paradox of the agent of reconciliation and transforming love becoming the most hidebound and reactionary body in society (a point repeatedly made to me during this research by many people in small businesses, community groups, etc.) cannot be denied.

There is no reason to give in at this point. Sykes notes that as Luther at the Reformation stripped away the accretions of centuries of tradition from the Church in Germany, and 'his own movement of spiritual reformation gathered mundane impetus, there is enough evidence of his agony at the re-occurence of the paradoxes.'[28]

The logic of this position is that there must always be great suspicion of institutional pronouncements, yet they must be made. Nevertheless, it is possible to change an institution: the paradox of charisma/institution need not lead one to throw up one's hands in a world-weary or other-worldly gesture. In particular, change can be brought about in small instances. Those representing the institution may justifiably be alarmed at the threat to tradition that this poses, but tradition is a dynamic process, not a fixed and static deposit.

Recent studies of New Testament churches have shown how much the process of becoming an institution was matched by an intensity of language about relationships within the church community. 'The new social freedom of the church ... gave a welcome identity to some able, unconventional women.'[29] When norms were broken, Paul was placed in a difficult position himself. The charismatic figure par excellence, he none the less felt a need to contain disorder yet to affirm new status in the community. Beyond this, there is the continual stress on intimate language in, for example, the Second Letter to the Corinthians. The language is that of love, affection, intimacy and warmth. There was 'a resilient, intimate fellowship ... in a pluralist setting'.[30] So the **use** of language, and community, becomes a way of allowing a church to regain an understanding of change that is not restricted by the necessity of formal structures.

If we turn to look at the nature of risk, the same ambiguity becomes evident. As Rowan Williams says, it is easy to 'dramatise encounter with God, to be caught up in a silly rhetoric of faith as an "adventure"'.[31] Equally, John Habgood argues that churches must be concerned with the diversity of the gospel in a total environment. This makes church leaders prudent. Moral courage is not the same as risk-taking, he claims, and avoids the 'unspoken assumption that risk-taking is somehow good in itself, as if the Church has need of spiritual adrenalin to assure itself that it is alive!'[32]

Williams prefers to speak of the fact that there is no wholly innocent Christianity. The moment we speak of God in words and images is the moment we know we have no other choice than making a pattern of our own world, yet equally we are making a tribal fetish. Again and again the biblical record shows that the words used of God change their meaning as we read through the record. 'The fact of revelation may be bound more to the recognition of this critical energy than to any one crystallising or imagining of the God who reveals.'[33] Yet revelation is not simply the energy to make and remake the biblical record. We also know that our failure to speak properly will not silence God. God in the biblical story has the time to be present where we have not. In a fascinating description of child-rearing in some lectures a few years ago at the Royal Institute of Philosophy, the point was made that ultimately the parent can give more time and patience than the child in any display of anger or rejection. So God sets our painful attempts to act within the context of an abiding hope: we all have an interlocutor whose time and resources do not run out, who returns patiently to confront and probe every distortion we may project. We are authorized to commit ourselves by the hope that our commitments, however mistaken, will not block the liberty of God to go on addressing us.[34]

The faithfulness of God to those who are called by him does not mean however that God blesses everything and anything. There are places where God can be found in the world, hard though these may be to discover. The judgement of God is seen in the life and death of Jesus, 'healer and critic of the false "order" of his day'. So we are called to act as individuals, to take risks, 'in the precarious signs that are all we have to bind us together'.[35]

Moral courage is rooted in convictions and intentions, and is discovered by living through hard times. It is not displayed for its own sake. There has to be the weighing of risks and arguments: this is part of a sensible decision-making process. Yet what matters beyond this is a sense of purpose, the discernment of fundamental principles, the boldness that may be necessary.[36] There is another kind of courage in the long-term commitment to policies felt to be necessary. Risks do not come singly: the choice is between one risk and another.

The place of theology in relation to enterprise is, then, a subtle one. Theology is part of the culture in which enterprise can come to such a coherence that we speak of an enterprise culture or, perhaps more accurately, a series of cultures. Politically this can be helped or hindered, especially by what may be called the bureaucratic culture. It is not that bureaucracy is unnecessary; today's organizations need bureaucracy. Yet there comes a time when an institution fails to accept change: it has become institutionalized. Furthermore, it can in Christian terms become corrupt. Article 19 of the Church of England's 39 Articles says polemically that the historic churches have erred: so too by implication may the Church of England.

Theologically this leads into the nature of reformation, change and the struggle to express the life of the Spirit in the institution. It is not a matter just of power, but of responsibility: who acts on behalf of others? The entrepreneur in society is met by the religious leader, seeking both to reform and to be faithful to the institution she or he represents.

At times the Church appears anything but risk-taking. Yet Williams points to the patience of God in his faithfulness, and Habgood to the necessity of moral courage. The enterprise culture can at one level be dismissed in terms of a greedy materialism, which must be denounced by the Church as the final excrescence of capitalism. There is in fact a much deeper problem, which is the possibility of any change at all. Yet the risk-taking, moral courage and reformation of the Church spoken of as utterly necessary by such theologians as Williams, Habgood and Sykes (all of them holding leadership positions in the Church as bishop or archbishop) show how much the enterprise culture puts a challenge to the Church's conservatism.

Conclusion

'Enterprise' is not an easy term to define. It has a specific role in economics, and it plays a key role in Schumpeter's theory of economic change. Equally, although he avoids the term because of its political implications, Handy's management theory is all about the practice of enterprise.[37] The devolution of responsibility, the need to take risks when we cannot be sure of the outcome, the ability to communicate with others, the necessity of combining self-reliance with team work: all these form part of a family of concepts that make up 'enterprise'. The motivation for enterprise is also ambiguous. There clearly can be negative, even destructive, aspects to the phenomenon. Even if the motivation is creative and positive, it may never be realized. That is why enterprise education is crucial: the work of the Durham University Business School is now recognized internationally, from Hungary to Bangladesh. Part of their work in schools will be taken up in Chapter 3. There are also some parallels in Christian education, as in some forms of experiential learning.

It would be disingenuous, however, to deny that the term 'enterprise' had no political meaning. That is why this first chapter makes, in effect, a digression: to look at how the term 'enterprise' (or, even more so, 'enterprise culture') has grown in the last ten years in Britain. It became a watchword of the mass media, exploited by politicians – as much part of the rhetoric of the 1980s as feelings concerning the Falklands conflict or the 'green movement'.

Any theological evaluation must attempt to grapple with the institutional reality of the Church, and its conservatism. I have sought to do so by means of the idea of charismatic change, which is a sociological term, and the necessity for this to be embodied in an institution. But this cannot be the end of the story. Institutions must grapple with the necessity of their own internal change, however painful this may be. In doing this, two beliefs will be helpful: one is the idea of the faithfulness of God to his people; the other the idea of moral courage. It may seem as if the Church has almost nothing to say about the enterprise culture. Trevor MacDonald and I discussed this point on many occasions: it is only fair to add that Trevor's criticisms in no way compromised his fierce loyalty to the Church of England. Yet institutions can and do change; the change required of the Church is difficult, to be sure, for it requires on the one hand criticism of the greed and materialism which can so often mar the enterprise culture, while also realizing that the innovation and flexibility shown in many small-scale enterprises is not always recognized by the officials of an institutional Church.

Notes

1. The best account of this period is by P. Riddell in *The Thatcher Decade*, 1989. See also M. Ball, F. Gray and L. McDowell, *The Transformation of Britain*, 1989, and G. Causer (ed.), *Inside British Society*, 1987.
2. The political literature is of course vast. An overview is given by H. Young in *One of Us*, 1989, P. Jenkins in *Mrs Thatcher's Revolution*, 1987, and R. Skidelsky (ed.) in *Thatcherism*, 1988. Lord Young's autobiography is entitled *The Enterprise Years*, 1990.
3. The best summary of church attitudes to social responsibility is given in A. Hastings's *A History of English Christianity 1900–1985*, 1986. Ronald Preston is one of the leading theorists. See his books: *Church and Society in the late Twentieth Century*, 1983, and *Religion and the Persistence of Capitalism*, 1979. More recently, there is J. Atherton's *Faith in the Nation*, 1988. Finally, there are of course *Faith in the City*, 1985, *Not just the Poor*, 1986, and *Living Faith in the City*, 1990 – all from the Church of England.
4. F. A. Iremonger, *William Temple*, 1948, and A. Suggate, *William Temple and Social Ethics Today*, 1987.
5. D. Anderson (ed.), *The Kindness that Kills*, 1984.
6. 'Enterprise' and 'small businesses' are surveyed in a number of books. See M. Brinks and J. Coyne, *The Birth of Enterprise*, 1983; M. Casson, *The Entrepreneur*, 1982; R. Scase and R. Goffee, *The Entrepreneurial Middle Class*, 1982; L. Weiss, *Creating Capitalism: The State and Small Businesses since 1945*, 1988; J. Boswell, *The Rise and Decline of Small Firms*, 1973; H. Miller, *The Way of Enterprise*, 1963; O. Gelinser, *The Enterprise Ethic*, 1968.
7. J. Schumpeter, *Capitalism, Socialism and Democracy*, 1943.
8. ibid., p. 83.
9. ibid., p. 132.
10. ibid., p. 133.
11. J.K. Galbraith, *The New Industrial State*, 1967.
12. Schumpeter, p. 63.
13. C. Seidl (ed.), *Lectures on Schumpeterian Economics. Centenary Memorial Lectures, Graz, 1983*, 1984. See especially P. Swoboda, *Schumpeter's Entrepreneur in Modern Economic Theory*, and P.J. Hammond, *Is Entrepreneurship Obsolete?*
14. On definitions of enterprise, see P. Burns and J. Dewhurst (eds), *Small Business and Entrepreneurship*, 1989, especially the articles by S. Birley, 'The Start-Up', J. Dewhurst, 'The Entrepreneur', and H.H.

Stevenson and W. H. Sahlman, 'The Entrepreneurial Process'.

15. M. Harper, 'Hardship, Discipline, Entrepreneurship', *Cranfield Working Paper 85–1*, 1985, cited by J. Dewhurst in 'The Entrepreneur', in Burns and Dewhurst (eds), p. 79.

16. The Bolton Report, *Report of the Committee of Inquiry on Small Firms*, 1971, cited by J. Stanworth and J. Curran in 'Employment Relations in the Small Firm', in Burns and Dewhurst (eds), p. 160.

17. A. Gibb, *Enterprise Culture*, 1990, pp. 27–8.

18. S. Birley, 'The Start-Up' in P. Burns and J. Dewhurst (eds), p. 11.

19. A. C. Cooper, 'Strategic Management: New Ventures and Small Business', *Long Range Planning*, 14.5, 1981, cited by S. Birley in 'The Start-Up' in ibid., p. 9.

20. J. Ritchie, *Concepts of Enterprise and Education*, 1990; A. Gibb, *Innovative Approaches to Entrepreneurship Education*, 1990; D. A. Kirby, *Entrepreneurship Research in the United Kingdom*, 1990; J. Ritchie, *Explaining Enterprise Cultures*, 1989.

21. W. Hollenweger, 'Ethnic Education', *Theology*, September 1987.

22. L. Green, N. Todd, M. Allen and D. Tytler, *A Thing Called Aston: An Experiment in Reflective Learning*, 1987; L. Green, *Let's Do Theology*, 1990. See also the *British Journal of Theological Education* (1987 onwards) for many other examples of experiential learning.

23. This section follows J. Ritchie, *Explaining Enterprise Cultures*, 1989.

24. V. Havel, *Living in the Truth*, 1989. The whole question of whether people can be enslaved by power, sex and money in an enterprise culture (or any other culture) is explored with great force and insight by Stephen Sykes in his article entitled 'On Power, Sex and Money'. He makes great use of Havel's understanding of 'living in the truth'.

25. Gibb, *Enterprise Culture*, p. 17.

26. C. Bermant, *Point of Arrival: A Study of London's East End*, 1975. Innovation can be right or left wing politically. See also Lord Young, *The Enterprise Years*, 1990, pp. 3–5.

27. I follow closely in the next few paragraphs the argument of one member of my support group, Mr Trevor MacDonald, of British Steel. I am very grateful to him for his cogent analysis of bureaucratic/enterprise cultures.

28. S. W. Sykes, 'Lutherans and Anglicans on the Catholicity of the Church', unpublished paper for the Anglican/Scandinavian Dialogue, Finland, 1986.

29. D. F. Ford and F. Young, *Meaning and Truth in 2 Corinthians*, 1987, p. 205.

30. ibid., p. 198.

31. R. Williams, 'God and Risk' in R. Holloway (ed.), *The Divine Risk*, 1990, p. 21.

32. J. Habgood, 'Church and Risk', in ibid., p. 36.

33. Williams, in ibid., p. 19.

34. Williams, in ibid., p. 21.

35. Williams, in ibid., pp. 22–3.

36. Habgood, in ibid., p. 36.

37. Private conversation with the author, February 1990.

2

Small Firms

Government policy 1979–91

The Conservative government under Mrs Thatcher consistently claimed that they had created a new self-confidence in business. Lord Young, already cited in Chapter 1, gave his October 1985 lecture to the Conservative Party Conference (the Conservative Political Central Lecture) under the title 'Enterprise Regained'. He drew on the controversial thesis of Correlli Barnett, which was supported by Martin Wiener, that the decline of Britain this century was as much a cultural decline as an economic one. Peter Riddell, the economic and political editor of the *Financial Times* during the 1980s, describes the attempt of the Thatcher government to promote enterprise in his book *The Thatcher Decade*.[1] It is significant that he devotes a chapter to this attempt, entitled 'Enterprise Culture', as well as chapters on economic policy, privatization, and the labour market. In other words, the enterprise culture, 'popular capitalism', indicates a different cultural transformation.

Riddell shows clearly the measures taken by the government to promote this cultural change. He argues, I believe correctly, that there was also a cultural dimension to a supply-side view of the British economy. In this analysis the problems of the British economy lay in its rigidity, so that laws and taxation 'stand in the way of change and stifle enterprise' (speech by Sir Geoffrey Howe as Chancellor, June 1979).

There were a whole range of initiatives taken by the government in the decade that followed. They included tax cuts; deregulation of government legislation; promotion of competition in mergers policy and dealing with restrictive practices in professions and businesses; liberalization on such different fronts as bus routes, advertising by solicitors, telephone services and domestic air routes; many small business initiatives such as loan guarantee schemes; industrial aid being switched from overall support of assisted areas and nationalized industries to innovation and technology transfer; and many schemes to link education and industry. As Riddell says, 'The very breadth of these initiatives makes it difficult to assess their contribution to the revival of enterprise.... The overall picture has, therefore, been mixed. There has undoubtedly been evidence of a revival of entrepreneurial activity, especially in the service sectors and in small business, and of a recovery of managerial self-confidence in much of manufacturing industry.'[2]

The conclusion that Riddell reaches, in June 1989 before the recession of 1989–91, was (in his words) of 'impressive evidence of a revival of entrepreneurial activity'. There was an average net increase of 500 new firms each week since 1979 after deducting closures, according to VAT returns. In 1987 there was a rise of nearly 900 new firms a week. Secondly, there was 'a rise of around 1 million in the number of self-employed people during the 1980s to more than 3 million by late 1988, over six times the increase in the previous 30 years. This total was equivalent to more than 11 per cent of the employed labour force'. There was also a great growth in the venture capital industry (from almost nothing in 1979 to more than £1 billion in 1987) and the unlisted securities market (which began in 1980 with £12.5 million invested, and in 1987 was £191 million). The government-backed loan guarantee scheme helped 19,000 companies in 1981–7, and 3,000 companies raised £750 million in 1983–8 in the business expansion scheme, which offered tax relief to investors in unquoted trading companies.

Each initiative has also had its critics. So great was the emphasis that the government laid on creating an enterprise culture that the final picture contains many failures and partial successes, as well as significant results. The Small Business Research Trust in 1988 noted that the business expansion scheme tended to lend more and more to the retail, property and leisure sector: only a quarter of the finance invested in 1985–6 went into manufacturing. The National Audit Office in August 1988 concluded that about half the businesses set up with government help displaced existing companies; 44 per cent of new entrants would probably have gone into self-employment anyway without the £40 a week (for the first year) Enterprise Allowance paid to unemployed people wanting to start their own businesses; of those new businesses that lasted the year (and 16 per cent did not), a quarter failed after the allowance was withdrawn, mostly within about four weeks. After three years, 60 per cent of the initial start-ups survived, with two-thirds not employing anyone else. Yet it could be argued that there are bound to be failures as well as successes in an entrepreneurial society, and that over all the gains were fairly sizeable.

The 1990–1 recession affected large businesses, but the worst-affected area was small businesses.[3] Small businesses are defined as those with up to fifty employees and a turnover of up to £5 million; many of them of course were founded in the 1980s. Several surveys reported a doubling of business failures in 1990–1. In the South and the Midlands it became the worst recession for fifty years. A few escaped, such as those in areas of stable demand or with a high export turnover. There were many reasons why small businesses were so vulnerable. Banks were forced to take higher risks or close firms; markets were often niches in the home market, and there was little diversification; reserves were low or non-existent; management became overstretched. Above all, small firms that grew on government contracts, or by sub-contracting, suddenly found the tightening of corporate belts led to an enormous crisis. Also, the fall in consumer demand wiped out thousands of firms. Falling sales, high interest rates, sharply falling profits and falling balance-sheet values led to an enormous crisis. At the start of the recession, base rate was at 15 per cent: small firms had to pay 18 per cent, in most cases, and had to earn at least that on their capital. By the end of 1990, many were actually making a loss. The fall in the property market meant the security for bank loans was eroded as well. The result was catastrophic.

Certainly in 1990–1 it seemed as if the enterprise culture had finally collapsed. The crucial question was posed by Alan Mayhew, a civil servant with the European Commission, who until 1990 was in charge of DGXXIII, the directorate dealing with small-firms policy. Could the cultural change that was evident in the 1980s be maintained in spite of the recession? It was striking that large numbers of firms continued to be formed even in 1991. Small firms already in existence in 1990–1 should be able to survive in 1992, and thereafter. It is difficult to evaluate just how destructive the 1990–1 collapse has been. The likelihood is that the growth of small firms in the service sector will not be so rapid, and the overmanning in that sector (which many hinted at in the late 1980s) was exposed by the recession. Nevertheless, it remains likely that small firms will continue to grow in the 1990s, with more attention to export markets and manufacturing than before.

Small businesses

a) Industrial relations and motivation

Many small businesses were very critical of government. Mike Fisher, who co-founded Whale Tankers and remains the managing director, spoke of the problems of regulation. He was very critical of the Employment Protection Act, Health and Safety at Work Act, etc. He argued that it got in the way of job creation, and that the enterprise culture was still regarded as crooked. Planning had blocked the expansion of his firm. His position was unusual: he paid high wages, additional loans at low interest for mortgage repayment, a special rebate for holidays to encourage people to travel, and provided BUPA medical cover. Yet he was opposed to trade unions, government regulation, and local planning. In some ways his firm displays a nineteenth-century vision: he refuses to borrow or lease, the firm grew slowly, and he did not wish to be quoted on the USM. Nor would he sell out to a competitor. His mottos is: 'Treat people properly; pay them properly; expect them to work properly.' His firm, which is one of the leading European producers of specialist waste tankers, employs 140 people with a turnover of £10 million. There are landscaped grounds (awarded recognition by the RSPB for wildfowl) in memory of a former colleague. There is also a complete company philosophy: freedom is all important, so no one is forced to do overtime or support company social activities. Secondly, there are links with the local community, through schools, fund-raising for charities, and work-experience links. Thirdly, the whole firm is divided into teams of four or five who build vehicles together under a job-controller. Quality is built into the working practices. All this has been achieved in twenty years by someone who began working for Rover at Solihull, and remembers how bad the quality of production was there.

It is a model story of entrepreneurial activity. Few people in the Church would support his aggressive and deeply critical attitude to government: 'government subsidy is like blood-letting: it is no cure and it kills off any patient which gets it'. 'Government simply gets things wrong – police, British Rail, the Social Charter.'[4] His views on how government affects business are deeply felt.

The same reliance on the workforce came through repeatedly in other conversations. United Engineering in Lincoln was a buyout from part of Clayton De Wandre, which made vehicle parts, especially heavy lorry-braking equipment. Peter Boyd and Keith Hunter said, 'Industrial relations are very, very good: many will want to join when we expand. We have a good workforce, a good reputation, not too strict, but they respond fairly well ... we had, and to some extent do have, the feeling that we will show the former owners we aren't beaten: we will show them.' Equally, they were critical of government and the former management they had worked for: 'We didn't even get a grant from the council or government for taking on the factory, painting it and getting rid of the dead pigeons!' This company now has employees investing and buying out a director. It remains a small company, with eleven employees, and eventually accepted a takeover from an outside party. Nevertheless, this allowed it to expand into new premises. Peter Boyd and Keith Hunter both put the survival of the company down to motivation, and the regulation of their products.[5]

Some companies have, of course, been in business for many years. Harkers of Stockton has recently celebrated its centenary. It has a turnover of £6 million, and employs 150 people. In contrast to Whale, it has an informal closed shop with the AEU. It works in precision engineering, and was bidding for a Boeing AWACS off-set contract the day I visited. The firm is family owned, and this gave it the freedom to invest up to 20 per cent of turnover in new machinery.[6] It was one of the very few on Teesside to survive as a family engineering business. Malcolm Harker argued that the craft skills culture still existed in Germany, but in Britain it had become very weak. His comment on the Conservative Party was sharp: 'a heartless lot of financiers'. The City was 'only financial manipulation, oiling the wheels of wealth distribution'. He believed that the only real creation of wealth was by manufacturing. He had only come into the family business because he was expected to; nevertheless, he had turned round the management structure, and had moved from conventional engineering to very hi-tech sub-contracting. Exports were now 50 per cent of turnover, and he was investing heavily to ensure that the firm survived. Despite this, he viewed the future with some concern.

There are many examples that could be given of industrial relations, and of the attitude of small firms to government. Clearly, there were small firms that were enormously helped by government aid; and equally, in the absence of unions, there can be exploitation and poor industrial relations. Yet I would echo Peter Lawrence's comment in his book on management: 'The small firm is really dreadfully vulnerable.... It is often scruffy enough to attract local government attention ... at the same time, unlike the big company, it does not have any clout, it cannot bite back, so that it is generally vulnerable to interference.'[7]

b) *Innovation*

Another feature of small firms founded in the 1980s is innovation. Of course there are many examples of firms manufacturing the same product over generations, yet there were enough firms exploiting the gaps in the market by innovation in the 1980s to make the point. Such people as Alan Sugar of Amstrad exemplify this very well, but since there have been many interviews with him, it may be better to look at less obvious examples.[8]

Mark Casson's substantial work on the entrepreneur argues that 'product innovation is probably the most important form of entrepreneurship, at least in a long-term perspective. A key element in many product innovations is the achievement of product versatility.'[9]

The present study looked at many examples of innovation. First there was MICRO-SYS, a software company in Warwick University Science Park. Then there was Korda, which operates as a mixture of consultancy, venture capital and innovator. A third was Domino, a multinational printing company developing microprocessor-controlled high-speed ink-jet printers. All three examples were very different, yet they exemplify the speed of change and their reliance on growth by producing further change. (They thus give illustration to Schumpeter's theory of entrepreneurship.)

MICRO-SYS employed (at the time of interview – it has since retracted) sixteen people in writing software. Its turnover in 1989 was £1 million. It presented a professional image: 'We have a strict company philosophy of being smart and polite.' Money was a big incentive, as was motivation. 'No one goes home until they have solved their problem that day, and I go home last. . . . It is symptomatic of our professionalism. Our basic constraints aren't money, but time and our personal talents. . . . We are a totally graduate company, with several doctorates. The problems are the lack of flair; rigidity creeps in, and creativity is lost.'[10]

A very different company at Warwick is Frank Grunfeld's Nima. He had been there since 1984, as one of the original occupants of the Science Park. He makes an instrument that coats materials via molecules for the electronic industry. He praised government assistance, but was critical of universities in Britain today: underfunded, with staff holding on to tenure. Nor did he feel Science Parks worked; there was little real co-operation between the university and the Science Park. Frank Grunfeld only makes eleven instruments a year, selling worldwide. What sustained him was the 'green ethic', with the freedom to be creative and yet be self-supporting. He represents an unusual innovator: self-employed, at the leading edge of technology, and not wishing to grow any further.[11]

Both Domino and Korda were certainly growing when I visited them. Although Domino has had mixed fortunes, it has grown from nothing in 1978 to £32 million turnover in 1988, 53 per cent up on the previous year.[12] There are now subsidiary companies in Germany, the United States and Holland, with 600 employees in the group, yet it is run from Cambridge: only a quarter of its sales are in Britain. One of the problems identified by its managing director, Alan Barrell, was the pressure of the City. Like Harkers, he made a sharp division between manufacturing and recycling wealth: 'The danger is that we may create wealth, but where is it going? We won't create the basis for a new Industrial Revolution. Much is sold abroad, like Acorn to Olivetti. The founders did a good job, but they are now out of it, and very rich.'

Korda was explicit in its management ethos. It sets up small businesses, both through consultancy and seed capital. 'We are creating opportunities, either in America, Europe or within an hour of London'. They have holdings in three firms that they have set up; others have been established, but are now independent. The three firms are a microbiologically enhanced oil-recovery business; an agricultural biotechnology business with a turnover of £11 million; and a drug discovery company, with £6 million turnover. The way innovation is managed is important. 'A culture of consistently long hours leaves one exhausted already. Those who stay are very bright; like a sense of adventure and acquiring new skills ... we seek to create an environment full of novelty, a perpetual seminar; fun; openness.' Carolyn Hayman, who runs the company with her partner Alex Korda, pointed to Korda's strong contrast with the civil service and accountancy firms where she began her career twenty years ago.[13]

c) Training and cultural change

I have argued in the previous chapter that the enterprise culture represents a cultural change that the Church must address. This change is seen most forcefully when the issue of training and corporate culture is looked at. It is found within both large and small companies, and even inside the civil service. I interviewed senior executives from Rover, British Steel, the Property Services Agency, the Driver and Vehicle Licensing Agency, as well as training firms such as TMI and TEC. Similar comments came from academics who were also consultants, or those concerned with the relationship of education and industry. There was a striking degree of similarity in the views expressed.[14]

Training was seen as the key to changing a company's performance. While this can be measured in economic terms, many of those interviewed alluded to wider concerns. David Scrimshire of TEC spoke of the great brake on change: the British class structure. Brought up on a Welsh council estate, he felt that many managers were still too removed from their workforce. The United States was, not surprisingly, a model for his company. So too had been the 1960s vision of 'getting on in society', and he was still fulfilling his dreams of these years. Having been a university lecturer in engineering, then moving into industrial consultancy, he finally ended up running a successful training company. 'We work with companies getting off the ground, needing advice to grow further. His commitment was to motivate and empower people, not in a political sense but an industrial one: 'giving managerial skills to the shopfloor'. Like some other small businessmen, he felt the Conservative government lacked any real rapport with the working class or with manufacturing. What he was most critical of was the trivializing effect of television, and the deadening impact of education: 'Comprehensives destroyed the working class's chance of doing better, and the media is run by people who glorify the working class, sex and violence.'

David Scrimshire's views were put more vividly than anyone else's, but they were not atypical. Vernon Smith of British Steel (Industry) said that creating new factories in old steel areas was a moral challenge. John Northcott pointed out that, 'enterprise is not the same as the creation of small businesses, or entrepreneurship. It is a quality, activity or project which is found in a culture'.

John Briffett of Rover spoke of the plateau in productivity that was reached in 1986–7. A new approach had to be tried, which reversed the aggressive management strategy. Managers had to stop making others change out of fear. It was not simply a humanitarian ethic, but a commitment to 'the cascade principle': each layer of management would train and motivate the rest. What was interesting was that this policy treated each part of the Rover Group as a medium-sized company. It was a change to motivate its workforce, and to communicate better. 'Managing better is working harder at communication.'

Similar stories were told by the chief executives of the executive agencies now at arm's length from the civil service in the 'Next Steps' programme. 'Those who work in agencies are pleased to see an emphasis on quality of service.' The constraints noticed by Stephen Curtis, who ran the Driver and Vehicle Licensing Agency at Swansea, were the failure of customers to ask for higher standards, and a lack of imagination in his own management.

Patrick Coldstream describes the changes in British industry in recent years. 'They must offer goods and services . . . that are better thought out . . . and more subtly organized than those of the competition. . . . Employee and employer, therefore, share the gathering interest in seeing companies transform themselves into learning communities, where members recognize each other as continuing learners.' He continued:

'As people's choices are widened by prosperity, education and the flow of information, so we should hope that they will press more insistently for learning through work.'[15]

d) Difficulties

It would not be true to say that every company inter-viewed was successful. Some were struggling to survive in 1989. Others were growing slowly, or did not want rapid expansion.

The manager of the Middlesbrough Enterprise Centre, Jack Corbett, was blunt: 'the quality of those given premises here now is falling'.[16] More office ventures succeeded in his Enter-prise Centre than manufacturing ones. In eight years, 36 out of 119 manufacturing firms survived: only ten employ over a dozen people. After five years, fifty-three out of sixty-two office ventures still remain. Manufacturing was harder, and successful managers made redundant by large firms (ICI, British Steel) tended to go into the service sector. Many manufacturing firms found it difficult to leave the Enterprise Centre, just as the end of the Enterprise Allowance (one year after start-up) was also a critical period.

Peter Drummond of Heritage Upholstery said that he 'worked for himself. There are many problems with doing this: long hours, overdraft, insecurity'. The quality of YTS trainees was, in his view, poor: there was no commitment or interest. He enjoyed working for himself, and would not go back to working for someone else again. But 'there are lots of one-man bands in upholstery now'.[17]

Others were much bleaker and asked not to be quoted directly. The owner of a small courier service said, 'You are always, always on demand. It's a hard grind: if I had any sense, I'd leave'. He had endless opportunities to expand, but he would be 'sunk with unpaid bills'. Again he enjoyed working for himself, but he felt as if he was out on his own. Government grants were hard to get: 'I'm not going to be passed from one person to another.'

Brian Whitfield, managing director of a tarpaulin and groundsheet company, actually chaired the local Small Business Club. Yet his comment was, 'It's been a constant struggle. . . . We have diversified, but none of our moves have been really profitable.' He felt that many small firms would not talk about their difficulties with banks: the banks still wanted too high a return. He had also asked for better training for employees in small firms. There had been such schemes, but they had been dropped. 'It's the loneliest job in the world, sitting alone in your office as an employer, making decisions. I have a phrase – "the lonely entrepreneur".' Again, as so often, he felt that the government's philosophy was one thing: its actual practice was another. As chairman of a Small Business Club he was in no doubt that attitudes to self-employment were changing, but 'at the moment it's more out of necessity than anything else that people work for themselves'. He also doubted whether many of the unemployed would ever succeed in business, although there would never be jobs for all the ex-shipyard workers in the retail and leisure developments in Teesside. As a magistrate and school governor, he saw growing vandalism, high unemployment, and many parents abandoning their responsibility for troublesome teenagers. Brian Whitfield gave a sober view of the problems of the enterprise culture in the north of England: 'Enterprise is good for those moving into self-employment from education and paid employment. For anyone else it can be a delusion.'[18]

e) Values and aspirations

Most people interviewed spoke at great length about their values and aspirations as small businesspeople. It is very often difficult to draw the interview to a close. The format of the interviews was simple. After asking details about the firm, its relationship with the local authority, banks and government grants, I asked why the person had decided to become self-employed. Thereafter, I discussed with them their values and aspirations; how far these had been met and what the constraints on them being realized were; their relationship (or their company's links) with the local community; and finally what, if any, were their religious views: a vast amount of information.

Clearly, money did matter for many people: 'My objectives are a higher income, reputation for quality workmanship, and quality of life', said Marcel Fielden, an architect with a small firm employing five people. 'I have achieved quality of lifestyle, but I have not yet earned the level of income I would like as a reward for the work which I have put in.'[19] MICRO-SYS and others also spoke of the power of money, and their wish to move to performance-related pay.

There are, however, other values. One of the clearest was Frank Grunfeld, who spoke of the 'green ethic'. He had deliberately refrained from growing larger, and felt endless growth was unsustainable. He also supported local charities, local schools, and took students on work-experience during the summer.

This leads into an important issue about small firms. Many entrepreneurs expressed their values through them. A significant number of those interviewed considered large firms to be uncreative, hostile to flexible patterns of work, and hierarchical. A second group saw small firms as allowing them the time and energy to develop other areas of their lives: they could control the hours they worked (though this was only true of successful entrepreneurs). A third group used small firms as a 'forcing-house' for creativity. By putting people together under pressure, a small group could achieve a quality that no large firm could match. A fourth group related the firm to the community, or sold products that were socially useful; alternatively, they could become co-operatives. Finally, many small businesspeople expressed the values of independence and flexibility. They felt that in theory the government supported them, but that in practice the government was constrained not just by economic factors such as the balance of payments, but by an ideology that was suspicious of the small entrepreneur. This was a paradox: in theory Mrs Thatcher should have been sympathetic, but she was often seen as having been taken over by the world of government and big business. Several made the point that she had never been self-employed herself, and her husband was used to holding substantial directorships.

Carolyn Hayman spoke of the stifling ethos of corporate firms in the 1970s, who would not allow flexible workpatterns for mothers with children. She also argued for the 'small firms philosophy' to be applied throughout local government, where sub-contracting for all services could supply a variety of types of provision: the National Childbirth Trust could contract to deliver a certain number of babies for a health authority. Private consultancies could also steer the public sector in certain directions. In this philosophy, small firms are a deliberate way of breaking up the uniformity of old standards, encouraging diversity and new opportunities.

Others did not place the firm at the centre of their life. D.J. Turkinson left ICI and started a small publishing firm, Plimsoll, which gives financial analysis from Company House on certain types of companies. Despite rapid growth, he put the Church at the centre of his life. If the company involved spending time working at weekends, he would find a way of changing it. The paradox here is that success allowed more time away from work. Other examples could be given.[20]

Yet another group was different again. Stable Block Design, also in Middlesbrough, had grown in one year from an £80,000 turnover to a £250,000 turnover. The firm was run by two local men who, after college, had first worked in London and the United States. They then returned to the North-East, and had just won a contract to design a new sewing machine for Singer in Taiwan. Their philosophy was simple. Each week the dozen people led a self-criticism session. If a person fails, they have a month to improve, or they leave. Their continual training, learning of languages, and employing the best designers meant that they wanted to expand into Europe. Their attitude to the North-East was ruthless: it was finished, and they would leave, with a bright future ahead of them.[21]

The opposite extreme could be found in managers who gave much time and energy to the local community. I have already mentioned Brian Whitfield, local magistrate, school governor and chairman of the Small Business Club. Another example is Domino, where the then managing director, Alan Barrell, expressed his Christian convictions through a host of activities: Cambridge Youth Theatre, raising money for youth workers, taking part in the local festival, supporting the local church, employing handicapped people. Domino had a deliberate policy to involve the workforce in supporting the community. Other high-technology firms tended to oppose this policy, arguing that the nature of their work made it difficult to be drawn into local links.

For some small firms, community and business almost became one. Lincoln Wholefoods is a small shop in a Victorian terrace, doing mail-order and home-delivery orders. It was started two years ago by an unemployed couple. They have expanded by listening to their customers, who are part of the neighbourhood. Also part of the locality was the local church, which took up much of their time. 'We don't want to grow into a chain of shops.... I get into as many community activities as I can handle anyway.'[22] Thermica of Hull reflected on its attempts to recruit the long-term unemployed into the firm, and the difficulty of rebuilding positive attitudes to work among them.[23]

However, by no means every small firm espouses conscious values – although it is striking just how many in this survey talked about them. John Briffett, who is a member of the Salvation Army, said that it was 'far easier than in the past to be known to be a Christian in the motor industry. Total quality involves honesty, integrity, not managing as we used to by fear'. Examples of a complete commitment to values in small businesses are rare, but I was often surprised by managers who supported community projects in Nicaragua, or who advocated employee share-ownership, or were concerned about the environment.

Theology and values

Each of the individuals interviewed in this chapter expressed two different but closely related arguments. One was what their work meant for them personally. It became quite clear that many self-employed people, as well as those in organizations and large industrial corporations, found the meaning of their work very important for them. This was partly because it was seen as a challenge to their own professional expertise. It was also because a series of values could be expressed in their work, which therefore became a focus for such ideals as freedom, creativity, justice, etc. Employment often replaced other worlds that might have served as a focus – such as local or national politics, community organizations or churches.

Secondly, the meaning of work mattered because through work a new social order might come into being. How far Britain will develop an extensive small-firms sector remains to be seen, and is much debated. Nevertheless, changes in this sector have altered the industrial characteristics of many northern towns in England, including Hull where I live. Small firms now have a definite place in the economic life of Britain. The future social order will also be affected by the training policies of many larger firms, as will the possibility of employment for many young black people.

It is not, however, the case that this reveals simply the human determination to stamp his or her personality on the world. Such an argument would be too extreme. Instead, the world is made up of relationships and communities. Any account of work that sees it solely in terms of private worlds, individual experience, and the search for subjective values will be utterly flawed. I met a few businesspeople who talked in this way, but it was not the norm.

The theological question that this raises is how this search for personal meaning and value in terms of relationships and communities might be evaluated. This applies either to the personal search or to the creation of a new social order made up of small productive units, economically independent of one another or interrelated in a larger company or organization.

The world is not 'a matter of indifference' for God himself. It represents an object of his interest, to which he is passionately committed: 'His world in heaven and on earth is the object of his will towards good; it is the counterpart of his love for freedom; and in both these things it is the fulfilment of his hope for a free response to his own goodness and love....'[24]

Equally, it is important to emphasize that it is the whole created world that God desires and loves. It is not simply the Christian Church. The salvation of Christ is the salvation of the entire universe, and Christ is the goal for all creation. Christ has been the unity of creation from all eternity, where he mediates and holds together creation as its wisdom. The New Testament sees creation as having an inner unity, because it is ordered by the wisdom (or *logos*, or word) of God. The well-known passages of John 1, Colossians 1.15–17 and Ephesians 1 work this out explicitly. Finally, one should mention that this is not a static vision of the world. The experience of the Spirit as indwelling in the world means that there is a hope for the transfiguration of the world. The presence of the Spirit leads to new ways in which the divine energy quickens the reality of creation.

This trinitarian vision of creation gives us the key to interpreting the values and aspirations expressed in the preceding pages. It is a trinitarian vision since the world is created by the Father to be the object of his love and desire; it is ordered by the Son in terms of an inner coherence and moral value, where the glory of God is expressed in the fulfilment of human beings; and it is transfigured through the Holy Spirit.

If the world can be seen as the creation and dwelling-place of God, what values might be expressed which would be in harmony with this vision of order and transformation? One such value might be that of freedom. Another might be that of creativity. A third would be found in new forms of relationship. All of these have been expressed by those interviewed in this chapter, although there may not be the same understanding of these terms as Christian theology would suggest. Discerning whether or not new cultural changes can be seen as relating to God's ordering and renewal of creation requires critical investigation.

The nature of freedom, creativity and relationships expressed in the Christian faith can be spelled out fairly clearly. The recent papal encyclical, *Centesimus Annus* issued in 1991, spells out a Christian conception of freedom, which consists of 'entering into that relationship of solidarity and communion with others for which God created him. Indeed, it is through the free gift of self that man truly finds himself'.[25] Freedom is thus an integral part of community, leading to groups who relate together in new ways. Moltmann points out how Christian freedom involves mutual recognition and respect for others, whereby the other person is not seen as the limitation of my freedom but the expansion of it.[26]

Freedom in relationship to community encompasses both new forms of social order and new expressions of personal meaning. Freedom can also be related to creativity, where the future is seen as the search for new possibilities. This is not a humanist programme, because the activity of God lies in liberating men and women from captivity to what constrains them by the action of Christ. Galatians 5.1 expresses the rule of the Son 'through the freedom for which he has made us free'.

Freedom, community and creativity are thus all interrelated in a Christian understanding of the world. It is this that makes it possible to speak of the world as having a coherence and order given to it by God, although this is not a static coherence. Therefore the organic, hierarchical view of civil society that characterized much Roman Catholic and Anglican thinking earlier in this century must be repudiated. This led, especially in Roman Catholic thought, to a reluctance to accept basic freedoms and democracy. Freedom was seen as too individualist, and corrosive of the community.[27]

However, the activity of God in creation is not one that preserves order at all costs. Instead, the presence of God in creation is one in which relationships are formed through a struggle to respond to God and fellow human beings. The biblical account, especially in the story of Israel in exile, is one of conflict and disagreement, where the future goal was not clearly perceived. Struggle and uncertainty marked every step.

There is then a conflict between preoccupation with personal gain, and the nature of divine activity. God's own self-giving is not concerned with self-preservation. 'He who did not spare his only son but gave him up for us all, will he not also give us all things with him?' (Romans 8.32.) There is a close connection between the divine self-giving in Christ, and the gift of salvation, freedom and new life. Contrasted with this is the person who hoards possessions, as in Luke 12.15, 'A person's life does not consist in the abundance of possessions.' The search for fulfilment through possessions is a form of self-destruction, in which loneliness is the final result.

Jeremy Paxman's book *Friends in High Places* is a vivid account of how the values of the Old English Establishment have been subverted by greed and the search for greater wealth. He is especially critical of the way in which private education appears in many cases to have abandoned the search for coherent values. While this is certainly not the case in every school, Paxman makes a telling case, contrasting the old values of the City of London with the frenzied activities of recent years. The biblical story of the landowner building larger and larger barns is ultimately a story of folly. The real values lie in aspiring to the values that have run through this chapter – a proper freedom, creativity and the search for community.

D.W. Hardy points out that 'the relationality of God is not an inert relationality, whose character is established once and for all. It is always a dynamic relationality, comprised of a social dynamic'. God does not simply see, know, love, or judge. The problem with this view is clear: God retains his independence. Instead, 'God expresses his own well-being by forming the well-being of his people, and by acting to maintain that the social practices of his people are orientated to him.'[28] The inner life of God is his relationality. The movement of this to human beings gives the very possibility of new patterns of social behaviour. God's being then is one that seeks relationships, and brings human beings to fulfilment.

Paxman's book shows how the Old Establishment centred on Oxford and Cambridge, the armed services, the aristocracy and the professions embodied a paternalist sense of responsibility for those lower down the social order. As the Establishment was fundamentally changed in the last decade, some new values were sought. He describes new developments in education, industry and the professions. This chapter has also sought to give some description of this change. Nevertheless, there has also been a relentless search for greater wealth, for its own sake.

The theological critique of this change has often been expressed by leaders in the Anglican Church. Archbishop Runcie was not in fact especially critical of Thatcherite policies. Runcie supported the development of a greatly enlarged voluntary sector. As Adrian Hastings says in his recent biography of Runcie, the Archbishop of Canterbury argued that 'humanity and the churches need to share freely, locally and in as individual a way as possible in the case of those who require special assistance. He is far more deeply a suitably responsible primate for Thatcherite Britain than a critic of Thatcher's policies'.[29] What Runcie attacked repeatedly was the idea that wealth was the sole aim of economic life, and the belief that economic prosperity carried no responsibility for those less fortunate. Developments such as Business in the Community, where industry accepted a role in regenerating inner-city areas alongside local and central government, were supported strongly by Runcie. Criticism was offered of those who pursued wealth for its own sake.

Consuming and possessing without limit can be seen as a form of pathology. We are all subject to a lack of time, resources and energy. This results in the fundamental scarcity of human life. Possessions can give a false sense of security against such anxiety, if they are taken on their own terms. The alternative to this is the sense of well-being that comes from a recognition of God's self-abundance. It offers a far more satisfying option that can respond to the fundamental scarcity of human life.[30]

How then might we evaluate the interviews and stories of the preceding pages? Their concrete nature stands in sharp contrast to the theoretical reflections that follow them. The trinitarian argument shows that the creation of value and its holding together is part of the work of Christ (to unite all things in him, things in heaven and on earth – a spirit of wisdom and of revelation in the knowledge of him: Ephesians 1.10 and 18). Such values are many, but include freedom, community and creativity. The second part of Chapter 7 is entirely devoted to elucidating this theme further, but it should be said now that all three are interrelated. Freedom involves 'not only choice but access to material and social conditions, freedom from domination, and a conception of the realization of projects, the cultivation of capacities, and the formation of character over time'.[32] Individuals are social beings, where reciprocity entails respect and concern by each person for the other's aims as having value in their own right. This raises the question of values and the social order, which will be taken up in the next few pages. Freedom, creativity and community form a whole, embodied in countless small firms and community groups visited on this project. A second point to be made is that this coherence is neither static nor free of conflict. Many small firms are anything but stable or peaceful organizations, and this sense of creative but potentially destructive chaos is familiar in many descriptions of entrepreneurs. There is also a conflict with other bodies. Most memorably, Whale Tankers invited a government minister to unveil a plaque on a new extension which commemorated a decade of local government interference with the company! Many other managers expressed similar struggles with the parent company, banks and government bodies. Internally there were companies where an autocratic owner/manager was confronted by workers seeking recognition.

A third point of significance is the ambiguity in many of these interviews about greater wealth. Paxman expressed it as Tom Brown's Porsche-Days. It would be naïve to deny that some entrepreneurs are not going to become very wealthy. The question is whether this is the primary aim of their activities, and what values are displaced as a result. Frank Grunfield's 'green ethic' stands at one pole; at the other there were those who wanted as much wealth as possible. Affirming enterprise will certainly lead to greater social and economic inequality. Nevertheless, a Christian vision will also be about affirming those without wealth, or even without work. The tension between these two options is a real one, and the pursuit of wealth must always be related to the common good of society. The theological reflection on the search for unlimited wealth concluded that this was a sophisticated form of pathology.

These reflections on values in community, conflict and dynamic existence and the pathology of unlimited wealth are a theological means of describing the trinitarian presence of God in the world, and of establishing theological interaction with the world. Theology cannot be limited to supporting new initiatives – whether as community ventures from the Left, or economic initiatives, usually from the Right. There needs to be a normative role for theology. However, I agree with John Atherton when he argues that it is impossible to move directly from the Bible, or doctrine, to detailed guidelines for living. Although I have used Jurgen Moltmann as the starting-point of these reflections, it is necessary to attend to the 'whole great sphere of life which lies between basic ideals and detailed practices'.[33]

The linkage between theological language about God and the analysis of the situation is one that has occupied the attention of many theologians in recent years. Wogaman, in *Economics and Ethics: A Christian Inquiry*,[34] speaks of theological entry points where such concepts as vocation, stewardship, grace and creation offer a theological perspective. While this is good, the problem is that the concepts remain rather idealized and static. There is little sense of God's present action in the world, nor of a trinitarian understanding of it. It is true that Wogaman speaks of grace as God's gift, but the dynamic sense of this term is not brought out. Grace is certainly important in economic justice as a reason for rejecting the idea that 'people should simply get what they "deserve," nothing more, nothing less.'[35] What is needed is the awareness that the recognition of God's presence may bring about a new human orientation, which is not denied even where there is misdirection. 'It is simply that the dynamic order which God has introduced into the human relation with him remains itself even where the eyes of human beings are diverted to lesser (and more controllable) substitutes; and, remaining itself it brings the possibility of ... recognition and reorientation.'[36] While Wogaman talks of the interaction of God and the human community, the emphasis is on theological ideas or concepts: 'the core meanings of faith', in Wogaman's terms. I have instead tried to argue for an understanding of Christianity not in terms of ideas or concepts, but of values that are sustained in the world by the gracious activity of God. These values do not of themselves generate any worked-out implications for society, and are both conflictual and dynamic. They therefore preclude any easy transition from belief to social pronouncements about contemporary issues.

If the argument was to be pressed further, there would be a need to see how the social analysis given by a particular institution could be related to this awareness of the sustaining activity of God. At this point I would argue in the same way as Atherton, Preston and others. 'The interaction between beliefs and situation' can generate 'middle-range imperatives for social involvement.'[37] These are not detailed policy options – *Faith in the City* concentrated upon these. Atherton points out the weakness of this approach, for it failed to distinguish between middle-range imperatives and policy options. Detailed options gave the impression of placing the report on one side of the political arena only.

This is a caution for this analysis as well. If *Faith in the City* 'disenfranchised conservatives of the social markets kind', in Atherton's words, there would be no gain either in writing a report on small businesses which only appealed to the political Right. I was repeatedly struck by how diverse the values of those who run small businesses were. It is also important to re-emphasize that the concept of enterprise goes beyond small firms. It includes education, community ventures, and will undoubtedly spread through the public sector.

Ethical reflections are discussed in Chapter 6. I would plead the tentative nature of this discussion, which does not reach the stage of middle-range moral imperatives described by Atherton. There is a clear reason for this. So far as I know, there has been no previous work on this subject from the Churches, or indeed many surveys of the 'enterprise culture' at all. Chapter 6 thus raises some of the ethical issues that would need to be discussed. A further linkage of these to the Christian faith would be necessary for such imperatives to be worked out. That is a task that is important, and one that I hope to work out in a forthcoming book on business ethics. It would take too long to work out here.

In conclusion, the values expressed in small firms are not inimical to Christianity, and may well resonate with them. This is of course an enormous generalization, but I would justify my claim on the basis of visits to some thirty firms across England, and discussion with another two dozen individuals involved in promoting or writing about this area. I have also read widely in the social and economic literature. Vernon Smith's comment was significant. 'Enterprise is not the same as the creation of small businesses ... It is a quality, activity or project which is found in a culture.' Innovation, creativity, sensitivity to those one interacts with, risk-taking and a search for responsible freedom are all facets of enterprise. In turn, this can be related back to the dynamic sustaining of values by the work of God in Christ.

Notes

1. P. Riddell, *The Thatcher Decade*, 1989.
2. ibid., pp. 74 and 86.
3. W. Rees-Mogg, *The Independent*, 8 July 1991.
4. Interview, 20 June 1990, Whale Tankers, Ravenshaw Lane, Solihull.
5. Interview, 24 January 1990, thanks to the industrial chaplain, Rev. Noel Beattie (who had an excellent relationship with the firm), United Engineering, 49 Beevor Street, Lincoln.
6. Interview, 22 January 1990, via the industrial chaplain, Rev. Ray Owen, Harkers Engineering, Church Road, Stockton. As in the previous note, Rev. Owen's links with Harkers were close.
7. P. Lawrence, *Invitation to Management*, 1986, p. 87.
8. J. Bevan and J. Jay, *The New Tycoons*, 1989, ch. 10: Alan Sugar, pp. 177–95.
9. M. Casson, *The Entrepreneur*, 1982, pp. 391–2 (and the section on 'Schumpeter on Innovation', pp. 373–6).
10. Interview, 16 November 1989, University of Warwick Science Park.
11. Interview, 22 March 1990, University of Warwick Science Park.
12. Interview, 31 January 1990, Domino, Bar Hill, Cambridge.
13. Interview, 17 January 1990, Korda, Farringdon Lane, London EC1.
14. Rover Group, interview with John Briffett, 25 January 1990. British Steel, interview with Trevor MacDonald, member of project support group, 8 November 1989; and many subsequent meetings and written comments.
    British Steel (Industry), interview with Vernon Smith and John

Northcott, 8 November 1989. See also the account of their work in P. Usher, *Putting Something Back*, 1989.

Property Services Agency, interview with Patrick Brown, 15 May 1990.

Driver and Vehicle Licensing Agency, interview with Stephen Curtis, 19 June 1990.

TMI, interview with Roy Brighton, 22 March 1990.

TEC, interview with David Scrimshire, 16 November 1989.

Full Employment UK Ltd, interview with Peter Ashby, 1 February 1990.

Sue Birley, interview, 1 March 1990.

Charles Handy, interview, 8 February 1990.

Patrick Coldstream (Council for Industry and Higher Education), interview, 18 January 1990.

15. P. Coldstream, *Higher Education, Industry and the Journey of Learning*, 1991.

16. Interview, 11 December 1989, via Rev. Ray Owen, Silver Street, St Hilda's, Middlesbrough.

17. Interview, 11 December 1989.

18. Interview, 22 January 1990, Cowpen Lane Industrial Estate, Billingham, Cleveland.

19. Interview, 22 December 1989, Vanguard Suite, Broadcasting House, Middlesbrough.

20. Interview, 11 December 1989, Vanguard Suite, Broadcasting House, Middlesbrough.

21. Interview, 11 December 1989, PO Box no. 25, South Bank Business Centre, Middlesbrough.

22. Interview, 24 January 1990.

23. Interview with Graham Nielsen, 9 March 1990, Thermica, Chamberlain Road, Stoneferry, Hull.

24. J. Moltmann, *The Trinity and the Kingdom of God*, 1981, p. 99.

25. *Centesimus Annus*, 1991, p. 41.

26. Moltmann, p. 216.

27. C. Curran, 'A Century of Catholic Social Teaching', *Theology Today*, July 1991.

28. D.W. Hardy, *The Foundation of Cognition and Ethics in Worship*, 1991.

29. A. Hastings, *Robert Runcie*, 1991.

30. M.D. Meeks, *God the Economist*, 1989, p. 176.

32. C. Gould, *Rethinking Democracy*, 1988, p. 53.

33. J. Atherton, *Faith in the Nation*, 1988, pp. 133–45.

34. J.P. Wogaman, *Economics and Ethics: A Christian Inquiry*, 1986, pp. 34–5.

35. ibid., pp. 34–5.

36. Hardy, p. 23.

37. Atherton, pp. 142–3.

3

Enterprise Beyond Industry

This chapter will examine two aspects of enterprise beyond small firms. Both developed greatly in the last decade. One is the realm of enterprise in education. The other is community enterprise. Neither aim at producing self-sustaining profitable ventures. However, both use the qualities of enterprise (innovation, risk, persuasion, self-reliance, wealth-creation) as ways of developing the skills of those who participate in the particular venture. Finally, there is now a growing literature developing around both areas. Two examples should be mentioned in particular. One is Linking-Up, the Church of England's response to the collapse of employment in the inner cities. This initiative, put together by Chris Beales and John Atherton, was funded by the Department of Trade and Industry, private bodies and the Church of England. The other is the work of the Enterprise in Education unit of the Durham University Business School, which now writes educational programs for countries as diverse as Bangladesh and Hungary. It was developed out of the British Steel (Industry) plan to revive both job prospects and the culture of enterprise in former and existing steel towns.

The influence of culture

There are many aspects of community enterprise. In one sense enterprise is not a technical term at all. If a local community takes initiatives, and lives by change, 'wheeling and dealing', then it has enterprise. Dick Hobbs's wonderful study of East London, entitled *Doing the Business*, is subtitled 'Entrepreneurship, The Working Class and Detectives in the East End of London'. It is dedicated to his family, 'to those too expensive for wages. To skulduggery'. There is a very serious point here. Hobbs's story is of a community that will not die. Despite the collapse of the docks, and well beyond the redevelopment of Docklands geographically, the East End of

London survives by change and exploiting whatever is there. 'Denizens of East London, by virtue of their action being ascribed to a common culture, can be understood in terms of their use of an essentially entrepreneurial inheritance ... Entrepreneurship emerges as the core characteristic of East End Culture.'[1] It might be small firms, criminal behaviour, educational advance or community organizing.

The contrast with many other areas is striking. Peter Dodd's research for his project was published as *The Influence of Culture upon Enterprise*.[2] He examined the Black Country, Southampton and Tyneside. He notes how much the culture of Tyneside is hostile to entrepreneurial activity. Partly this was because of the feudal feel of great industries like Armstrongs, which employed 26,000 in 1914, and was very hierarchical. Partly it was because there were few small firms, and the whole culture of the North-East was conservative. Only young people in the North-East are able to escape from the spell, and to consider self-employment. Even there, a survey for Livewire on young entrepreneurs nationally by Project North-East found in 1979 that the voting intention of those in the North was twice as likely to be for the Labour Party as in the South (25 per cent North; 10 per cent South). This is not so much a deep commitment to socialism, but a reflection of the culture's conservatism. Equally, the growth rate of small firms in the North-East is much lower there than elsewhere, despite a strong network of agencies.[3]

Community enterprise

Community enterprise is a form of community development that has flourished in the 1980s, both outside and inside the churches, especially after the publication in 1985 of the report *Faith in the City*. Community enterprise is defined as 'an organisation with social as well as commercial aims and objectives and is owned and controlled by people who live in a defined locality or who share other forms of community interest'.[4] It can own and develop community resources such as land, buildings and machinery. Alternatively, it can be a financial service providing revolving loans within a community and attracting outside capital. It has particularly spread in the inner urban areas of the United States, as an attempt to halt urban decay where the problems are too great for one individual to overcome. In any case, there are great benefits for a community in working together rather than relying on working for an individual. In Britain the churches have particularly developed this work through the William Temple Foundation in Manchester.[5] John Atherton, originally from the William Temple Foundation, then helped to create a national scheme for the churches called Linking-Up. Outside the churches, there has been a particular interest in housing development, especially in Glasgow. Linking-Up has worked in many areas, such as a community cafe, taxi service, recycling waste paper, training and credit unions. Its main role is not to undertake these ventures, but to support the development of ideas and initiatives by consultancy work.

Three interviews with people are given below. Each reflects a different aspect of community enterprise. In one way or another, all are part of the Church's work in the community enterprise.

Derek Seber[6] is an Anglican clergyman who works for Linking-Up. Using a theology of mission that interprets mission as including bringing about social change, he interprets Jesus's speech in Luke 4 as being about sight to the blind in terms of community empowerment. He assists those working to organize communities by showing where funding and training is available. Beyond the work of setting up community structures, Derek Seber seeks not to work on behalf of others, but alongside them. He argued as follows:

> Church Urban Fund is too ... much concerned with outreach. It isn't community development with the poor.... Yet the local church could be significant in our common life: in local areas, it meets weekly, with a good turnout and can be representative of the community. Indeed there is a Marxist revival of interest in grassroots religion now.... Local churches thus are playing a role in this process in Britain ... and Linking-Up assists churches in economic development. It is there to generate income in a local community and to prevent outflow: community businesses and enterprises; credit unions, etc. All this exists in the hope that other questions will be raised thereafter, for those involved in the process (questions of power, ultimate decisions, etc.).

David Everett,[7] another Anglican clergyman, also worked for Linking-Up. He began to help people set up their own businesses, without government aid or Church support, instead of them being unemployed. His work now involves building credit unions, creating ethnic employment with Somali groups, as well as language teaching, and identifying tenant groups who could start and run their own community enterprises. He also assists with the Bridge Project, which has many small starter-workshops in craft design, and has a turnover of £300,000 a year. The work with the Somali community involves dialogue with Muslims as well. David said:

> We are all agreed in Linking-Up on the need to educate churches to the changing economic realities in which they have to operate.... Either you have to generate income yourself, or it may mean you go down the road of contracting for services. The churches still have a grant-aided mentality ... not surviving in the harsh reality of the commercial world – this goes back to attitudes to wealth-creation. With my 'green' hat on, I am interested in small-scale initiatives.

Steve Charters[8] managed the Bridge Project. Examples of his work include a Somali restaurant, a printing press run by the mentally handicapped using equipment surplus to the local authority, and small craft-based activities. Steve commented:

> Our philosophy is to work with the very disadvantaged.... Control of one's future, ownership, participation at work are the key issues. Look at Liverpool housing co-operatives or Scottish community businesses – people working for themselves. The vision is that of guild socialism from the last century, and people co-operating with each other. In religious terms, I link the priesthood of all believers with the idea of self-reliance. The problems are both a shortage of resources, and how hidebound some local authorities (and central government) are.

Theology and society

The difficulty of relating a Christian ethical vision to the work of community groups and community work is that the task seems to be uncontained. While it is possible to write about social transformation, and the participation of those without work or status in society, in terms that speak of their liberation from the forces of evil and oppression, there is a real sense in which the ongoing task presses upon one. Michael Keeling puts the point well in his recent survey of Christian ethics:

> In the twentieth century we have taken the enormous step of letting the whole social context become the agenda for Christian action.... Yet it has now become clear that science and technology are incapable of producing a lasting moral vision.... For moral vision arises from the intuitive and poetic capability of the human spirit, of which religion is also a part. In the next century there must be a new moral vision, this time for all humanity.[9]

Both those involved in reshaping education and in community activities are seeking precisely that new moral vision which involves a vision of the whole. Keeling points to the paradox that science and technology enlarged enormously our conception of human possibilities, while at the same time proving incapable of generating a lasting moral vision.

No individual can live well without the sustaining structures of a community; in fact, they can barely live at all without these supporting institutions. That is why there is such a thing as society. Hence traditional moral argument has claimed that the good of the nation, or the common good, is greater than the individual happiness of one person. As a result, individuals have been asked to sacrifice money, time, even life itself, for the good of the community.[10]

Such an argument is not easy to sustain today. The common good is not easily ascertained in a pluralist society, although there have been attempts to re-establish it. More cogently, the common good is related to justice. Justice is about the flourishing and well-being of all its members in fundamental ways.[11] As Jean Porter says, any community that 'allows some of its members to sacrifice the well-being of others to their private interests with impunity, forfeits its claim on the allegiance of its members'.[12]

It is commonly held by many community groups that the well-being of the poorest groups in our society has been sacrificed on behalf of others. It is also the case that many of the sustaining structures have broken down, and there is little sense of tradition at all. All this means that it is difficult to have confidence in any vision, let alone a vision of the whole. Keeling is right to suggest that this is one of the crucial issues for the next century.

Human flourishing demands a sense of hope. The importance of community groups is that they can fill the place
of sustaining institutions, and provide a communal resource
while new institutions emerge. That will be a long and painful
process. Community groups increasingly act in ways that
recognize the reality of the market-place, and yet provide
hope. The alternative is an ever-pervasive nostalgia for the
good old days. The Christian contribution to this difficult
period in urban regeneration is both to draw on its own
resources of hope, while recognizing and blessing such secular
examples of hope as may exist in the city:

> Human beings have always been tempted by nostalgia.... But
> God leads his people forward. The future is always unknown and
> therefore potentially frightening.... But to be afraid of the future
> is to choose death. The faith which springs from the resurrection
> of the crucified Jesus gives birth to a confident hope which no
> disappointment can deny.[13]

Enterprise and education

The relationship between enterprise and education is very
broad. I was helped greatly by three people who put the
whole matter in context for me. Patrick Coldstream, Director
of the Council for Industry and Higher Education, charted
the relationship between these two areas of society in recent
years.[14] Judi Cotton is the co-ordinator at the Enterprise Education Unit, Durham University Business School.[15] Finally, the
Reverend Ray Owen was for ten years an industrial chaplain
on Teesside. As well as his work with small firms, mentioned
in the previous chapter, he has also worked a great deal to
promote enterprise in education.

It is important to say what this concept involves. There
are two elements, which are interconnected. One is the
question of enterprise in the curriculum, an aspect that has
been especially promoted by British Steel (Industry); Durham
University Business School (DUBS) project developed out
of this. The other is more controversial, and concerns the
enterprising nature of the school in its management. Judi
Cotton emphasized to me that while she approved highly of
local management in schools, she did not feel that opting out
of the state system was a helpful development. Criticism of

opting out as a policy for schools has come from the National Society, which is a voluntary body which works in close connection with the General Synod Board of Education of the Church of England. They argue theologically that the moral issues that surround 'the type of ethos they want to maintain in the school community' are based on Christian principles. Such principles include altruistic service to those around it, this being a true reflection of the service of Christ, and growth in the knowledge of God. The booklet *Free to Choose?* puts the question of the enterprise culture in terms of 'supping with the Devil', and associates the question of enterprise in the curriculum with the growth of City Technology courses.[16]

Yet the defence of enterprise in education offered by those from British Steel (Industry) and elsewhere would be far more positive. Sue Birley, a professor first at Cranfield and then at Imperial College, who also runs her own consultancy company, said that schools were the reason why enterprise was such a difficult concept in Britain.[17] She said, 'The other cultural constraint on enterprise is the dependency and failure built into our culture. Schools insist that you ... take no responsibility for oneself. Failures should be encouraged, not punished. Instead you should be enterprising wherever you are. Young people are more interesting these days – they are into politics, caring for things.' She instanced Livewire for young entrepreneurs, and many pressure groups concerned with the environment, world poverty, etc. Her definition of enterprise was simple: 'creativity; doing things in a new way; responding to different options which become open to you'.

The DUBS model has involved 90 per cent of secondary schools and colleges of further education in the North-East, and has now moved into primary schools. A partnership between the private sector (British Steel (Industry), National Westminster Bank, Marks & Spencer), government and the university has allowed the Enterprise Scheme to be launched. It is not simply a matter of planning how to set up a business. In fact, this subject-based approach – looking at accounts, marketing etc. – is probably unhelpful. A second approach, which is less common, concentrates on process: building creativity, problem-solving, decision-making. DUBS uses this, but changes it somewhat. There is an objective, which might range from designing a guided tour around a historic site to setting up a school newspaper. 'Enterprise' is involved in bringing out overlapping managerial, technical and enterprise skills.

Yet this model does not affect children only. Since it is designed by teachers, and evaluated by them, it can become part of pupils' personal development programmes. As one evaluation put it:

> The success or otherwise of a child's participation is not related to the bottom line of the business he or she has helped to set up. It is rather a measure of the personal development he or she has undergone, and which will be of help with problems they will face after school.[18]

As I listened to educationalists talking about this objective in education, I remembered the Anglican chaplain to the Chinese community around St Martin's-in-the-Fields, London, speaking of Chinese culture: 'It results in a strict view of work. It is best to work for oneself. Independence matters, not making wealth.' The Reverend G. Lee was critical of this philosophy in its purest form: it led to little co-operation, and he made a link between the complete commitment to independence and the problem of finding help if a business fails. He was often involved in counselling because restaurant owners would never share difficulties with one another. He noticed how younger Chinese, brought up and educated in London, found it easier to work for Western firms, and achieve professional skills. It was as if two completely separate cultures were both changing very painfully. In the North-East, teachers were struggling to instil new qualities in their pupils: 'self-awareness, understanding, care', and achieving 'the best possible goals in their own life .... It had become apparent that one of the factors holding up economic regeneration in the North-East was the need for no less than a cultural change among young people.'[19] In London, the Chinese community was atomized into total families, or clans. It was a disgrace to receive benefits, and the only true value was in working for oneself, and then for one's family. Working for other Chinese, still less for Westerners, was not admirable. The constant need to challenge oneself, as in gambling or expanding a business too fast, meant that the Christian concept of work as related to service was alien. Yet this traditional Chinese understanding of self-reliance was also breaking down, and seeking ways of self-expression that put less premium on independence as the cardinal virtue.

Finally, some mention must be made of local management of schools. (There is also substantial work now on enterprise and higher education, omitted for brevity.) Local management of schools, as the *Financial Times* put it, 'requires heads to change their role totally; they will have to learn even faster than their pupils. It means they will have to take on far more administrative responsibility.'[20] The problem is quite obvious: there is far less time for directing the school by the headteacher. This in turn requires much more delegation by headteachers. The *Financial Times* survey found staff were consulted far more, and the environment became much more open. One head made the point forcefully:

> We're starting from a base where people are just not used to the environment of decision-making. If someone is going to take on this extra work and responsibility there should be some comeback and feeling of achievement, but if one is in a situation where the LEA is constantly looking to save money, that's demoralising.

If enterprise in schools, either in the curriculum or in the running of the school, is simply a way of installing the need to grow as many small businesses as possible, it will defeat itself. Equally if local management of schools becomes a management strategy which ensures that schools are situated in affluent areas, are in competition for resources with schools in deprived areas, or ensures that educational budgets are reduced, then this initiative will also fail. These are the dangers of changing a centralized approach, with a curriculum that did not emphasize the achievements teamwork could bring, into something much more flexible. The opportunity, however, should not be missed. Patrick Coldstream put the choice like this:

> It has been common for inspiring thinkers about education ... to use metaphors for teaching which are to do with initiating learners into their inheritance.... But the proper possession of the inheritance gives autonomy to people.... It seems to me that our students are to lead lives which will present them with an unprecedently rich and rapid series of changes and choices ... [we need to] lay emphasis on education not only as initiating learners into an inheritance but also as equipping them ... to

make choices confidently on good information and so to create their own future.[21]

Notes

1. D. Hobbs, *Doing the Business*, 1988, pp. 181–2.
2. Industrial Christian Fellowship Theme Pamphlet no. 44, September 1990.
3. Project North-East, *Young Entrepreneurs Report*, June 1989, p. 13.
4. F. Spreeckley, *Developing Community Enterprise*, 1989, p. 2.
5. I am grateful to Tony Addy of William Temple Foundation and Paul Bagshaw in Sheffield for very helpful interviews on their work.
6. Interview, 21 May 1990, Linking-Up Offices, Manchester.
7. Interview, 4 June 1990, Linking-Up/Church Action with the Unemployed Offices, Bethnal Green, London.
8. Interview, 11 June 1990, Bridge Project, Bethnal Green, London.
9. M. Keeling, *The Foundation of Christian Ethics*, 1990, p. 235.
10. J. Porter, *The Recovery of Virtue: The Relevance of Aquinas for Christian Ethics*, 1991.
11. B. Jordan, *The Common Good*, 1989; J. Atherton, *Faith in the Nation*, 1988, pp. 31–47.
12. Porter, p. 177.
13. *Faith in the City of Birmingham*, 1988, para 6:39, p. 129.
14. Interview, 11 January 1990.
15. Interview, 20 May 1991.
16. C. Alves, *Free to Choose? The Voluntary Principle at Work in Education*, 1991.
17. Interview, 1 March 1990.
18. J. Cotton, *Enterprise/Education/Experience*, 1990; interview with Rev. G. Lee, 7 December 1990, London.
19. Harrison, pp. 1–2.
20. 'Local Management in Schools', *Financial Times*, 4 June 1990, p. 10.
21. P. Coldstream, *Higher Education, Industry and the Journey of Learning*, 1991, p. 14.

4

Ethnic Enterprise

One area that changed a great deal in the 1980s was that of
ethnic enterprise. The stereotype is, of course, the familiar
one of Asian shopkeepers who work for long hours and
succeed where others have failed. An alternative stereotype
is that of the highly successful Asian millionaire, portrayed
in *My Beautiful Launderette* and other films of the 1980s. The
reality is a great deal more complex. Ethnic enterprise is
interwoven with racial discrimination and it often makes
little sense out of that context, except in a few cases.
It is also a phenomenon that has increasingly gathered
attention. Rather late in the day, in 1990, the British Council
of Churches Community and Race Relations Unit held a
residential consultation on the 'Economic Empowerment of
the Black Community'. There had been earlier initiatives,
however; in 1988 Fullemploy held a conference on Black
Business Development, attended by government ministers,
academics, trade unionists and businesspeople. Fullemploy
itself was founded to promote ethnic enterprise, and it
established a reputation in the training field. Finally, there
have been a number of academic studies, especially the 1984
collection of essays edited by Ward and Jenkins.

Ethnic communities in business

A typical example of ethnic enterprise that flourished in the
1980s was that of Hansib Publishing. Hansib is run by Arif
Ali, and publishes two of the leading black newspapers, *The
Caribbean Times* and *Asian Times*, as well as many educational
and reference books. The interview that I had with him
at his office in June 1990 represents the viewpoint of a
successful entrepreneur, and one who is also very involved
in society:

Black people have started their own businesses in recent years, and we have pushed this.... In the 1960s only a few were working in small businesses ... now it's much more common. As a publishing business we have assisted people into self-employment.... The publishing business also acts as a teaching school – we take people on for a while, give them confidence, and they move elsewhere.... Society is the problem – we have been given opportunities in this country, but not as much as we'd have liked.... Black businesses do keep their links in the black community.... I'm hopeful about the future, although we need tougher government action on racist attacks and job discrimination.... Businesses enable people to gain self-respect and get into the mainstream. The churches can also help to open up society.

It is interesting that Hansib has not become a co-operative. Arif Ali had been one of the founders of the co-operative movement in Guyana, and tried to find work with one in Britain. Rejected because of his race, he nevertheless founded his own co-operative. However, this venture also failed, and he established the publishing company as a conventional business. The company, as demonstrated in the extract, acts as a training ground for young people seeking to break into the labour market. It thus has a social purpose beyond itself.

Most Asian and Afro-Caribbean firms started out as small traders and middlemen, either on market stalls or in cottage industries. Nearly all started from scratch, 'building up sales volume very slowly over many years'.[1] However, such traders had a considerable advantage in knowing their own home market, although the majority did not venture beyond that base. Shortage of finance was not a problem: for Asians particularly, their families in their country of origin were able to help. Afro-Caribbean firms tended to look to partners for help. Both were unique in hardly using government help at all. Many had not heard of the government's schemes – it is a striking example of how separate government promotion of an enterprise culture can be from the grassroots. Also, the gulf between government provision and cultural reality is shown in the motives of those who had started their own business. Unlike the average immigrant from their country, they had not come to Britain to look for a manual or skilled job. They had emigrated hoping to study in higher education, to escape political regimes, or to start their own businesses.[3] However, few became graduates, and fewer still made a career of higher education: instead, the generation that came to Britain in the 1950s and 1960s became owners of small businesses.[2] Higher education, even if in theory committed to improving admission rates for minority groups, remained inaccessible for most immigrants. Their talents went into starting businesses instead.

Many Asian shopowners have long working hours, poor conditions and small economic rewards. It is certainly not the case that these factors are willingly accepted. They are tolerated because of the moral demands of religion or family values: it is not good to be dependent on another section of society. There are also problems in finding jobs anywhere else: racial discrimination in the labour market is well documented. So there continues to be very high rates of formation in retailing firms among the Asian community: up to 22 per cent in 1984, with a 12 per cent failure rate of all firms. Competition is severe, and the majority of small shops are located in inner-city areas. Obviously these are not places that are growing in wealth. So from this point of view, Asian shops are trapped into greater competition among themselves in the independent retail sector.[4] 'The burdensome hours, high levels of family assistance and other manifestations of commitment so frequently noted are as likely to be indicators of a vain struggle for survival as the basis of ultimate success.'[5]

As the 1980s proceeded, some of the scepticism among academic researchers about small business growth for ethnic minority groups receded somewhat. It is fair to say that this suspicion was a reaction to the rags-to-riches stories of Asian shopkeepers in the popular and quality press, and that there certainly was a much tougher side than many of the journalists allowed. There was also an awareness in academic studies that the Pakistani ethos was like the 'Protestant work ethic': self-sacrifice, self-denial and an emphasis on hard work and saving.[6] The culture of entrepreneurship was regarded as deeply ambiguous: was it an example of self-help, or a sign that Asians could not survive in the wider society? Would it not be better, argued many reserachers, if individual enterprise was transformed into a community venture, or if the talents of entrepreneurs were employed in more conventional career patterns?

Nevertheless, the late 1980s saw an increased interest in ethnic entrepreneurship, moving away from the retail stereotype. Four examples can be cited: Fullemploy, Evangelical Enterprise, the British Council of Churches conference, and the Asian panel of the Prince's Youth Business Trust. They represent the very diverse world of ethnic enterprise in the 1990s.

Ethnic community enterprise

The British Council of Churches conference drew together many black organizations in Britain, and black US Church leaders.[7] It began with the high unemployment rate among black people in Britain: the rate for Afro-Caribbean men was twice that of white men in 1965, with the Asian figures being worse still. Black people are concentrated in semi-skilled and unskilled jobs, and tend to work in low-paid industries such as hotels and catering. There was a particular problem among black women. The British Council of Churches conference was critical of the path of individual enterprise, arguing instead for more equal employment opportunity policies, and contract compliance policies. In this area, public bodies, including government, would only consider tenders from private firms if they implemented such policies. They especially advocated the development of community enterprise, imitating examples in the United States, in housing and community retail stores. An interview with the Reverend David Haslam, one of the staff on the Community and Race Relations Unit of (what was then called) the British Council of Churches, put the point clearly:

> We decided not to go for individual entrepreneurship ... it reflects an individualistic model which is unattractive. Instead we decided to go for a community approach. The economic empowerment of the black community will give them a basis to fight the many discriminatory features of British society.... [In the USA] the churches provide training; low-interest loans; housing; a commitment to community wealth-creation. Some businesses are co-operatives, but they are even more difficult to work in the USA than in Britain. As well as wealth-creation, US churches also chase companies on employment policies. A second

area where US churches work is the Project Equality programme. They publish a buyers guide for the churches, and list firms with bad practices. Churches there act as consumers and shareholders. It opens up the whole area of business ethics. We hope in five years time to have black-controlled training programmes, and black pressure on businesses.

Other groups, such as Evangelical Enterprise, have moved much closer to working with the government. Evangelical Enterprise is a partnership between the West Indian Evangelical Alliance and the Evangelical Alliance. Other evangelicals, such as the Evangelical Coalition for Urban Mission, have been much more critical.

The largest example of black-led training programmes was Fullemploy.[8] It had a high profile in the 1980s, although it finally closed after a lengthy financial crisis in 1990–2. Linbert Spencer, the chief executive in 1990, emphasized the commitment to training, with over 1,000 government-funded places. It trained people for employment and self-employment, and also acted as a consultancy to major employers such as banks, high street stores, and the BBC. Linbert Spencer did not feel that the Asian shopkeeper working long hours for low wages offered much of a model to follow. Asians needed to break into new markets, and Afro-Caribbeans needed capital. He also stressed the need for local authorities to place orders with black companies. However, an even more basic need is to increase the skills of the workforce, and to ensure that racial prejudice does not prevent the employment of those who are qualified. Fullemploy itself was a role model, by winning management consultancy contracts from private businesses, instead of just relying on government grants. 'The 1970s urban aid all went to generate social welfare, which helped to create a climate of dependency; black people couldn't develop capital to free themselves. The government could and should now aid people to get started, and provide resources for community infrastructure.' Spencer noted how many Asian banks there were (this was before the collapse of BCCI, which also served the Asian community), but few Caribbean ones. India and Pakistan have more wealth to help communities in Britain than Carribean countries do.

WM and P is a small company in Brixton, and is the only black-owned company in public relations and advertising. By 1990 it was still expanding. Again, it stressed how much of a role model it provided. It also acted as a mediator between large retail companies and the black community. A quotation from them expresses their strong feelings:

> But in the past we've endured hostility from local councils at individual entrepreneurs, and even failure to pay bills.... Many small companies were subsidized by the GLC, but the GLC controlled the grants so they remained dependent on their cash.... When the GLC went, they went with it. Now things are changing, and slowly local councils are changing their attitudes.... It's simply not good enough to support community enterprise. My brother is in computers making it big in San Francisco: the printer who does our posters is black and drives a Ferrari. This is black success. It's not just money.

Finally, however much it may have been over-sold, the reality of Asian enterprise must be mentioned. Many Ugandan Asians have achieved considerable success, although others have found it harder.[9] What now threatens their commercial interests is the clash of cultures in Britain. 'Asians brought up in Britain often want to have their own houses and independent lives. This threatens the pooling of family resources, which is important in helping Asians to start successful businesses with relatively little capital.'[10] There are certainly some very wealthy Asian businessmen. Nazmu Virani is the archetypal immigrant who became a successful entrepreneur. He arrived at Heathrow in 1972 as a 24-year-old refugee from Uganda. He was almost sent back with his family because he lacked documentation. Today his family is (in 1990) worth over £100 million, having moved from renting a grocery store in Dulwich to owning twenty-three hotels and 700 pubs. Along the way he found English banks reluctant to invest in his business. His success, like so many other Asian entrepreneurs, is the result of five factors: the closeness of the family relationship; the unofficial networks in the community; the growth from British companies into international empires by the children of the founding entrepreneurs; the determination, created by a struggle against prejudice; and the setting up of small Asian banks.

How should ethnic enterprise be assessed? It is a complex phenomenon, encompassing community businesses, church involvement, small traders and successful entrepreneurs. Racial prejudice recurs constantly. G.S. Bakshi, in Robert

Chesshyre's *Return of a Native Reporter*, made the point explicitly:

> Prejudice against coloured people and lack of enterpise were, he believed, intricately linked in the conditioning of the British working class. At home, in the days of empire, they were treated as 'white coolies', much as black natives in the colonies. They were kept ignorant ... trapped by economic necessity. What the factory owners required were human machines who would go to the factory in the morning and be content with the pub in the evening. A class was created which was almost without initiative. But in the human pecking order, there was still one inferior being – the coloured man.[11]

On this analysis, the empire encouraged industrial inefficiency, providing a market for inferior goods. It also nurtured racial prejudice and a distrust of enterprise. Today in many inner cities there is a flourishing 'alternative enterprise culture' in drugs.[12] It is clear from the analysis of Toxteth and Moss Side in 1991 that there is a deep despair in these communities, a decade after the 1981 riots. Racial prejudice remains high, and housing is also bad. Yet there has been a change: Peter Ogunsiji, a black businessman repairing cars in Cranby (the local name for Toxteth, Liverpool), says, 'Half these kids selling drugs are born entrepreneurs. Give them half a chance and they will be running the Stock Exchange.' There is a demand for self-help schemes and seed money for enterprise.[13]

Theology and ethnic enterprise

Most of the Churches have been critical of the enterprise culture, and ethnic enterprise is no different. Greg Smith, of the Evangelical Coalition for Urban Mission, is typical in his reaction. He is critical of taking models

> from the USA enterprise culture.... The Right talk about empowerment in economic terms and in terms of breaking the culture of dependency, but the Bible seems to mean something rather different. There undoubtedly are positive evaluations of creativity, stewardship and hard work in the Scriptures but we must not equate these too easily with the values of an enterprise culture where only a few benefit at the expense of the have nots.

Greg Smith argues that dialogue with the government may well have been a dialogue with the deaf, citing the effect of benefit changes, the redevelopment of Docklands and the depression of those who live there and the high unemployment.[14]

Perhaps the answer lies with Adeole Solanke, who was one of the finalists in the 1989 Livewire young entrepreneur competition. 'I feel I've done what many people, especially young people, women and blacks, should perhaps do ... operate as independently and professionally as possible.' It is striking that many black entrepreneurs retain links with their local community, including community projects, and are often close to the Labour Party.

This means that alongside the poverty and high unemployment of Moss Side and Toxteth, with the despair this engenders, there is also the possibility of a particular style of enterprise: either a community model, often advocated by the Churches, or individual enterprise, as shown in many individual examples and exemplified by many successes from Fullemploy.

This raises a theological question. Can a theology that is aware of racial prejudice be sympathetic to enterprise, or must enterprise be seen as part of the New Right, as Greg Smith seems to suggest? The most notable theologian in this area is Ken Leech, who has long written about social concern, race, spirituality and Anglo-Catholic theology. It is interesting that in *Struggle in Babylon*,[15] sub-titled 'Racism in the Cities and Churches of Britain' and published in 1988, Leech surveys the reality of class and urban conflict, without even mentioning economic production. This is not to deny his deep socialist commitment, which he has shown in many books on the Christian Left. Leech is quite correct to point to persistent inequality, especially in the growth of poverty in the 1980s. Yet it is not clear why the violence and urban conflict of the inner city, in which black people are so often victims, cannot be reconciled with self-employment. *Faith in the City* spoke of a 'pervading sense of powerlessness and despair'.[16] One of the most striking points about self-employment is the feeling of self-control, without denying the objective reality of inflated property prices,[17] difficulty of raising capital, etc.

Leech associates Catholic spirituality on this issue with the offering of bread and wine in the communion service.

Such an offering sees the bread and wine as symbols of the industrial process, in which not merely the use of wealth but the creation of wealth is important. Wealth-creation is concerned with how wealth is made: 'it is impossible to offer to God the fruits of injustice and oppression, as Irenaeus saw in the second century'.[18] One implication of the challenge to the false values of society by the vision of the Kingdom of God is an alliance with Marxism which is worked out in specific locations. This is to see Christianity as part of the culture of resistance, in which worship is a living foretaste of the coming age of justice. Yet, as Leech himself says, there is also the view of grace working in and through human potential: 'the power to transcend the limitations of nature ... a high and optimistic view of human potential'.[19] Could this not be found in examples of enterprise? If racial oppression is bound up with the capitalist system, and there can be no compromise between the Church of Christ and the idolatry of wealth (to quote an earlier Christian socialist, R.H. Tawney), then it certainly will not be enough to look for examples of racial harmony.[20] What this chapter has sought to explore is how ethnic enterprise has sought to be socially responsible, while finding in self-employment a new sense of self-worth. There are many examples of small businesses with exploitation and sweatshops, and equally there are frequent examples of small shops that only earn a fragile living. However, what appears to be the case is that alongside the continuing high unemployment there are also examples of hope and initiative. Partly these will be community ventures, partly individual self-employment. Wealth-creation in itself does not advance the gospel's proclamation of divine self-giving, nor the unity of the human race. What it can do is create a sense that people are fashioning their own destiny, which then must be transformed in Christ. This could lead to a failure to criticize what is wrong in our society, yet there is no reason why self-employment should lose its cutting edge. Nor need self-employment be related to self-reliance without God: it is too easy to equate financial independence with spiritual independence. There must instead be a renewed understanding both of the unity of the human race, which God has loved and restored in Christ, and of the possibility of transformation in social as well as personal life. Certainly this vision has inspired some of the entrepreneurs mentioned in this chapter.

Last of all, there is the inter-faith dimension. Asian entrepreneurs are often deeply committed to their own faith: one
example is the Hinduja family, the richest Asian family in
Britain, who are devout Hindus. Dialogue between the world
faiths is often biased in Britain because Christians do not meet
Hindus or Muslims on equal terms. Christianity remains the
established religion in Britain, and many Asians and Hindus
remain poor and marginal immigrants. The support that Asian
entrepreneurs give to their own faith can only make inter-faith
dialogue more realistic. There are still few Muslim or Hindu
centres in Britain able to engage in dialogue with the prevailing
culture, as the Rushdie affair showed clearly. If the Christian
Churches are to engage in a Decade of Evangelism in the
1990s, that must include a dialogue with other faiths: and
in that dialogue, Hindu and Muslim entrepreneurs can play
their part, alongside other leaders of their community.

The transformation of Britain into a multiracial society in
the last four decades has been deeply painful. There has
been much experience of poverty and of rejection, including
some from the Churches themselves.[21] Those who attempted
to respond to this situation often did so through public bodies.
Many of these initiatives failed simply from under-fuding,
such as education or housing. Yet the interviews with WM
and P, Linbert Spencer and Arif Ali also reveal a desire
to regain some of the initiative themselves. In this light,
wealth-creation becomes a symbol. It is not a criticism of
public funding and local authorities, but rather it is seen
as a partnership. As the immigrants to Britain in the 1950s
and 1960s have become stereotyped, there is a danger that
racially based categories will become commonplace: the
under-achieving Afro-Carribean, the hard-working Asian. It
is precisely because enterprise can challenge such stereotypes
that it is to be welcomed. So it is important that the diversity
of enterprise should be maintained, both in the community as
a whole and in individual stories of achievement. Ultimately
the Christian gospel points to the renewal of all humanity
and the created order itself. It is a renewal that transcends
ethnic and tribal limitations. In this renewal Jesus expresses
the creativity of God: but that is a Christian claim that must
be taken up in the dialogue with Hinduism and Islam in
the coming decade. So perhaps the most profound hope of
ethnic enterprise must be for Hindu and Muslim theologians

to fashion their own theologies of wealth-creation, and social criticism, which can be set against the Christian tradition.

Notes

1. P. Wilson, *Growth Strategies in Minority Enterprise: Case Studies in Corporate Growth of Asian and Afro-Caribbean Business in Britain*, 1987, p. 1.
2. ibid., p. 14; cf. R. Ward, 'Ethnic Business and Economic Change: An Overview', *International Small Business Journal*, 4.3, spring 1986, p. 10: 'Yet while the findings of the Kerner Commission, convened after the American riots of the 1960s, led to extensive practical support for black business, the report of the Scarman Tribunal, set up to investigate the racial disturbances in Brixton, England, 1981, has had much less effect. Governments and local councils of varying complexion have indicated their support for minority enterprise, but effective public intervention has so far been confined to a small number of Labour councils.'
3. P. Wilson and J. Stanworth, 'Growth and Change in Black Minority Enterprise in Britain', *International Small Business Journal*, 4.3, spring 1986, pp. 13–27.
4. D. McEvoy and H. Aldrich, 'Survival Rates of Asian and White Retailers', in ibid., pp. 28–37.
5. T. Jones and D. McEvoy, 'Ethnic Enterprise: the Popular Image', in J. Curran and J. Stanworth (eds), *The Survival of the Small Firm*, vol. 1, 1986, p. 207; cf. also R. Ward and R. Jenkins (eds), *Ethnic Communities in Business*, 1984.
6. The point is explicitly made by P. Werbner in 'Business on Trust: Pakistani Entrepreneurship in the Manchester Garment Trade', in Ward and Jenkins (eds), 1984, p. 169.
7. British Council of Churches Community and Race Relations Unit, *Consultation on the Economic Empowerment of the Black Community*, 2–4 February 1990, St Albans; British Council of Churches Community and Race Relations Unit, *Future Investment: The Economic Empowerment of the Black Community. Report of a Visit to the United States*, April 1985; *Evangelical Enterprise Works*, 1989. There is a critical article by D. Tyers, 'Evangelical Helpmeets or Hinderers?' *City Cries*, summer 1989.
8. Fullemploy Group, *Business Development. A Serious Option for the Black Community? The 1989 Consultation*, 1989; Fullemploy Group, (with E. Gretton), *Black Business Development in Nottinghamshire: Report for Nottinghamshire County Council*, 1988; Fullemploy Group, *Annual Review*, 1989.
9. Surveys of Asian enterprise are found in Ward and Jenkins (eds), 1984; and in R. Ward, R. Waldinger and H. Aldrich, *Ethnic Entrepreneurs*, 1990. Newspaper accounts are given in *The Independent*, 28 December 1989 ('Leicester's Asians turn exile into a commercial success'), and by A. Roy in the *Telegraph Weekend Magazine*, 25 August 1990 ('The Quiet Millionaires'). R. Chesshyre's *Return of a Native Reporter*, 1986, is an account of his return to England after four years as *The Observer's* Washington correspondent. There is a section on Asian businessmen.

10. *The Independent*, 28 December 1989.
11. Chesshyre, p. 252.
12. *The Independent*, 6 July 1991, a survey of Moss Side ten years after the riots there.
13. *The Independent*, 5 July 1991.
14. D. Tyers, 'Evangelical Helpmeets or Hinderers?', in *City Cries*, no. 19, summer 1989, pp. 6–8.
15. Sheldon Press, 1988.
16. 1985, p. xiv.
17. See K. Leech, *Struggle in Babylon*, pp. 32–3.
18. K. Leech, *The Anglo-Catholic Social Conscience. Two Critical Essays*, 1991, p. 7.
19. ibid., p. 7.
20. K. Leech, 'Religion and the Rise of Racism', in D. Ormrod (ed.), *Fellowship, Freedom and Equality*, 1990, p. 66.
21. Leech, *Struggle in Babylon*, pp. 196–8.

5

Self-employment and Attitudes to Work

Introduction

The enterprise culture is thought to be made up of a distinct set of attitudes, values and motivations. In reality, those who are self-employed do not fall into such a clear-cut group. Nevertheless, an analysis of the ideology of self-employment does reveal sufficient differences to merit such an evaluation.

The usual stereotype is held to be that the employee tends to value security while the entrepreneur will take calculated risks, and is innovative and change-oriented. In this chapter the attitudes of entrepreneurs will be explored, giving particular attention to the views of young people and women. Are there distinctive values associated with those who are self-employed? What is significant is how these values relate to an understanding of human beings who are open to the world. Central to this entire study is the view that this openness is implicitly and deeply religious. In exploring what is unknown and potentially challenging, there is raised the question of the basic trust that supports our life.

Openness and change in human beings

The experience of transcendence is that we are open to our world. The basic tenets of self-employment, such as independence, freedom, creativity and change, question normal working patterns. This chapter will show how starting a business was a positive response for many women after a traumatic personal event had challenged their lives. What is 'transcendent' is that this event had opened up further questions, and this led to self-employment. When self-employment had begun, yet further questions were revealed, which touched very deeply on issues of personal integrity.

Among young people there was also much less concern with job security, a greater concern with risk-taking and a desire to 'be their own boss'.

Such concerns will be substantiated by a considerable number of surveys cited in this chapter. The thesis here is that there are three attitudes to self-employment in Britain. The first epitomizes the entrepreneurial attitude so commended by the government of the 1980s: seeking higher profits, greater market share, professionally directed and technologically sophisticated. A second embodies the virtues of the traditional self-employed, charted by sociologists at the beginning of the decade. Such virtues are loyalty, perseverance, thrift and concern for tradition and order, and are most typically found in the small shopkeeper. It is, however, the third group that is most interesting. This sector is comprised of those whose motivation and lifestyle is not solely that of maximum profits and market-share. Yet it is not a group that rejects risks and looks for stability. Instead, it values creativity, independence and flexibility. (Having said this, there is also of course a desire for economic success.)

This is, it is true, a generalized definition of the three groups. What substantiates the claim that they are distinct are a series of surveys of those who began small businesses this decade, and my own visits to entrepreneurs. It is the third group that concerns us here. Such people seeking self-employment are concerned about income and reward, and yet their motivation ultimately goes beyond this. It is possible that studies of co-operatives would show the same pattern in Britain. The famous co-operatives of Mondragon in the Spanish Basque country also show this concern for non-material values.

If we return to the theme of this section, which is openness or transcendence, in theological language, a profile emerges of human beings as responsible, free and transcendent. Being a person means a conscious and free relationship to the world: someone who is responsible for themselves.

A common feature of the interviews in this book is the inability of people to halt the process in which they are caught up. As the Roman Catholic theologian Karl Rahner puts it:

> Basically he is always still on the way. Every goal that he can point to in knowledge and in action is always relativised, is

always a provisional step. Every answer is always just the beginning of a new question. Man experiences himself as infinite possibility because in practice and theory he necessarily places every sought-after result in question. He always situates it in a broader horizon which looms before him in its vastness.[1]

Rahner is writing of the human condition, but the quotation expresses precisely the way in which the desire for autonomy, responsibility and independence in people lead them to take a decisive step, such as that of self-employment. Rahner also offers three reasons as to why (or how) people ignore this experience of openness. Again, this echoes many of the conversations that occurred in this research: the feeling of being unable to control one's destiny; a very frequently expressed wish that the decision to become self-employed had been taken years earlier when there was more energy and time; the scepticism about the constraints deeply embedded in contemporary employment. Rahner's three explanations for evading the experience of openness and questioning are:

1. A decision by the person to delimit their world, so that they commit themselves to that concrete part of life which can be controlled by them. What goes on beyond that world is one in which they have to live, but they do not worry about it. In so far as they do reflect on it, they accept that there is much that cannot be changed. What matters are personal relationships.
2. There can also be a recognition that there are ultimate questions not merely about the self, but about society, and existence as a whole. This question can be thought about, and discussed in an intellectual way, but the final decision is to postpone the answer with a sensible scepticism.
3. There is also a despairing involvement in the world. It is worth quoting Rahner directly at this point:

One goes about his business, he reads, he gets angry, he does his work, he does research, he achieves something, he earns money. And in a final, perhaps unadmitted despair he says to himself that the whole as a whole makes no sense, and that one does well to suppress the question about the meaning of it all and to reject it as an unanswerable and hence meaningless question.[2]

As a theologian, Rahner is exploring a more fundamental

question than the decision to deny or to hold a religious faith. His concern is with the way in which it is possible to accept responsibility for oneself, and to express any commitment. Rahner's argument is that in the ongoing search for personal responsibility and commitment, transcendence is not the experience of some definite, particular objective thing experienced alongside other objects. It is rather a mode of existence, a way of living, prior to and permeating every existence. It is instead the openness to life as such, and is always in the background of our life.

Freedom then is not the power to be able to do this or that. It is the power to decide about oneself and to actualize oneself. This does not mean that life in society and history are irrelevant. Rahner's argument is not the same as the 'New Right' philosophy of von Hayek, where all that matters is the ability to choose and this must not be impaired. Hayek offers a negative definition of liberty, set over against socialist and other definitions of freedom as the freedom to become certain things: the freedom from want and need, etc. Rahner's analysis of freedom avoids this political debate on freedom, which concerns either freedom simply to choose, or to study at a university, train to achieve skills, etc. Instead of the Right/Left debate on freedom, Rahner argues that the ultimate locus of freedom is the person themselves, and their own self-understanding and self-awareness. A bare 'freedom to choose' ignores the importance of self-interpretation, and the way in which personal freedom is not a neutral power that one has and possesses as something different from oneself. Rolling back the frontiers of the state or setting people free from bureaucracy may be important, but the centre of the argument lies elsewhere. Rather, the point is as follows: I am who I am because of what I have done, and what I can do: it is my own history, my story, my self-possession. The 'Left-wing' account of freedom, where people can realize their talents, abilities and endowments, is also of great importance, but unless that self-realization enables the person to look at themselves and know themselves, this is not a person experiencing themselves. Free action, however, is not just something that takes place only in the hidden depths of a person, apart from society. Freedom is made real, or becomes concrete, in particular decisions, in thousands of concrete decisions. Nevertheless, there is a unity about these decisions. The identification of the person with their work is a common feature of self-employment, but it remains that individual person who expresses themselves.

Freedom, then, is about the experience of ultimate self-responsibility, which never ends so long as that person's own history continues. It is not an individual, isolated psychic occurrence, but a freedom that relates someone to others. On the basis of this freedom, this awareness of self-possibility, the notions of accountability and responsibility in civic life, politics and employment are built. Equally, the fact that we have a personal life rests on this self-awareness. Our life is placed in our own hands; we are left to ourselves, both with our knowledge and our actions. As Rahner says, 'It is being consigned to himself that he experiences himself as responsible and free.'[3] Equally, it is not the case that empirical psychology will point to a particular datum in human behaviour called 'freedom and responsibility'. It may be that we will experience this nature of our existence: it is especially the case that those starting self-employment felt that their independence had been constrained, or they had suffered a personal trauma. Nevertheless, whether or not this experience occurs, the fact remains that a person is confronted by themselves, and is both person and subject.

Two final points remain to be established. It would, on the basis of the argument so far, be possible to argue for a person acting in society in and for themselves. Such a person would be interrelated with others, through their actions, and would achieve a certain interdependence. They would not simply be an isolated individual, nor would the experience of freedom be internal and psychological. Responsibility would be acknowledged through the decisions which that person took. Nevertheless, the experience of openness and ability to change that self-employment offers to many people goes beyond this argument.

We need at this point to introduce a new term. That term is best expressed as 'mutuality'. While not denying anything that has been said so far, mutuality is a relationship in which each person recognizes the other person as free and capable of self-development; each acts with regard to the other person in ways that respond to the needs of the other and enable self-development; each person takes mutual enhancement of the other as a conscious aim.

Once mutuality is added to transcendence, and the experience of freedom, it is not sufficient to be aware of the aims of the other person as important. Instead, the argument moves on to common activity. The strongest form of common activity is where individuals join together to effect a given end, and where the shared end is freely chosen together. The weaker, and far more usual, end of common activity is co-operation to bring about a goal chosen by someone else. Common activity is different from individual activity, even when aggregated together. Many small businesses and community enterprises exemplify this common activity. Once again the freedom of agents is the constitutive feature. It is certainly true that not all small businesses are like this: many can be highly exploitative paying low wages and denying workers their basic rights. The Low Pay Unit has shown this. However, at best, small businesses can extend to those employed in them – full-time employees and part-time workers – some of the independence and flexibility that is sought by those founding small businesses. Similarly, community enterprises may also offer the possibility of self-development to those working in them.

A complex idea of freedom as mutuality, common activity and self-development still requires the active participation of those engaged in this task. It is not enough simply to provide facilities for self-development. First, such an approach has tended repeatedly to become paternalist. The provision of state help easily slides into a decision that the state knows what is best for individuals. At its worst the state has seen itself as embodying the 'higher consciousness' of society, seeking social progress. Secondly, this provision of assistance has often been seen by individuals as requiring allegiance to an organic whole, which is society, or the nation state. Much of the drive to self-employment precisely rejects this argument. There is, of course, such a thing as society but it is made up of individuals. However, simply reducing society to individuals with freedom of choice will not enable the mutuality I have argued for to happen either.[4]

The next point that must be established, albeit briefly, is the religious significance of the argument so far. The drift of argument is like this. There is in human beings a basic freedom, or openness to the world, which substantiates all other civic and social freedoms. This freedom is embodied in the responsibility we have for ourselves and our own destiny. It is not to be equated with a Right-wing argument for free choice alone, for what matters is the realization of this freedom in human action, which leads on to interdependence. Nor is it the same as the provision of positive freedom, where one can attain a higher good. This can all too often be coercive. Instead, it is about self-understanding and self-awareness. Freedom, and transcendence, is not a state that will be always recognized. Nevertheless, it is part of the human condition. There is a danger that it can become purely individualist. That is why I have also emphasized the necessity of mutuality, and common activity, as the expression of this freedom.

Denys Turner has argued that the individualist freedom portrayed by the theologian Don Cupitt is really the result of cultural change. Advanced capitalism turns religious language into a meditation on the nature of freedom. The Dominican theologian Fergus Kerr is most forceful on this, however. Don Cupitt's vision of the individual who constructs his own life is the ultimate expression of pure liberalism: 'the person who prides himself on being the Captain of his own soul is the buccaneer of the free-enterprise market economy, the free-booting entrepreneur who imposes his own rules on the immense void of faceless sea'.[5] Kerr, however, equates Don Cupitt's extreme account of freedom with the free-market. Rahner is a better guide.

It is clear that most people who engage in self-employment will not offer the analysis of freedom given above. It is, however, in my belief, a possible defence of self-employment. Equally, few people who are self-employed see any connection with religious belief at all. Yet in a previous chapter the theology of risk and faith was clearly shown. However, there is a more basic reason for raising the question of religious faith that the fact that Christian belief may itself be risk-taking.

The reason is contained in the ambiguity of the word 'transcendence'. Transcendence offers a person the choice of one's own self, as one acts in freedom. If this is accepted by a person, then true self-understanding and self-realization is possible. All this could imply simply a noble humanism, but a Christian will want to argue that the freedom that a person becomes aware of is in fact given to them. Whether the freedom that can be experienced is seen to be received, and not one's own, becomes the religious question. Does the person create their own unlimited space into which they will move, or is this space in fact a disclosure of God? Salvation is not a strange, mythological term, but is the final validity of a person's self-understanding before God. In the act of accepting freedom and responsibility, a person can achieve true self-understanding. Salvation is thus about the deepest roots and origins of a person's existence. What confronts a human being is the mystery of their own integrity, freedom and relationships. Further, these relationships are set in a world we did not choose to inhabit, although it is in and through them that we discover our freedom. Transcendence therefore refers both to the ultimate mystery and freedom of a person's openness, and to the ground (or origin) of that freedom: the absolute mystery called 'God'. It may be, as Rahner speculates, that human beings in the West will cease to believe in 'God'. Marx felt that the atheism he espoused would become such a feature of everyday life that the very word 'God' would disappear. If, however, the word 'God' remains, then it is not simply an accidental word. It asks about reality as a whole, about the basis for freedom, integrity, self-worth and independence. It is, then, presupposed in everything that follows in this chapter.

This does not mean that the search for new values in self-employment is religious. It is only implicitly so. The question of what freedom is, in a world apparently determined by vast social forces, becomes a real one. Beyond the search for freedom, there is the question of a religious understanding of freedom. Religious freedom is the capacity not to go on behaving in new ways, but to make a choice that is final, definitive, ineradicable. It relates to another term: 'eternity'. In our passage through life, we form ourselves, and by our choices we shape our own eternity.

All this is a long way from the decision to start one's own business. Nevertheless, one must start somewhere. The choice of self-employment in this decade is part of a search for new values in society. Out of these values can come a concern for freedom, autonomy and self-realization. At the heart of this freedom is the question of what sort of existence this self-realization actually has. Is it simply a matter of a particular stage of someone's life, or is it deeper than that?

These questions will be raised again in this book. A Christian understanding of humanity and personal existence finds

that transcendence is the essential nature of our life. Transcendence is the openness and searching that mark out human
life. Such is the theological reason for an interest in the
attitudes and motivations of the self-employed to which we
now turn.

The attitudes of the self-employed

Catherine Hakim's work on self-employment shows the
variety of attitudes espoused by those who are self-employed.
The British Social Attitudes (BSA) surveys for 1983 and 1984
show that only 10 per cent of the self-employed belonged to a
trade union. Yet in 1984, 53 per cent of full-time employees and
26 per cent of part-time employees belonged to one. Indeed, 56
per cent of the self-employed said they had never belonged to
a trade union, whereas only 26 per cent of full-time employees
made this claim. Nor did the pattern vary much between men
and women.[6]

This could be held to show that the self-employed tend
towards individualistic rather than collectivist values. Thus
Leighton writes of the 'philosophy of self-employment:
independence, flexibility, choice and freedom'.[7] Again the
1984 and 1985 BSA surveys contrasted the very different
evaluations of their jobs offered by employees and the
self-employed. Employees spoke primarily of interesting
work that used their skills, then of job security and good
pay. The self-employed spoke of flexible hours (44 per cent
of respondents), the absence of supervision (41 per cent) and
profitability.

Surprisingly, only 17 per cent of the self-employed mentioned freedom. There are several reasons why this might be
so. First, it is striking that 30 per cent of the self-employed
in 1984–5 had been employees within the past five years.
This is not a long time in which to change deeply held
attitudes. Those who opt for self-employment reject tenets of
employment such as security, but freedom is clearly a more
intangible notion. Another survey by Payne in 1984 looked at
young people (23-year-olds).[8] Here young self-employed men
ranked 'being your own boss' as the most important factor in
deciding how to choose a job, then pay, then security. It is
striking that young male employees ranked these three aspects

in the reverse order. A second point worth emphasizing is that women, especially married women, consistently prefer flexible hours and convenience in a job to ideals of freedom, security, etc. (Women's attitudes to self-employment will be examined in more detail below.) Thirdly, freedom and independence is still closely tied to the work ethic. Freedom is not an ideal that sets the individual free to wander where he or she will, but is related to the importance of work for self-identity and self-worth. The 1985 BSA survey found no difference between the unemployed, the self-employed and employees on this score. Over two-thirds in all three groups said they would continue to work even if they had a substantial unearned income. Also, two-thirds in all three groups said paid work (if they had it) meant much more than just earning a living. There was not much variation either in the attitude of the self-employed and employees to doing their best at work, regardless of pay – although the self-employed emphasized it slightly more.

Finally, there is the question of how far freedom is a practical reality for many self-employed people. As one of those interviewed by Hakim puts it, 'It leaves life flexible ... though it's all psychological. Physically you're tied to work twenty-four hours a day when you're self-employed, but you feel as if you've got control over when you start and why you're doing it.'

As the 1980s began, such studies of self-employment as had been done by sociologists stressed how little entrepreneurial spirit was present among small shopkeepers. Many preferred security, and would have given up if they could. However, this is not the attitude found in later surveys of the self-employed. (It is ironic that many of the classic 'petty bourgeois' self-employed in the decades after 1945 did not exemplify the culture of risk and independence at all.)[9]

These surveys suggest that there has indeed been a change in the 1980s in the way in which starting up a business has been viewed. Flexibility, absence of supervision, and far less concern with security are what seem to have been the deciding factors. It is not a shift in attitude that looks for increased leisure – quite the contrary, in fact. It is, though, a very *sudden* change in priorities – one that has taken many people out of the employed workforce in less than ten years.

A 1987 survey asked what is perhaps the crucial question:

why did you start your own business? Interviews with those who had become self-employed in the previous four years (those called 'new entrants') showed that there was a marked emphasis on simply *being* self-employed. This was considered more important than any particular business idea. Again, 41 per cent stressed the importance of independence. This was of course a group that had just entered self-employment, and excluded more traditional self-employed people, such as small (and perhaps ageing) shopkeepers. Self-employment was seen as a challenge, giving freedom when to work and whom to work for.[10]

Certainly between one-fifth and one-third of these new entrants said that they had become self-employed because they could not find an employee job, or because they had been made redundant. This sector were less ambitious, seeking only a job. This is the shadow side of the change in attitudes mentioned above: where people feel forced to enter a world they would not otherwise have chosen. Not unexpectedly, this group have the highest drop-out rate.

Much more work remains to be done on the motivations of the self-employed, especially the new entrants. Nevertheless, there does seem to have been a shift in attitudes, especially among women and young people. This change is quite surprising, given that these two groups have traditionally been much less likely to become self-employed than adult men. Of course, the lack of employee jobs during high unemployment, and lengthy government promotion of an enterprise culture, must also have been significant factors.

Also noteworthy is the significance of family in self-employment. Even excluding family businesses as such, including farms, pubs and shops, one government survey in 1987 found that over half of the spouses of those working from home were also in business on their own account. The survey of 'new entrants' in 1987 also confirmed that they had a network of family, relatives and friends around them. In contrast, those who gave up were *less* likely to have such a network. Most new entrants do not employ anyone else, but, of those who do, over half employ a member of their family.

This is related to the significance of working from home. Four-fifths of new entrants in 1987 worked from home, as did three-quarters of those using the government's Enterprise

Allowance scheme. A typical example might be someone who supplies goods (food, clothes) for a shop or restaurant run by someone else in the family.

This change in attitudes with regard to self-employment is not yet fully understood. What does seem to be happening is that for some people there is a positive choice not to work for someone else. The decision is strongest among young people, and those who have recently started out on their own. It is closely tied both to working from home and with one's family, which enables paid work to be more autonomous and flexible. Whether it is part of a wider change in social and political attitudes remains to be seen. It is clear, though that self-employment is not seen by most new entrants as being the result of a scarcity of jobs at a time of high unemployment. The fact that those who start self-employment place the influence of family above the influence of government promotion suggests that deeper cultural changes are taking place than political rhetoric would allow. If employment is being related to personal independence, self-expression and networks of families and friends, then a profound shift is taking place in the way the individual sees their destiny despite the constraints of society. If that is so, then this will be of significance both politically and in religious practice.

Before such themes are explored further, it is worth looking more closely at one survey of self-employed women.

Women's attitudes

There has been a sustained rise in the number of women starting businesses in the United States and Britain. In the United States, the number of female small-business owners grew by 74 per cent in 1975–85, and now make up 37 per cent of all small-business owners. In Finland and Sweden, over 25 per cent of owner-managers are female. However, the trend is sharpest in Britain. In 1981–7, male self-employment went up by 30 per cent, but female self-employment went up by 70 per cent. This is an increase comparable to that in the United States, but it was achieved in only six years rather than a decade. However, the overall percentage of females among the self-employed is still lower in Britain, with only 25 per cent of the self-employed being women.

It is noticeable how few studies there have been of British female entrepreneurs. Even by the late 1980s there had only been five studies, one of which was funded by the Department of Employment. Another of these set out explicitly to look at ethnic women, and their experience of racial prejudice in Britain.

Women have a complex pattern of employment. Some work until the first child is born, and resume when the youngest child is of school age. Other women have a more continuous working life, combining paid work with young families. Nevertheless, the position of employed women in the labour force has remained unchanged. Most women work part time, in the service sector, and in low-paid, semi-skilled positions; some are still unskilled. Only 5 per cent of all working women were managers or employers in 1965. The figure had not altered in 1980.

Therefore the rise of female entrepreneurs represents a significant change. As Schwartz put it in 1976, it is 'a new female frontier'. The change should not be over-emphasized, though. 'Hotels, catering and distribution' accounted for 42 per cent of female self-employment in 1984. 'Other services' accounted for a further 30 per cent of female self-employment. Not surprisingly, men were more likely to be self-employed in the construction industry: 26 per cent of self-employed men and only 1 per cent of women worked in this sector. Thus the old stereotypes of employment still partly exist.

Nevertheless, the change has happened. This study is not concerned to provide an over-view of female entrepreneurs in Britain, but to ask what their motivations and values are. Again the desire for independence was found strongly by the Carter and Cannon study of 1988.[11] 'Independence' meant different things to different people. For young women aged under twenty-five, it meant greater career opportunities, and an escape from the confines of being an employee. Similarly, older career women decided on self-employment after repeatedly encountering a lack of recognition by their employers.

Independence can mean other things, though. Carter and Cannon found several young women who feared that they lacked the ambition to succeed in conventional jobs. They drifted into small-scale self-employment – typified by one person who was unemployed after leaving college until her family bought her machinery for printing sweatshirts. The desire for high profits was rejected: self-employment offered a way of earning a modest living, while not having to accept the traditional authority figures perceived to dominate most employment. Unlike young males who strongly emphasized self-expression in their own business, this group saw self-employment as a way of financing their own lifestyle outside of working hours without the tensions usually found at work. Independence also meant the ability to combine having a family and being at work. Many women in the surveys spoke of the lack of comprehension of male managers at the demands of young children and work. Other women were returning to work by becoming self-employed after a period devoted to motherhood. It was important to this group that the business remained small and not too demanding until such time as the family had grown up and the venture could become a full-time occupation. This strategy once again shows the importance of the family in small-scale businesses. In this case, though, it is not a family-run enterprise, but an adjunct to family life, where 'proprietorship offered short-term independence from motherhood'.

Finally, there were women who had a family background of small businesses. These were often older women, who identified strongly with male role models of independence. Carter and Cannon quote one respondent: 'I always thought that I could do well on my own and my family have always had businesses.'

As we have already seen, the influence of the family in small businesses turns out to be of enormous significance. Several women in the Carter/Cannon survey cited a change in personal circumstances, such as marriage, divorce or pregnancy, as the impetus to the re-evaluation of their working lives. Nearly one-third of the sixty respondents stated that starting a business was the result of being 'a victim of some traumatic event', either personal or at work. Self-employment was seen by them as a positive response to the situation.

Carter and Cannon also noted:

> A major difference between male and female owned business lies in the criteria upon which success is judged. Women generally regarded success in terms of how well the business met individual needs rather than in conventional terms of profitability and income gained.

Business ownership fulfilled its objective for the vast majority of women in this survey by providing independence, control, and personal satisfaction. It may well be that as the business prospers, more conventional economic criteria of success will be adopted, since individual needs have then been met.

However, successful business ownership is not a matter of a well-managed launch and steady growth for most women. There are problems relating to sources of support. The patronizing attitude of bankers towards prospective female entrepreneurs was frequently mentioned. So too was the danger of working from home, presenting an image of a 'bored housewife with little interest in profits'.

Despite denying feminist views, many post-launch problems were specifically mentioned by women as relating to their gender. Some women suggested that men would be reluctant to work for a female owner. A large number preferred in general to employ women rather than men: they made better employees, being more adaptable and less likely to challenge the owner's authority. Older women tended to adopt a maternal style, where all employees were seen as part of a family. For others, being an owner was stressful whenever personal relationships at work became intertwined with decision-making – a not infrequent occurrence. Especially when businesses were started as a response to perceived discrimination in previous employment, self-employment was seen as a means of gaining control over status. Goffee and Scase noted that delegation could prove problematic, especially when allied to a 'superwoman' complex of succeeding in spite of all adversity (mentioned by several respondents).

Finally, it is important to mention again the relevance of family and networks in starting a business and achieving 'independence'. There was repeatedly an emphasis by respondents on the ambiguous attitude of close relatives to starting up in business, characterized by one comment:

> It's my in-laws ... they say that there is no market and that I wouldn't make any money out of it. I really feel that it goes deeper than that ... most of all what is behind it is that I am their only chance of having grandchildren because my husband is their only son, and I think that they feel that I should be concentrating on that.

Others, however, attributed their success to family support, which increased their confidence. The moral support from spouses was identified by many as a major asset. A few said that family relationships deteriorated, especially in the minority of cases where husbands joined the firm after a successful (female-led) start-up.

However, few women said that relationships with their children had worsened. The longer women had been in business, the more positive they were. They felt more self-assured, and spoke of the role model that they provided, especially for daughters. Not surprisingly, there were many more problems for those in the sample who had young children, especially where the business was run from home.

Friendship and forming networks were perhaps the biggest changes in personal life. Among young women this was often a deliberate strategy: building up friends through business who could also provide advice and support. Indeed, no fewer than 43 per cent of the Carter/Cannon survey reported earning less income in self-employment, although 70 per cent said that the quality of their life had improved.

In summary, self-employment for women is growing fast. A 70 per cent rise in six years is remarkable. Women entering self-employment are too diverse a group to allow single explanations of their motivations. However, it is clear that women's self-employment is to do with much more than a search for profits and market-share, although this may become more dominant later on in the business. There are certainly persistent themes – such as the closely interrelated areas of family responsibility and self-identity. Perhaps the most compelling aspect of this survey is how many women felt that they were providing a positive role model for both their children and other women. Given that still only one-quarter of small businesses in Britain are owned by women, there is clearly room for much more change in this area.

Self-employment is one strategy among others pursued by women as a means to greater independence and respect in society. Traditionally, women and young people (aged under twenty-five) did not feature in self-employment in Britain. Here, perhaps most of all, there is evidence of the profound cultural changes that this decade has seen in self-employment. The rise in women's self-employment marks one more challenge to the conventional stereotypes of women at work.

Young people's attitudes

After Mrs Thatcher had been Prime Minister for a decade, a number of newspapers surveyed the group who were too young to vote in the 1979 election, but who were now aged 15–28 in May 1989. This group, known as 'Thatcher's children' in the press, were those people who had no adult knowledge at that time of any government but hers. There were 11 million aged 15–28 in May 1989, all eligible to vote in 1992.[12]

The Independent's survey, in association with the BBC, was evaluated by Peter Kellner. Some 392 people in the 15–28 age group were specially polled, as were 860 adults over 18 as a representative quota of whom 236 were aged 18–28. This provided a total sample of 628 respondents aged under 28, and 624 over 28. The material aspirations of 'Thatcher's children' were common to all classes in the sample. Home ownership, private pensions, foreign holidays and meals with the family were the hopes of all young people on reaching 40, and well over half of the respondents felt they would own a home and have a private pension scheme by then. About one-quarter also aspired to owning stocks and shares, private health care and private education by that age. Only a few (13 per cent) did not wish to own their own house, although one-quarter were not sure they would be able to afford it by the time they were 40.

Young men were less concerned with job security than those over 28, although the majority of young men still opted for job security over a successful career: the figures were 58 per cent security, 40 per cent success for young men, and 74 per cent security, 21 per cent success for all those over 28. However, it must be remembered that this includes employees as well as the self-employed. Peter Kellner commented on the irony of young people growing up at a time of mass unemployment but who are nevertheless far less concerned about job security than their parents or grandparents. Also, a majority of young people rejected the idea of negotiating pay and conditions with an employer by means of a trade union: they preferred to rely on themselves. However, it is not as though this generation was unconcerned about all issues. Out of a list of ten things they worry about, AIDS was by far the most prominent, just above nuclear war and drugs.

A smaller percentage of those over 28 were worried about AIDS, with such issues as drugs, the environment, nuclear war, poverty and terrorism being greater concerns. Neither group listed poverty in the Third World as being of much concern to them.

It is, however, in the area of self-employment that the real changes have taken place. Some 40 per cent of all those under 28 wanted to run their own business, although that figure breaks down to 48 per cent of young men and 33 per cent of young women. Why was there this difference, given that women are also opting for self-employment? Perhaps it was that 68 per cent of all young women still preferred job security, some 10 per cent more than the equivalent male sample; equally, they were more fearful of nuclear war (49 per cent of young women; 36 per cent of young men). Peter Kellner proposed that the figures showed young women to be still wary of risk-taking. Similarly, it could be argued that the surveys of woman entrepreneurs in the previous section demonstrate that their entry into self-employment is not a risk-taking strategy but a search for independence, and a lifestyle that reflects their values.

Only 4 per cent of young people were actually running their own business, but 35 per cent of men and 26 per cent of women expected to do so in the future. Most felt they had the skills to do so, and 21 per cent of men (again, women were lower at 12 per cent) said they had seriously considered the option. Very few felt it was too risky an idea: only 15 per cent of all young people rejected the idea outright.

One of the underlying themes of this chapter has been the relationship of the entrepreneurial choice to public values. The earlier sociological research of Goffee and Scase at the beginning of this decade examined the views of the traditional self-employed, such as older shopkeepers, small family firms, etc. Not surprisingly, there was a high degree of Right-wing political and social attitudes among them. These attitudes coincided with a marked lack of entrepreneurial values such as risk-taking, innovation and change. In the new self-employed, these values came to the fore. What is very significant is that these new values carry with them no commitment to Right-wing political or social views. As Peter Kellner says, this generation of 15–18-year-olds, 'shows signs of becoming a more entrepreneurial generation than their parents. However, there is no evidence that they are more Right-wing in their underlying values.'

Many of the views of the young people were virtually identical to those of older electors. Some 62 per cent wanted a country where public interests were more important than private ones; and they preferred a more managed economy to a free-market one – with only 30 per cent actively preferring the latter. Equally, 54 per cent rejected the ideal of individuals being encouraged to look after themselves; 61 per cent preferred the protection of the environment to increasing the standard of living; 59 per cent opted for keeping people at work even if it was not very profitable. Only on one test was there a change: 48 per cent of the young people felt they preferred a country that allowed people to make and keep as much money as they could.

These are not views that oppose the collective provision of welfare. More detailed questions about housing, better public services and welfare revealed a willingness for the government to tax more heavily in order to maintain the social values and welfare state that they had grown up with. There is, however, a clear message in these statistics. Within an underlying commitment to comprehensive schools (which young people preferred far more than those older than them) and the welfare state, there is a desire to explore individual initiative and entrepreneurship. This appears to reflect a common desire to share in the prosperity that the last decade has brought for the majority of those in work. The issues that young people are concerned about are chiefly personal, such as AIDS and drugs, or global, such as nuclear war. Poverty, in Britain or the Third World, hardly touched them. Is this the reflection of a lack of concern for those who are disadvantaged?

This is not necessarily so, for the questionnaire asked what young people themselves worried about. If there had been a rejection of the welfare state, and collective state provision for the disadvantaged through higher taxation, this might have been arguable. Instead, young people quite overwhelmingly accepted the need for such provision. What concerned them personally, though, was a preference for 'being your own boss'.

As with the survey of women, these facts appear to show the beginning of a significant change in British society. In many young people there is admiration for the ideals of self-employment, risk-taking and a rejection of job security. What will be significant is how these ideals are responded to. They **are not** to be equated with a particular political philosophy, **nor** with a selfish individualism. It remains to be seen how these cultural changes will be reflected in political and social policies.

In an earlier article, Peter Kellner argued for a wider definition of wealth-creation than simply the satisfaction of private wants by private, economic activity in the free-market. Wealth-creation included our enrichment 'by things that economic statistics either ignore or fail to measure fully. One of the most vital tasks of the public sector is to preserve these common assets, and to protect them when they are threatened'.[13]

Such assets include a society that cares for the disadvantaged, a healthy environment, and the public provision of high-quality education for all. These ideals are not being rejected as interest in self-employment grows. Rather, there is an understanding of wealth-creation as embracing both entrepreneurial activity and the provision of high standards for the benefit of the whole of society.

Successful entrepreneurs: different aspirations?

One of the debates that continued throughout the 1980s was whether it was possible to identify companies that generated significant job creation. David Storey, of the Small Business Centre, Warwick University, has argued that 40 per cent of new businesses ceased to trade within three years of start-up. Furthermore, most firms that survive continue to be small. It is therefore sensible to identify which firms should receive assistance.[14]

The debate on whether or not it is possible to identify successful firms is not of concern to this study. Nevertheless, it is important to look at whether there is a particular type of entrepreneur who is highly successful. Success might be measured by job creation (one who had fifty or more employees after five years of start-up) or by high profit (achieving an average return on total assets of at least 37 per cent over six years). Storey thus analyses the difference between founders and directors of successful, as opposed to ordinary, new firms.

One immediate difference that can be identified is that the influence of the family is less significant in successful new firms. There is a paradox here: new firms are often started as a result of the influence of family or a network of friends, and the support of this network is crucial in continuing to survive, yet the most successful firms are different. Directors of fast-growth companies are likely to be professional directors, running several small companies, whereas other companies are family affairs or 'one-man bands'. Even more strikingly, the most profitable companies, which tended to be in mechanical engineering in Storey's sample, had technical directors with a background and training directly relevant to the companies' activities. Storey found that only one-quarter to one-third of high-profit or fast-employment growth had husband and wife teams on the board of directors, and only 13–16 per cent had sons or daughters on the board. Other new firms, which were not highly successful, had husband and wife teams in over half the cases, and sons or daughters in nearly two-thirds.

Those who do manage successful businesses also have different aims and objectives. While they may also be dissatisfied with their existing employer, it is the sense of market opportunity that is all important. Education, past work experience and age do not vary much between the successful entrepreneur and the ordinary small-business owner. Once established, successful entrepreneurs will compete much more overseas, not with local firms. They will stress quality and innovation to a high degree, and actively seek high profits, greater market share and long-term growth. (Other entrepreneurs will put a greater stress on job satisfaction, as has already been mentioned in this chapter.)

There would, then, in Storey's analysis, appear to be a particular type of aggressively successful entrepreneur. He or she will be far more professional, perhaps managing several businesses. This person will identify markets, and seek for the firm to grow in size and profits. Neither family background nor job satisfaction will be so significant. There are not many such successful firms, as defined by Storey.

We therefore find yet again that the 'enterprise culture' can be further refined in terms of attitudes and motivation.

There are the traditional small-business owners, who are often conservative in values and attitudes. Job security would be significant, and they may well feel trapped. A second group is the complete opposite, where cut-throat competition is the norm. While these latter firms are of great economic significance to the future of British society, their values are not typical. Far more typical than either of these groups is the small firm that emphasizes independence and creativity. These are the firms that grow steadily if not spectacularly, often employing young people or women. In this network of family and friends a new search for values at work appears to be underway.

Theology and social attitudes

A theology of self-employment is concerned with the values and ideals that inspire those who work in them: the ideology of work, in the technical phrase. This chapter has cited extensively the Department of Employment surveys, the British Social Attitude annual reports, and the work of individual sociologists. It is not a definitive analysis, but it does present a fairly clear picture of the cultural changes in contemporary Britain. While it is probably true that such changes have moved faster in southern and eastern England than elsewhere, nevertheless the consistency of the facts is impressive. There does seem to be an underlying reality, beyond the party political debate and the media discussions.

The issues that are raised by this change are many. What does it look like in practice? How far will it grow, and in what ways will it develop? What should the moral response be to this movement? Is there any reason for the Churches to be interested in this development? Following the Roman Catholic theologian Karl Rahner, I have argued that it is a definite cultural change that should attract the interest of theologians. There are other ways in which a search for freedom and authenticity might be carried on, not least in personal relations, but this one is one that should not be ignored. The other questions are ones that will be taken up in the ensuing chapters of this book. Together they contribute to a new understanding of a theology of creation and wealth-creation.

It is certainly the case that our society has developed an economic language that predominates over everything else. The American theologian Philip Turner argues that alongside this language there has been a shift from principles to values. Principles, he claims, are primary truths that form the basis for other beliefs and then give rules for ethical conduct. They are fixed, absolute and eternal. Values are, in Turner's view, less permanent and are subject to change and alteration. Increasingly we measure our lives, in Turner's opinion, by

> economic metaphors [which] dominate our moral discourse and our moral imagination. We calculate the relative value of our acts and practices as we balance our bank accounts. We try not so much to do the truth but to see that our actions have 'profitable' results. Because of the metaphors we use, we understand the moral life more and more as a matter of profits and loss. Money provides a primary metaphor for grasping our basic engagements.[15]

Turner's argument is persuasive, but it can be overstated. Dorothy Emmett, in *The Moral Roots of Democracy*, argues that the British system of social administration, at best, does embody a broader set of values and moral language than Turner might suggest. Perhaps this may be because Turner is writing about a different society, but it may also be the case that the situation is not as uniform as he suggests. Emmett appeals to the sense of the importance of fairness, generosity of spirit and respect of the other's point of view. Paxman's book, *Friends in High Places*, makes similar claims for the civil service, although he recognizes how much the sense of service has become weaker in recent years.

Emmett's study is cited by the report of the Church of England's Board for Social Responsibility, *Changing Britain*, which looked at the values of modern Britain. This advocates a way of combining the values in public life with Christian values, and is prepared to defend the use of values as a moral concept. While it does not discuss self-employment directly, it does examine the labour market, competition and the complexities of a pluralist society. It argues that the Churches can play a role in sustaining moral values. Turner, on the other hand, puts the primary emphasis on life within the Churches and speaks of the priority of inner freedom before the Christian can turn his or her attention to the public realm.[16]

Two other approaches might be mentioned from a Christian standpoint. One, associated especially with Robert Benne, advocates a greater espousal by the Churches of what he calls democratic capitalism. While there are important criticisms to be made, Benne repudiates the Christian socialism common in the Western Churches for the greater part of this century.[17] A fourth approach would still maintain a strong critique of self-employment and the values of enterprise. There are many theologians who could be cited here. Perhaps the most critical is Jurgen Moltmann, the German theologian who was strongly influenced by the Marxist philospher Ernst Bloch and his monumental work *The Principle of Hope*.[18] Moltmann is especially interesting since his espousal of a form of Marxism was always one that drew on the messianic, dynamic creativity of popular and grassroots Marxism. He therefore regards the capitalist enterprise as deeply flawed. In his book, *On Human Dignity*, there is a chapter entitled, 'America as Dream'.

Turner, the Church of England report *Changing Britain*, Benne and Moltmann offer four different responses to the search for new values in self-employment. Turner looks to the Church as a whole, and individual congregations in particular, to provide an alternative set of values to the dominant economic ones. *Changing Britain* believes a synthesis of Christian and secular values is still possible in the public realm. Benne has a subtle position: he advocates a tension between the gospel and the world, but also an espousal of free-market capitalism. Moltmann is deeply critical of the whole capitalist position, and advocates a Christian socialism. (He has never explicitly adopted a Marxist position in economic analysis, but it is certainly close to the critical position of several of his books, especially *On Human Dignity*.)

These four standpoints offer a useful way into the debate on self-employment, since they represent very different resolutions of the development of economic life in modern Britain. Moltmann is the most straightforward. He sees the development of free-market capitalism as destructive of the environment, and as creating a permanent underclass of poverty. While few expect any answer from the Churches, Moltmann replies that the true Church embodies, 'the reality of the experience of rebirth to a living hope ... the sacrament of God's future and the future of the world ... I do not know any reason for being a Christian other than his divine experience of conversion, rebirth to a living hope and the presence of the kingdom of God in the Spirit of God.'[19]

Moltmann sees the creating God as having a counterpart in the working human being: both in the joy of work and in the self-giving of people through work. Moltmann finds a parallel to the biblical accounts of God rejoicing in his work and the self-renunciation of God. Human work, then, is participation in Christ's lordship, and a form of co-working with God.

But the nature of work remains undefined. Moltmann sees the Calvinist emphasis on work as enterprise as disturbing the balance of the world. For Luther, a person's occupation was a vocation that became a home, where one found the meaning of social existence. For Calvin, the nature of work moves towards the inner voice of God. Faith and the calling of God were demonstrated by the very way in which one worked. This understanding became transformed in the secular society of the twentieth century into the regulation of one's own life by self-examination. Moltmann finds the final development of this concept of work in a description of the contemporary entrepreneur. 'Diligence, initiative, perseverance, willingness to take a risk, a feel for economic opportunities, saving, investment of profit in the enterprise mark the entrepreneur in the industrial age.'[20]

Moltmann rejects this as contempt for the social world: work is not exhausted by its subjective meaning. However, it is not simply the individual entrepreneur whom he criticizes. In a later chapter, 'America as Dream', he offers three definitions of America. The first is promise, the second is covenant, and the third is experiment. Promise leads to the vision of unlimited possibilities, freedoms, powers. Moltmann sees this as a secular manifestation of the desire to build the Kingdom upon earth. In technical terms, it is a messianic eschatology: the drive to realize the last things (*eschatos*) through a deliverer (or messiah). There is a future hope that can be combined with faith in its own realizability on earth. This stems from the Exodus story of the Old Testament, and the experience of the entry into the freedom of the promised land. 'The Puritan Pilgrim fathers experienced and interpreted as an exodus their emigration from European oppression into the freedom of the American wilderness.'[21]

Over against this understanding and promise, Moltmann stresses the reality of the present. He interprets the provisionality of American life as the great weakness of its existence, even if it appears as strength:

> To live with a dream and a hope of its realization is something great and extraordinary. But this life in dream is also something very unreal. One lives in the future, inquires about the realm of possibilities, and thereby depreciates what is real and present.'[22]

What is real and present is the reality of work. 'Through their work in the world human beings can and should correspond to the creative activity of God, from which the world emerged.'[23]

However, two powerful criticisms of Moltmann's own analysis may be mentioned. The first is that he repeatedly uses an uncritical Marxism which regards the Western secular discussion of business ethics and contemporary problems in economic activity as part of a bourgeois culture. Moltmann lapses back into general discussions of the need for humanity to reflect their created being. 'Anything that burdens or destroys the natural environment must be dismantled, or must be banned.'[24] This generality is not helpful, and he has been criticized for failing to provide moral and theological categories that assist choice.

The second criticism is theological. Moltmann views the work of human beings as co-operative with the work of God. Writers both from the New Right, such as Michael Novak, and those from the Marxist Left, such as liberation theologians in South America, value the present reality of work far too highly.[25] Throughout this book the argument has been that the search for new forms of employment create and embody new values. These values can reflect the harmony established by God in Christ, but they are not to be seen as co-creation with God of the world.

The issue has profoundly important consequences. Human beings can find great significance in work, but it is not the only reality in their lives. There are entrepreneurs who let the whole of their lives be swallowed up in work. Nor is the time spent in other activities simply to be seen as 'not work': recreation, community involvement and family life all have independent and worthwhile value. As Barth puts it,

'The life which is obedient to the command of God is much
more than work.'[26]

Humanity is the final object of God's creation, not his
co-partner in the world. The story of Genesis expresses this
in mythological form where human beings are not present
during much of the creation. Furthermore, the creativity of
human work can be expressed in freedom, and not as a task
or obligation. At its simplest, while we certainly do need to
create new forms of social life that will solve the pressing
problems of our planet, we are not given our ultimate value
by this. As Barth puts it, 'Without any works or merit he may
rest with God and then go to his work. . . . The sabbath is the
sign of the freedom which God the Creator has assured to be
gracious to his creatures.'[27]

The implication of this argument is enormous. The entire
Marxist argument rests on the idea that work is a social activity
through which human beings express their essential nature.
Through work, human beings create a new society and find
their true selves. Not surprisingly, it was a theory developed
by many theologians this century, who argued that, 'Socialism
is the only possible economic system from the Christian point
of view.'[28] This is not just an argument of economic efficiency.
It stemmed from the view of many theologians that human
beings, made in the image of God, were workers, and that
the redemption of the world must include the transformation
of work into a harmonious expression of the nature of human
life. Moltmann starts in this tradition, and sees work as
co-creative with God. Therefore for him, 'all work in the
world is . . . filled with the hope of the kingdom of God'.[29]

It is possible however to give a very different place to the
significance of work than this. Human beings are people
in relationships, as Turner and the Church of England's
Changing Britain argue. What matters is the quality of these
values and relationships, not the experience of work above
all else. Barth's exegesis of Scripture is sometimes strained,
and he puts too much weight on the argument that Jesus
did not work as a carpenter after he began his messianic
ministry. Equally, he downplays the significance of Genesis
1.28 overmuch, so that it hardly seems to be a command
to cultivate the earth at all. Nevertheless, Barth's argument
is significant. Human vocation is about the community of
men and women on earth in which work plays a significant

but not overwhelming role. Above all, the significance of human beings does not simply lie in their work.[30] This is surely echoed in many of the comments made by those interviewed in this project. Self-employment is a means by which new communities and values are created. It is not the final existence of life. Moltmann's criticisms of American life may have validity, but his utopianism yields little basis for ethical choice, and tends to collapse into generality. More significant is how much Moltmann over-values work as the expression of who we are. While this is consistent with his interest in Marxism, it is difficult to reconcile this perspective with his new environmentalism. This is especially marked in his most recent book, *Creating a Just Future* (1990). He attempts to reconcile environmentalism with his view of work as fundamental by speaking of work in terms of social participation, but the argument is not developed at all.[31] Moltmann's criticisms then conceal an over-large valuation of the necessity of work, if people are to be fully human.

Turner and *Changing Britain* offer a surer perspective. Turner conceives of Christian social ethics as a Church-led discourse, which then must be translated into the world's terms. It begins with the common life of the Church, which expresses the new existence of the Kingdom of God. Christians will struggle with this challenge, but they cannot be content with this. Out of the reciprocity and dialogue in the Church there should come 'a vision of the sort of common life God intends not merely for the Church, but for society as a whole'. It is not as though Christians are trying to mould society into the life of the Church. Rather, it is that in struggling to live the new life of the Kingdom within the Church's life, there may be a vision of what life in society could become in the Kingdom. Others in society will also have their values and aspirations for society. It is clear that many of those interviewed in this study expressed in fairly tentative terms some new vision of social life based on their experience of the changing society which made up Britain in the last decade. Turner expresses the co-operative activity of Christians in a passage worth quoting in full:

> Life together among Christians can also give them motive, skill and power to enter the general life of society and there

seek with all people 'of good will to bring about a pattern of social relations which more closely approximates the form and quality of life that will be obtained in God's kingdom. Thus Christians can recommend and work to bring about approximations of their vision which are accessible to all people, without making specific reference to religious belief. They can hope to provide good reasons that in no visible way rest upon specifically Christian foundations or require direct use of a Christian vocabulary. Because their social vision rests upon the law of life itself, Christians may hope that the world will prove more patient with the social vision they wish to recommend.[32]

Lying behind this aspiration is Turner's recognition that the pluralist and secular character of modern Western civilization has no wish to accept the authority of the Christian Church, or anyone else. There is both a wide dichotomy of values in modern urban life, with an emphasis on the factual, pragmatic nature of society. Experts gather the data, the manager applies the expert's conclusions, and the therapist assists individuals in coming to terms with this social world.[33]

As with Moltmann's neo-Marxist analysis of capitalism, I have doubts about taking this entire picture wholesale. Turner seems to be embracing the viewpoint of the philosopher Alasdair MacIntyre without qualification, and *Changing Britain* offers a more subtle understanding of the nature of values in society. There is also the consideration that Turner and MacIntyre are writing about the North American context, which appears more secular and pluralist than Europe, in spite of greater Church membership in North America. However, Turner's two-stage argument does offer an important way forward in considering how the Churches might respond to the values expressed by other groups in contemporary society.

Turner recognizes that society does need a set of beliefs, values and purposes that give some moral reference point. If moral concerns become private opinions, and each moral argument is seen in terms of the pressure group that may espouse it, there can be no moral dialogue at all. In a similar vein, John Atherton attempts to justify the notion of the common good as a basis for social discourse.[34]

Turner and Atherton both begin with the nature of the

Church. Turner seeks a way of regarding wealth within the Christian community. The initial starting point is the inner freedom portrayed in Matthew's account of the Sermon on the Mount. The 'poor in spirit' possess an inner freedom, which can be compared to the 'lilies of the field'. This inner freedom means that relationship with God can form the basis of human life. It is not that poverty or wealth is not a highly significant factor, but none the less here is a unique sort of freedom. (I take up the theme of poverty in the final chapter.) What is significant here is that the destructive power of poverty can be broken, in a way that is neither utopian nor idealist. Faith sets the Christian free from the internal dynamic of economic life.

This hope serves as the basis for a Christian ethic which should then recognize the importance of the Church as a communion of believers. We are not individualists but bound together in a new relationship.

In Paul, as in Luke, the poor are cared for within the Church. Money is a means of proclaiming and demonstrating the love of God within the new community. As Turner says, 'The implied interchange of gifts and resources between congregations and individuals, and the implied presence of rich and poor one to another, would reflect the life of God ... the nature of the life of the church on a local, national and international level would be transformed beyond recognition.'[35] This might be spoken of as the stage beyond inner freedom, which could be called the creative hope or spark for life on earth. It is intrinsically related to both worship and the common life of the Church. Atherton sees worship as the reflection of vision and the means for the promotion of vision. Discipleship is inspired by Christian insights which are worked out in promoting a new form of society. Beyond this action, the experience of our social involvement is fed back into worship. There is an interaction between prayer and involvement. Worship, even when it is flawed in terms of its exclusive language or imperfect theology, provides the means by which the dynamic activity of God can be recognized.[36] Furthermore, worship can become formative for those who participate in it:

Wisdom *is* seen to have a creativity set within it.... The movement of God towards humankind, so near to them in love, requires that they recognize him – fear the very one who is nearest to them in love.... Correspondingly, the hope for God which is found in fear provides a creative spark for all human understanding and life. The way to wisdom is through a proper relation (fear) to God, from which there springs a creative hope for life on earth.[37]

A working out of the creative possibility that this argument offers is the generosity that could be practised. Hospitality and generosity can be exercised because wealth is given by God as a trust. So too the creative hope offered in worship can lead people and community groups to practise a remarkable simplicity, or to take risks when financial prudence might advise otherwise. The argument here is not that it is Christian to be imprudent, but rather that the temptation of money is its power to require complete security in wealth.[38]

If the Church can possess what might be called 'generosity', 'vision-building' or the 'creative hope' for society, how might this be spelt out in its life? The immediate challenge is to the idea of human flourishing as standing alone and self-sufficient. Here there would seem to be a direct challenge to much of the pervasive individualism in the rhetoric of the New Right over the last decade. The strong individual who builds his or her company has become one of the folk heroes of the last decade, as Chapter 1 noted. The individual who stands on their own does not have to relate to anyone else, 'for the world is a place where everyone must struggle to improve his/her position by maximizing assets in every way'. The truly strong person in this analysis is the one who is 'impervious to the threat posed by others'.[39] The strong person is so because of where he/she stands, which is usually in control of some company or heading part of an organization. Hence economic life, especially in the City of London, has tended to display a series of takeovers and coups, where the person in power is ousted by someone else. It is hardly surprising that in recent years the City of London has been spoken of as ceaseless conflict, or a jungle, whether in the period of its prosperity or in the sharp retrenchment in the last three years. The complexity of this situation is seen from within as a series of shifting alliances.

The Christian vision is far more easily spelt out in the small companies and some large organizations described above. The vision of the interrelatedness of the Church, where each member is dependent upon one another and each contributes to the common good, should afford images and values that can be set against any description of economic life as made up of sheerly impersonal forces.[40] John Atherton is the one who has spelt this out in the greatest detail. While recognizing the provisionality of any attempt to express the common good, and opting firmly for the necessity of arbitration or conciliation between conflicting viewpoints, Atherton nevertheless believes that it is possible to express what a society built on relationships might mean.[41]

What it would mean for the Church is a commitment to strengthen the social, and economic, relationships that do still exist. There would seem to be two means by which the Church in particular can work on these issues. On the one hand, there is the sustaining of many small ventures in the community and in education, in which the Church already is involved to a considerable degree. This will be taken up in the next chapter, but something of the underlying framework may be given here. On the other hand, there can be a dialogue between the Church and those in employment – those in powerful positions. That is at the heart of this book.

Participating structures enshrine the vision of people living meaningful lives, with the opportunity to affect decisions which are taken on their behalf. Some of the changes in firms like Rover and organizations like the DVLC at Swansea reflect this concern. Participation in the political sphere involves a commitment to democracy, and the extension of participation into intermediate groups, such as voluntary organizations. People can learn what it means to participate, and also are protected from too great a reliance on centralized state power. In economic terms it might mean greater share ownership, employee participation and profit-sharing.

The Christian social perspective emphasizes rights and responsibilities. The Churches will be primarily concerned with promoting the value of relatedness and participation, rather than pressing for detailed policies. The aim is to 'express that strong sense of mutuality and interdependence which arise out of the Christian understanding of the Body of Christ and the common good'. The aim is to communicate to those who are excluded, and to those who are unjust, 'our Christian recognition of them as children of God and fellow heirs of the promise of the kingdom'. At the same time

it is important not to escape into fantasy. When Michael
Novak describes the corporation as a sacramental body,
enduring abuse and yet maintaining its role of suffering
servant, there can only be inflated theological rhetoric. The
value of theology is precisely that it can act as a release
from the social pretensions of contemporary life, and show
where these illusions might lie.[43] Rather than building new
theological edifices, which may not promote the search for
values in economic life, theology 'can challenge us to keep
our intrinsic and instrumental values in the right relationship
so that the priorities we build into our personal economic lives
and our social policies will undergird the deeper meaning of
existence'. This will often prove difficult, as those involved
in economic life reassess priorities.[44]

The dialogue between the attitudes of the self-employed and
theology also has to take into account the vast majority who
are not self-employed. The speed of change, especially in the
last decade, may create feelings of complexity and insecurity,
especially where others are concerned. 'People often express
alarm about the morality and stability of others around them,
even though in response to questionnaires their own personal
stability seems assured.'[45] We are never certain whether we
have chosen the right option, but if there is only free choice
there can be no escape from uncertainty. We often escape
the reality of choice by claiming the necessity of so acting.
Change can threaten the ability to communicate uncertainty.
Thus there is a strange dichotomy in each society, common
to the industrialized West. There is an exaltation of the strong,
solitary individual. There are also those who seek to create
new forms of relatedness. Thirdly, there are those who are
increasingly isolated by poverty or illness. Juxtaposed with
these differences are ones to do with the speed of change. The
vast majority of those interviewed above, not surprisingly,
welcomed change, and actively promoted it. Others simply
accept it as part of human existence, forgetting that, in the
not very distant past, stability was the norm. A third group
regards change very differently. Often they are those who
are isolated anyway. 'The experience of rapid, wide and
continuing change can be unnerving, and can put the moral
tradition under strain. Change can become so threatening that
people can no longer even communicate their fears about it to
one another, and feel isolated in them.'[46] A familiar experience

of mine is raising the changes of the last decade, including self-employment, with older or poorer groups. A pervasive sense of unease, which is not clearly articulated, demonstrates their unhappiness with the changes in modern society.

A dialogue with those caught up in the changes of the last decade will therefore depend on whether one is talking with those who have profited from the changes, or those who have suffered. Those who have profited do not simply include the affluent: they might be those in community groups, education, or those affected by new working practices. The quality of interrelationships for those who have promoted change will become deeply important. This raises the difficult issue of whether competition or co-operation is more effective. Advanced societies employ highly specialized individuals, with ever-greater divisions of labour and specialization of roles, which are promoted by competition. However, within an organization such as a small business, the need will be for co-operation, and this pattern of competition and co-operation is true of relationships between organizations as well. Organizations will engage in hard bargaining (in other words, competition) before the nature and price of co-operation is established.[47]

The theological contribution to this debate, which is one that occurs frequently in small organizations I have visited, is two-fold. On the one hand, over-simplification of the issue does not help. Sensitivity to the issue suggests that co-operation may be essential in, for example, the raising of children. The image of the unconditional love offered by God to Israel in Hosea 11 can act as a paradigm for human relationships that are affirmative and non-coercive. Competition equally may encourage inventiveness, and be a spur to motivation. It may appear that competition is unchristian, but within limits it expresses the full realization of individual talents. The Christian answer will therefore suggest that the truth lies in a tension between these values. Calls for a 'clear lead' are to be resisted, but that does not mean there are no ethical contributions that can be made.

On the other hand, the more there is rapid social change and moral complexity, the more certain it is that those basic moral values that underlie all others need to be strengthened and nurtured. In particular, the notions of person and community are moral concepts that should be respected.[48]

The concept of a person has already been spelt out in this chapter, and the idea of freedom is closely related to it. Within a Christian context, it can be nourished by the idea of 'inner freedom', which can resist the blighting effect of wealth or poverty. Morality thus becomes a matter of respect for persons, and the conditions of their flourishing. Personhood requires other persons in 'a relationship which is typified by freedom, and is expressed in mutuality, in equality of respect and in solidarity'.[49] When those in small businesses, large organizations, community groups or wherever talk of meaningful participation, theology can work on two levels. The key is Turner's distinction between the language of faith and the language of social vision. In terms of faith, the relationship with God is the most deeply personal of all. The value of a person stems from the fact that human beings are made in God's image, and therefore reflect the glory of God. The nature of a person's character does not diminish that claim: our actions do not make us cease to be human, for the cross demonstrates the forgiving love of God (Galatians 2.20). The resurrection makes possible not only forgiveness but the chance of life out of death, new beginnings out of failure. All this is taken up in the Christian understanding of *koinonia*. This Greek New Testament word goes beyond community, for it describes a relationship between people because of their common participation in the same reality. That reality itself has a diversity of meanings, yet which cohere together. It can mean economic sharing, sharing in the experience of salvation, or participation in the Church. Beyond that it meant a sharing in the life of the Spirit, and therefore it encompasses freedom of persons on the one hand, with mutual interrelatedness on the other.[50]

This is the language of faith. The reality of a firm like Whale Tankers is one of a search for greater independence from the state, while seeking to build up the community that is the workforce. Therefore notions such as fairness, justice, honesty and freedom of speech will be combined. The end-product will be some idea of what it might mean for a firm to work well, where freedom (from the state) and interrelatedness (within the company) can be expressed. Other terms that could be used are those of service and communication. 'We won't take fees unless we deliver value. It's an ethical point,' was the way Carolyn Hayman of Korda put it. We want to give 'managerial skills to the shop floor ...' said David Scrimshire. Not every firm succeeded in its aims. Thermica of Hull reflected on the culture of 'fiddling the firm' from those it recruited who were long-term unemployed, though this point was made neither as a generalization about the long-term unemployed nor as an excuse for not trying again. Brian Whitfield, chairman of the Teesside Small Business Club and director of a tar-paulin manufacturer, knew how little impact small firms were making on the unemployed teenagers of Cleveland.

Values then need to be nurtured. The Churches will have a pastoral responsibility for their own members, who may work in business, but the task of the Church goes far beyond this concern. Pastoral responsibility in Turner's description is still within the language of faith. The secular world cannot be addressed in such language, although there is still a residue of understanding when the Christian faith is articulated. Christian theology has always recognized the importance and necessity of speech beyond the confines of faith, and dialogue with this world. In the thirteenth century, Thomas Aquinas, perhaps the greatest theologian of the Catholic Church, regu-larly quoted Muslim philosophers who, like himself, were rediscovering the works of Aristotle. The Christian tradition has also argued that there is a natural knowledge of morality, and that in principle at least the human mind can affirm the values of human flourishing and well-being. For instance, the Ten Commandments 'are not arbitrary divine impositions, but rather the way that a particular culture has understood divine concern for the human creatures, the people, whom God is in process of forming'.[51]

Changing Britain ends by quoting Karl Rahner, who has already been mentioned in this chapter. Rahner writes that the task for the churches should be 'morality without moralizing.... We are moralizing if we expound norms of behaviour peevishly or pedantically, full of moral indignation at a world without morals, without really tracing them back to that innermost experience of man's nature which is the source of the so-called principles of natural law and which alone gives them binding force.'[52]

Benne advocates a form of free-market capitalism which is more thoroughgoing than any mentioned by the contributors cited so far. It is therefore worth ending this chapter with his attempt to translate the Christian faith into the language of secular philosophy, while also noting his warning. Using symbolic language, he writes that

> the Fall refers to the tragedy of our willing and acting as we exercise our freedom. Both [Benne refers to Paradise and the Fall] are symbols that attempt to interpret the tragic facts of our existence. The Fall particularly is an effort to hold together both the inevitability of our fate and our responsibility for it.... We are also aware of the unique circumstances and gifts of our being and the need to use them under conditions of scarcity in time and energy.[53]

Benne argues that this reflection gives rise to anxiety about our limits and possibilities. Anxiety prompts us to creativity while there is yet time to use our opportunities. We also use the occasion of our anxiety to make an idol of our culture.

The culture of democratic capitalism expresses both elements of this anxiety. The free market has given the United States an efficient economy, high living standards and human liberties. It 'preserves respect for humans as ends in themselves, as centres of self-transcending freedom'. It encourages 'voluntary human community without which human fulfillment is impossible'.[54] Yet at the same time capitalism markets hedonism and sensuality. Benne refers to an earlier American theologian of this century, Reinhold Niebuhr. Sensuality for Niebuhr is an inordinate devotion to mutable goods: pleasures of food, sex, play or drink. The character encouraged by sensuality is not marked by aggressive will-to-power but in using others for self-gratification. Sensuality negotiates everything, including job and organizations, as ends to pleasure. The pursuit of pleasure has no limits.[55]

Benne, like *Changing Britain*, returns to the need for morality without moralizing. Therefore he is insistent that the task of the Church is a dual one. On the one hand, it must continue to be faithful to the gospel that it preaches. On the other hand, it must also seek to understand the capitalist culture that surrounds it, speaking a secular language of the market-place and criticizing where necessary. Benne does not doubt the difficulty of this task. He knows that contemporary society 'has marginalized and privatized' the claims of Christianity to be of relevance to the 'evolving system of democratic capitalism'. However, he proceeds with care. He rejects uch of the *Christian Century*'s 1991 'Post-

Communist Manifesto', drafted by Max Stackhouse and Dennis McCann.[56]

This manifesto made a series of claims for theology and capitalism: 'Working to serve people's needs in the market-place may be a holy vocation in and for the salvation of the world.' 'Interests not guarded by theology and channeled by covenanted communities of faith march through the world like armies in the night.' Public theology must construct a 'cosmopolitan social ethic' in which 'democracy, human rights and a mixed economy are acknowledged as universal necessities'. 'Any account, including a Marxist one, of why things are the way they are that does not speak of theology and ecclesiology (the doctrine of the nature of the church) errs.'[57]

In so far as McCann, who was certainly a Catholic theologian deeply critical of capitalism in the 1970s, has simply shifted his views in the 1990s, this is merely a debate among American intellectuals. Reminiscent of the 1940s renunciation of communism by Koestler and others, it does not concern this book. But there is a much wider issue, which Benne correctly points to. Theology here is being conflated with political and social analysis, in much the same way as Moltmann does, only from a capitalist perspective. Benne denies that the mission of the Church is to encourage capitalism, however much it might be the only viable economic system in the final decade of the twentieth century. The mission of the Church is the preaching of the gospel. The danger of collapsing salvation into a particular form of creative action is that the universality and challenge of religious truth becomes compromised. Grace is not available only for those with politically or economically correct opinions.

There is also a danger that far too much is being claimed for theology. The analysis of contemporary capitalism needs to be undertaken by a public philosophy which is informed by a knowledge of economics, social theory and history. This in turn can be related to theology and Christian ethics. Christian ethicists, commenting on changes in economic life, use a public philosophy informed on the one hand by economic and social theory, and on the other by theology and Christian ethical theory. This debate can be carried on both by those whose primary knowledge is of economics and by those who are theologians. Both utilize the language of public philosophy, which goes beyond the professional discourse of economists or the assumptions of the language of faith.

Benne's analysis of how theologians might comment on economic activity forms the basis for this book. The attempt, in Benne's words, 'to draw a straight line between the Christian Gospel and human action in any economic programme, as well as the inordinate claims made for its clericalized model of public theology, deserve criticism'.

There is also the danger that wealth is separated from notions of worth and well-being. Jack Mahoney has drawn attention to the danger of theologies of wealth being seen as adversarial defences of political positions. This turns a theology of wealth into a right-wing rebuttal of radical Christianity. There are two dangers here. First, theology is rarely done well from an adversarial position. Secondly, it ignores fundamental ethical questions of wealth, competition and well-being irrespective of political ideology.

Mahoney distinguishes between the social use of wealth, which can be seen positively, and the personal or individual possession of riches, which is a familiar concern of the early Church. This argument is developed further in the final chapter. There is no clear theology of wealth-creation in the Judaeo-Christian tradition, which is why it is easier for Christians in the prophetic tradition to turn to the Old Testament. Nevertheless, a theology of creation needs to be worked out.[58]

The creation of wealth in society is therefore closely related to a social understanding of wealth. Wealth must be created socially to finance health-care, but health-care is a different form of wealth. Torrey writes, 'We valued the National Health Service on criteria other than its benefit to the economy, for people's health is a corporate and individual good unquantifiable in financial terms.'[59] Money is obviously an arbiter of worth, and there are ways of costing health and illness in economic arguments from cost/benefit analysis. Beyond that, however, the sense of well-being both individually and corporately from being healthy is (as I know myself) a value that transcends economic analysis. Fiscal wealth becomes the means to sustain personal well-being by health-care.

How theology and economics might be related has been the concern of this section. It is a matter of 'placing' economic activity correctly, and then seeking to discern what a public philosophy might be like. Apart from a discussion of Schumpeter and Galbraith early on, this book does not concentrate on economic theory. Far more I have examined economic activity, and the values of those engaged in it. The aim is the construction of a public philosophy in which theology can be seen to have informed the analysis.[60]

However, the response of theologians to the values of capitalism are very diverse. This section has concentrated on a number of representative authors, including Jurgen Moltmann, Philip Turner, John Atherton and Robert Benne. I have also looked at the Church of England report, *Changing Britain*. It is clear that all of them recognize the overwhelming importance that economics has in all aspects of life today. Given this fact, and the opportunities that economic activity can offer to some and deny to others, theologians adopt a set of responses that seek to maintain economic activity in its proper place.

But what is that place? Moltmann offers the paradox of both valuing work as expressing the essence of humanity, while condemning the free-markets as inherently destructive. Despite valuable contributions on the Trinity and human life cited earlier in this book, Moltmann appears to both over-value and under-value economic life in the free-market. It is neither so important as he suggests for who we are, nor so destructive either. There seems to be no way of generating a proper dialogue that yields workable moral criteria.

Atherton, Turner and *Changing Britain* all move between the language of faith and that of secular reality. Turner's is the most church-centred, reflecting much of his despair at the possibility of re-establishing a moral order in the diverse pluralism of contemporary society. Nevertheless, he insists on the importance of the Christian congregation moving beyond its boundaries. There are two aspects of his thought that are very useful. One is the notion that the congregation can develop a sense of responses to economic life even before it becomes involved in the world. Such responses include the idea of 'inner freedom', sharing between rich and poor, and generosity. The second aspect is the distinction between the language of faith and that of the secular world.

Changing Britain has made the most significant contribution to this task. As well as enlisting lay people working in industry, education, youth work and medicine, the working party contained a number of theologians and sociologists who were very aware of the gulf between the two worlds.

Preston, Mahoney, Halsey and Archbishop Habgood of York attempted to fashion a means of elucidating the complexity of moral issues in the secular world, while still allowing the Churches to be in dialogue with them. Although it met with a critical reception from many Christians who wanted a clearer statement of values, and from politically activist groups who felt that it ignored the social and economic problem of many groups, it remains a deeply significant attempt to bridge the two worlds of theology and secular life. There has been no other major attempt to mediate between these two realms of values, and it is a report that will have a significance beyond its initial publication.

Atherton and Benne both discuss the structures of free-market capitalism. Atherton concentrates on ways in which British society can remain participatory for all those who live within it. He uses the Christian language of the Church as the Body of Christ alongside the tradition of 'the common good', and seeks to find means by which these organic metaphors can be earthed. By far the most practical and concrete of all the theologians discussed, he suggests that the dialogue with those in employment must seek to find ways of working with the reality of the situation, not against it. He is therefore deeply critical of Moltmann. His position on the future of British society is both very critical about the growth of the long-term unemployed, while hopeful that a free-market system can still embody the common good that is an anticipation of the Kingdom of God. Something of the same ambiguity is found in Benne, although his book is more affirmative of capitalism and more concerned with theoretical issues of justice.

With this section, the empirical survey of the enterprise culture is concluded. I have examined the stories and values of those working in economic life, seeking to reflect on their goals and aspirations. Another two chapters looked at community enterprise, education and ethnic enterprise. Here the question is what sort of society these different manifestations of enterprise are set in and surrounded by. Equally, one can ask what sort of society it should be. Finally, this chapter described the attitudes of those engaged in self-employment, before raising the difficult question of whether the Church can communicate with these attitudes at all.

Two final tasks now remain. One is to ascertain what

moral questions the enterprise culture raises, and whether the outlines of an answer to this issue can be found. The final chapter returns explicitly to the theological task. The first part of Chapter 7 is historical, and looks back at what the Judaeo-Christian tradition has felt about economic life from the earliest times. The final section, properly for a theologian, seeks to ask how the activity of God relates to the growth of this new culture. By re-examining the theological tradition, a move can be made to constructing a public philosophy informed by faith.

Notes

1. K. Rahner, *Foundations of the Christian Faith*, 1978.
2. ibid., p. 12.
3. ibid., p. 14.
4. C. Gould, *Rethinking Democracy*, 1988.
5. S. Cowdell, *Atheist Priest? Don Cupitt and Christianity*, 1988, p. 75, quoting Fergus Kerr, Cupitt's Dogmas, *New Blackfriars*, vol. 62, 1981, pp. 204–14.
6. C. Hakim, 'Self-Employment in Britain: A Review of Recent Trends and Current Issues', *Work, Employment and Society*, vol. 2, no. 4, December 1988.
7. P. Leighton, 'Employment and Self-employment', *Employment Gazette*, 91. 5, 1983.
8. J. Payne, 'Young Self-employed Workers', *Employment Gazette*, 92. 11, 1984.
9. R. Scase and R. Goffee, *The Entrepreneurial Middle Class*, 1982.
10. J. Bevan, *Barriers to Business Start-up*, 1989.
11. S. Carter and T. Cannon, *Female Entrepreneurs*, 1988.
12. *The Independent*, 3–5 May 1989.
13. *The Independent*, 15 August 1988.
14. D. Storey, *Fast Growth Small Businesses*, 1989, and D. Storey, *Entrepreneurship and the New Firm*, 1982.
15. P. Turner, *Sex, Money and Power*, 1985, pp. 71–3. Turner is quoting W. Safire, 'Principle Versus Value', *New York Times Magazine*, 12 August 1984, p.8.
16. *Changing Britain: Social Diversity and Moral Unity*, 1987. Emmett's book is quoted on p. 18.
17. R. Benne, *The Ethic of Democratic Capitalism*, 1981. His response to the 1991 'Post-Communist Manifesto' in *The Christian Century* is given in the issue of 23 January 1991, under the title 'Ethics, Economics, and the Corporate life'.
18. See J. Moltmann, *On Human Dignity*, 1984. Moltmann's *God in Creation*, 1985, is less political. Criticism of Moltmann's work is given in P. West's 'Cruciform Labour? The Cross in Two Recent Theologies of Work', *Modern Churchman*, XXVIII, no. 4, 1986, pp. 9–15. See also

the same author's 'Karl Barth's Theology of Work: A Resource for the late 1980s', *Modern Churchman*, XXIX, no. 3, 1987, pp. 13–19, and 'Divine Creativity and Human Creativity', *New Blackfriars*, LXVII, 1986, pp. 478–84. Finally, there is the recent set of lectures given in 1987–9 by Moltmann, published as *Creating a Just Future*, 1990.

19. Moltmann, *Creating a Just Future*, p. 5.
20. Walter Raymond Foundation, quoted on p. 49 of *On Human Dignity*.
21. Moltmann, *On Human Dignity*, p. 153.
22. ibid., p. 160.
23. ibid., p. 40.
24. Moltmann, *Creating a Just Future*, p. 14. Ronald Preston has been especially critical; see *The Future of Christian Ethics*, 1987, p. 95.
25. The articles by Philip West are helpful here, although I am not persuaded by his argument that divine creation refers to the establishment by God of the truly just society. Creation must refer to the action of God in freely creating this world and choosing human beings to be the object of his love.
26. K. Barth, *Church Dogmatics*, 1965, III/4, p. 471.
27. ibid., III/4, pp. 50ff.
28. P. Tillich, *Religious Socialism*, 1978.
29. *On Human Dignity*, p. 44.
30. Barth, III/4, pp. 470–5.
31. Moltmann, *Creating a Just Future*, p. 11.
32. Turner, p. 9.
33. ibid., pp. 106–7. He is quoting MacIntyre's *After Virtue*, 1981, and *Secularization and Moral Change*, 1967.
34. J. Atherton, *Faith in the Nation*, 1988, pp. 31–47.
35. Turner, p. 87.
36. Atherton, p. 130.
37. D.W. Hardy, *The Foundation of Cognition and Ethics in Worship*, 1991, p. 26.
38. Turner, pp. 90–1.
39. Hardy, p. 32.
40. Turner, p. 95.
41. Atherton, pp. 66–101. Paul Ballard's *In and Out of Work: A Pastoral Perspective*, 1987, is written specifically for people working on such issues of relatedness. J.P. Wogaman, *Economics and Ethics*, 1986, has less on participation, but does address the questions of poverty and education as discriminating against those without work.
42. Atherton, p. 81.
43. Wogaman, p. 39.
44. ibid., p. 40.
45. *Changing Britain*, para 8. Stanley Hauerwas, in *The Peaceable Kingdom*, 1984, ch. 1, and M. Douglas Meeks, in *God the Economist*, 1989, p. 165, both discuss the complex relationship of being free to choose in our society, yet having no option but to choose. The area encompassed by 'choice' widens each decade, including now the option of relationships or marriage, children in marriage, and even, for a few individuals, whether to work beyond middle age or live off what one has earned thus far. Medical ethics also offers increasing choices.

46. *Changing Britain*, para. 8.
47. ibid., paras 91–103, especially para. 96.
48. ibid., para. 135.
49. ibid., paras 55–6.
50. ibid., paras 57 and 62.
51. ibid., para. 53.
52. ibid., para. 183, quoting K. Rahner, *The Shape of the Church to Come*, 1974, p. 66.
53. R. Benne, *The Ethic of Democratic Capitalism*, 1981, p. 29.
54. ibid., p. 173.
55. ibid., pp. 250–5.
56. Benne, *Christian Century*, 23 January 1991.
57. *Christian Century*, 16 January 1991. Dennis McCann's earlier books include *Christian Realism and Liberation Theology*. Max Stackhouse has written *Public Theology and Political Economy*.
58. J. Mahoney, 'Wealth in the Judaeo-Christian Tradition', in D.W. Hardy and P.H. Sedgwick (eds), *The Weight of Glory*, 1991.
59. M. Torrey, 'Is Money the Sole Arbiter of Worth?' *ICF Quarterly*, 1989.
60. M. Fogarty, 'The Churches and the Creation of Wealth', *The Month*, April 1989.

6

The Ethics of Enterprise

Responsibility and ethics

It is surely the case that the ethical aspects of the enterprise culture have earned most criticism. It has repeatedly been attacked for greed, selfishness, exploitation and a crude disregard for any interests but one's own. However, suggestions for an ethical framework are dismissed by many advocates of an enterprise culture as an attempt to stifle the spirit of enterprise before it has even been established in Britain.

My own surveys and interviews have highlighted the following facts. Although few of the people I visited attended a church, there were many discussions about values and goals. Since those interviewed were not selected on any prior basis, but simply through contacts, this was a surprising finding. Indeed, one senior Anglican clergyman, who had previously run a ministerial training course in the south of England, said that the decision of a woman in her forties to seek ordination and the decision of a woman of similar age and background to start a business were probably very similar ones. Both include a search for oneself, a desire to discover values that have an integrity because they have been tested in experience, a considerable tension with institutions which might be resolved by putting energy into the world of the small parish/small business.

From this perspective, which I found very illuminating, the question of ethics becomes very broad indeed. There appear to be two issues which, although related, must not be confused. The first issue is that of global and national well-being. Within this area, the following ethical questions for enterprise need to be examined:

1. Global poverty, and the issue of whether firms like Traidcraft can use the market to establish greater prosperity in the world outside the rich trading blocs.
2. Environmental protection, and the relationship of this to

business, government regulation and consumer education. Educational bodies such as ICOREC, working with the World Wide Fund for Nature, are important here. So too are those who seek to bridge the worlds of business, and the environment, such as the recent books by David Pearce, John Elkington and John Davis.

3. The growth of poverty inside Britain (sometimes, and perhaps not very carefully, swept into the category of 'the underclass'), and the place of community development. Some of this has already been mentioned, but Frank Field's writings should also be referred to.

4. The difficult question of whether the enterprise culture simply results in the growth of greater consumption. I have much sympathy with those who will not use the term enterprise because it has been devalued by a 1980s search for pleasure, greed and irresponsibility. Charles Handy made his point to me in an interview.[1] He said that it had also become a political term. He argued that entrepreneurs create wealth, but not necessarily material objects. If there is only the creation of financial wealth, then it will be ephemeral. Creating financial wealth, as in banking, need not of course be synonymous with greed: it can have very high standards,[2] but the 1980s have all too often seen the association of hedonism and financial skill. A different point is the growth of consumerism, which can be about greater protection in the market-place, or can go much further, as in the National Consumer Council, and the interests of those who are clients in health, education, transport, etc. The Citizen's Charter has picked up this aspect of consumerism. Consumer pressure for corporate accountability has recently been surveyed in the book *Morality and the Market* by N. Craig Smith.[3]

A different area altogether is the issue of ethics within a company. Here too there is great diversity, but the main disagreements appear to be these:

1. The question of conscientious dissent within the workforce, or whistleblowing. There have been several cases of this in the 1980s, involving such well-known firms as Guardian Royal Exchange where a manager disclosed financial transactions to the Inland Revenue.

His dismissal, and GRE's refusal to reinstate him despite
the ruling of an Industrial Tribunal, showed the need for
guidelines in this area.

2. The question of sub-contracting. Many small firms will
    take on work that previously would have been done
    inside a large company. The sub-contracting may involve
    the issue of workers alongside each other on the same
    site with different levels of pay, job security, or comp-
    ensation in the event of an accident.

3. The question, if it is an ethical one, of whether employee
    participation can be enhanced in the company by
    employee share ownership. This has been a matter
    of interest to all political parties in recent years. One
    report advocating its extension is from the Institute of
    Public Policy Research, *A Stake in the Company*.[4] Other
    researchers have raised the question of employee relations
    in the small firm.

4. Finally in this area there is the growth of ethical invest-
    ment trusts. This has been a fast-growing area of the
    Stock Exchange in Britain, and in the United States
    ethical investment is firmly established.

These two areas of social welfare and issues primarily concerning business are related, though, in a third sector – a
sector that has been especially promoted in this last decade.
This is the field of promoting business involvement in the
community. Business in the Community has taken a lead in
this area, as has the British Institute of Management. It is
large corporations who often can afford the greatest financial
involvement in social responsibility, but small firms, while
they may have less finance available, can have a very powerful
impact on their local community. Many firms interviewed
clearly saw themselves as having a responsibility to their
local community. Paradoxically, the 1990–1 recession tended
to make ethical issues inside the City of London appear with
much greater clarity as the financial boom slowed down, but
it also had the effect of making social involvement in the
local community by a small firm very difficult indeed as the
firm struggled to survive. One major study of this whole area is
from the Policy Studies Institute, *Companies and Communities*,
by Ian Christie and Michael Fogarty. Ian Christie was a
member of this research project's advisory group.[5]

However, it is not only through the idea of business involvement that the worlds of society, and industry and commerce, can be linked. The theme of responsibility has become an overarching concept which includes other themes such as citizenship, the environment, or ethics inside business. Vaclav Havel has invoked it as one of the main components of the regeneration of Czech society after the end of the era of communism. Responsibility implies the need for a strong individual ethic, but also a rediscovery of what it means to live in a community. As Geoff Mulgan argues in a recent article, responsibility as a term resists political appropriation. Arguments about responsibility 'challenge both the unfairness and amorality of the market and the diffusion of responsibility brought about by large-scale industrial socialism'.[6] Responsibility, especially in a Christian understanding, is not just about accepting where blame can be allocated. It is also about acting on behalf of others, and empowering others so that they are able to act in a new way. So this sense of prospective responsibility, where we answer for what we will do, is closely related to our freedom as people created by God. We are called to respond to God's call and 'the idea of responsibility [is the term] which gives us the most exact definition in face of the absolute transcendence of the divine judgement'.[7] Barth is arguing here that God sees us for what we are, and God's vision of humanity is a challenge to our lives. How we work within the world, reforming its structures in ways that enable others to be themselves, is the real task of Christian witness. It is not merely a life of accountability to God's pre-ordained law. Responsibility becomes a future, dynamic aspect of our lives under God.

Freedom in the enterprise culture can become rhetorical: 'the conquest of meaning by vacuity' to quote Mulgan's judgement on much recent political discourse.[8] Yet the freedom to do the right thing goes far beyond freedom without restraint. Bearing responsibility is a human task as much as exercising freedom, but Marxist philosophy is silent on this issue. It replaced the language of responsibility with that of power, and certainly exposed the way in which moral language, religious and otherwise, was intertwined with the defence of privilege and power. Nevertheless, when this necessary task is achieved, there remains the nature of responsibility. Christian theology has taken up the need for responsibility on behalf of others, especially in the writings of Bonhoeffer. The centre of ethics is Christ, where humanity is loved, judged and renewed. Out of this renewal can come a recovery of natural rights and obligations, the response to a particular situation, or long-term social action:

> Christian ethics involves a willingness freely to accept the role of deputy for others when a concrete occasion arises; it means doing whatever seems pertinent according to the facts of the situation and accepting guilt if the action turns out not to accord with the will of God disclosed in Christ. Responsibility is the Christian's vocation, urged Bonhoeffer, and this means obeying the call of Christ by responding with one's total being to the whole of reality.[9]

Responsibility as a concept has very specific implications, whether taken as accountability or responsibility for others. The link between power and responsibility is very important. It is also the case that many pressure groups, such as the Basic Income Research Group, see the crucial issue as enabling people to take responsibility in society when they are currently excluded from it. How then should the ethical framework be constructed around enterprise, so that responsibility might be enhanced? It is primarily a matter, theologically, of re-evaluating the nature of individualism. Much individualism in recent years is to do with a wholly internal accountability. The person is inner-directed, and can withstand any degree of social pressure. John Habgood notes that such people, who are often isolated and autonomous, are easily recognized in many of the industrial pioneers of the last century. They may also flourish in authoritarian religious contexts, 'driven by high ideals with clear goals for worldly or other-worldly success'. Other individuals are equally autonomous, but lack any internal moral sense. They fail to see any interdependence with others. Others again lack both a strong inner drive and a moral awareness. 'For them individualism primarily entails self-expression. The aim is to be different, independent, authentic, even idiosyncratic.'

Yet such a life can become empty, and simply become absorbed in self-expression through consumerism. To quote John Habgood again, 'Conspicuous consumption is one of the marks of success in the race for self-enhancement. But it can also be an expression of idolatry in the sense that our possessions help to define our ego. Feuerbach's derogatory comment that "man is what he eats" can be alarmingly true if "consumes" is substituted for "eats".'[10]

There needs to be a rediscovery of moral roots and a turning towards moral goals, in any Christian comment on the enterprise culture. The gospel illuminates human life, so that a new vision or perspective is opened up on human society. Condemning consumerism in itself will not be helpful, unless there is a realization that this passion stems from a lack of vision. The role of the Church, as Charles Handy and others said, is to applaud the good and bless whatever signs of hope and light there are. Responsibility is then bound up with handling questions of values, and asking what values established companies promote.[11]

Social ethics

The question of global poverty is one of the most intransigent issues of recent years. Nevertheless, companies like Traidcraft, and agencies such as Christian Aid, have worked to establish just and successful trading links with developing countries.[12] Indeed, Traidcraft might be said by accusers to be doubly suspect, as a 'Christian firm' might conceal much aggressive behaviour inside the company, as well as alienating people by the use of religious language.[13] Traidcraft was founded in 1979, and in its first decade sold £15 million worth of products from the Third World. Turnover is now approaching £5 million, and growing (in 1989) at 20 per cent including recycled paper products. It buys from small producers working in the poorest communities, and sells them in Britain by mail-order catalogues and the help of nearly 2,000 volunteers. It is clearly a very successful company, and empowers those who would otherwise have no chance to develop their own lives. It is a graphic instance of taking responsibility for others, in a way that nevertheless respects their freedom.

Traidcraft's objectives were worked out by its employees over a six month period in 1986. The executive directors let the staff have considerable autonomy in drawing up the mission statement, and there was an awareness that the ethical criteria by which the company operates should also affect its internal life. Just trade was defined as fairer systems; developing people's potential; more and better jobs; fairer relationships within Traidcraft; and efficient and practical structures.[14]

Michael Taylor's book is a closely argued discussion of whether it is correct morally to strengthen the poor against the rich, in terms of a Christian ethic. His book *Good for the Poor* has many examples of small co-operatives in rural villages which combine farming with financial help. Alongside this in the same village there might be adult literacy classes which are also a form of political and social education. Taylor questions whether building up the poor against the power of the rich might not be sub-Christian. There is little of self-sacrifice in it, nor much of forgiveness. Yet he argues that the realism 'which seeks to strengthen the poor to stand up to those who otherwise will continue to decide against them'[15] might downplay the more generous and creative side to human nature, but it assumes that people will behave badly if given the chance. Yet this realism is a form of love. 'Just as love will achieve no good if it adopts techniques of agricultural production or economic aid and development which simply do not work, so it will do more harm than good if it refuses to take the limitations of human nature into account. . . . Such realism is not the opposite or the betrayal of Christian love. It is a way of loving.'[16]

Whether foreign aid actually works is a technical issue that goes far beyond the range of this book. Taylor discusses Roger Ridell's book *Foreign Aid Reconsidered* in some detail.[17] A strong criticism of government aid is given by Graham Hancock in *Lords of Poverty*.[18] Both studies examine the corruption of Third World governments. Riddell comes up with inconclusive answers to the question of foreign aid, in the form of capital for investment, while Hancock is very critical of corruption. Nevertheless, Taylor argues that the international economic system, especially the world debt crisis, has a dire effect on the very poorest countries. Thus he argues that the way forward for Christians is both to appeal to the strong and to strengthen the weak. Appealing to the strong would mean fairer terms of trade for the Third World, and more control by the Third World countries over multinationals. Above all, it would mean reducing the debt that many such countries have incurred. Strengthening the weak means forming communities that can work together politically and economically to establish their independence. Stimulating economic growth and helping the poor are not contradictory objectives in the view of the 1990 World Bank Report, which cites examples such as Indonesia and Malaysia.

Enterprise then is not in itself harmful to the Third World. What is destructive is the way in which rich trading nations shut out poorer ones. What is also destructive is 'the pace of self-centred Western materialism' and the manner by which 'our own increasingly affluent lifestyles are a direct cause of the growing gulf between Third World and First.'[19] Adams's work at Traidcraft is an attempt to show how an entrepreneurial vision can help to relieve poverty, but, like Taylor, he would be the first to argue for the need for wider structural changes as well.

Environmental protection has much in common with the movement for world development. The very successful firm Body Shop promotes 'green manufacturing'. There is an awareness that luxury and affluence in the West will destroy, or at the least degrade, what we have inherited on our planet. Christians need to find a theological ethic that is environmentally aware, just as part of Taylor's book discusses the relationship of Christian evangelism and mission to world development. Traidcraft is an evangelical company, and the tension with Bishop David Jenkins (the company has its head-quarters in his diocese) is clear. Again there is a search for a new theological ethic of world development. Finally, there is the question of whether there can be an overall compatibility between the market and environmentalism. Is Body Shop simply an unusual company, or can companies embrace a business ethic that includes environmental protection?[20]

Those who have defended enterprise from a New Right position have argued that free transaction by private agents is not only more efficient but also morally superior to trans-actions determined by the state. Thus the state has no right to intervene, if the two parties are satisfied. This argument clearly fails in the case of the environment (including harm to animals, as in animal testing). A green policy might allow state intervention to protect the environment, but it may need to go further. Nicholas Ridley argued in *Policies against Pollution*[21] that 'it is an essential part of the free market philosophy that regulation by government is necessary to secure the public interest in environmental protection.... It is an ill

for which the operation of the free market provides no
automatic care.' However a green policy might influence
prices and public investment. David Pearce argues that there
is no need to halt economic growth. Again the argument, like
that on overseas aid, is both complex and controversial. Pearce
writes 'With wise management of resources it is possible to
drive a wedge between economic forces and their effect on
the environment.'[22]

There are a number of ways in which governments can
intervene. Environmental protection legislation can set the
base line whereby all companies have to come within that
limit of pollution. A second step is to have a 'pollution
tax', where companies are charged for any polluting at all.
The easiest way, as Pearce says, to avoid the taxation is to
install non-polluting technology. A 'pollution tax' might be
successful and raise no revenue at all.

A third step is for the state to stop interfering in the
market in ways that harm the environment, and instead to
tax 'ungreen' products. Markets must be made to reflect environmental costs, by withdrawing subsidiaries from polluting
processes (such as pesticides in agriculture, which are often
over-used in developing countries) and by letting some products carry a higher price through taxation.

This argument avoids resorting to massive regulation. This
may be necessary as a final position, but the bureaucratic cost
is high. It also moves away from state control as the answer,
for the problem with this position is clear. If the state both
owns the polluting operation, and also wishes to regulate it,
there is a conflict of interests. This conflict might be financial,
or in terms of employment, or political. It is easier to resolve
conflicts of interests through environmental economics. Green
economics develops techniques that value costs and benefits
as far as possible. Using financial values is only a technique,
but it does point to the need to trade off benefits from one
source against another. Beyond these evaluations we move
into issues that cannot be defined financially, such as the
benefits of future generations.

At this point theology can re-enter the debate, since the
fallacy is to think that our hopes must be entirely based on
ethics. John Zizioulas has argued that moral rules are hard to
follow if they are separated from religious beliefs.[23] Zizioulas
argues for a new ethos rather than an ethic, which would

embrace the mythological, the imaginative and the sacred. Perhaps human beings should then see themselves as called by God to be responsible for creation as servant-priests of creation: 'we must be the channel through which God's grace and deliverance is shared with all creation. The human being is simply and yet gloriously the means for the expression of creation in its fullness and the coming of God's deliverance for all creation.'[24]

There is also the involvement of companies and consumers. Body Shop has negotiated with anthropologists and Indian tribes to buy products that will support the local economy without damaging the forest. All their products are bio-degradable, and there is no animal experimentation. However John Davis's book argues that there will need to be a much more radical rethinking by all companies of what sustainable development might mean. His arguments range over labour-intensive versus capital intensive methods of production, and questions of repair and reconditioning. He wishes industry to switch to recycling and reuse. However, his book goes much further than this, for he tackles the whole question of responsibility and consumer affluence, which has been a theme of this chapter. Self-respect, self-fulfilment and transcendence are the ultimate human needs, and this will require a complete rethinking of how people are employed.[25] Much of Davis's argument on management in chapter 5 of his book is about the importance of small groups. He thus echoes the aspirations expressed repeatedly by those interviewed during this research for values that allow people to be autonomous, yet interdependent. But these are precisely the values that will also allow sustainable development.

The ethical challenge of the environment and of the Third World can be, and must be, met. However, there is a third challenge, which is equally severe.[26] Much of the criticism of enterprise sees it as entirely devoted to consumption, which destroys morality by the cultural contradictions of capitalism. This collection of essays from Lancaster University, *Enterprise Culture*, takes this position in its examination of the rhetoric of Lord Young.

Similar criticism comes from the psychologist David Smail, Professor of Psychology at Nottingham, in his book *Taking Care: An Alternative to Therapy*. Smail does not attack enter-prise directly, but he sees society as living in a state of adolescent longing, pain-avoidance and consumerism. This is combined with an acceptance in society of the values of expendability, competitiveness and cost-effectiveness. Smail says, 'The things that mean a lot to me are Christian ethics from a stoical point of view.... Self-sacrifice, loving your neighbour – these are valid claims.' There needs to be a public space to talk about morality, justice and love, alongside the pursuit of happiness, and its success as something that can be marketed. An uncaring, power-driven world is one in which people will find it hard to have any fundamental values.

Smail is not a Marxist, and he does not attack capitalism directly. What he does do is show that the cultural changes described in this book can be very damaging. Individual therapy is not sufficient: there needs to be a public change as well. This implies that a return to an older, traditional society is unlikely to work, even if some criticisms of enterprise argue in this way. Indeed it needs to be emphasized that human beings can achieve altruism and universalism, as well as a reason for self-interest. It is the former that needs encouraging, for self-interest is always a strong and compelling viewpoint.[27] Others are much more pessimistic: Paul Heelas's essay, 'Reforming the Self', sees the enterprising self as evolving into an authoritarian personality. He looks for a reaction against the whole movement of enterprise similar to the Romantic movement or the 1960s sensibility.[28]

There is no way of 'carving up morality into a private sector and a public sector. We are social beings ... it means that for the foreseeable future we are going to be involved in the stresses and strains of public life, as well as in that all-important and personal commitment and personal moral growth without which our role as Christians in public life would be merely fraudulent'.[29] Smail and Heelas pose a fundamental challenge to the concept of enterprise. If a personal and public morality can be sustained alongside the freedom of the enterprise culture, it will offer a way of moving away from older, hierarchical conceptions of society. I take up this theme in Chapter 7, and have written about it elsewhere.[30]

One final comment must be made about poverty. Much industrial mission work has seen in homeworking the exploitation of the most marginal sections of our society – Asian women: 'the lowest paid and most exploited workers.'[31] Yet those who exploit them are often seen as successful entrepreneurs. Others, such as Frank Coffield at Durham University, have criticized the whole development of enterprise as 'a farrago of hurrah words such as "creativity", "initiative", and "leadership"' which offers activity-based enterprise courses for those who will spend their lives as peripheral workers in 'part-time, poorly paid, temporary, dead-end jobs'.[32] Over against Coffield's criticism, Chris Beales's *Mainstream and Marginal* is a study of economic change in inner-city life in the United States. The answer to criticisms of exploitation and low pay offered in this report is participation. As Chris Beales writes:

> Identity will be a key consideration – the identity of the business or project as being a part of the local community ... and which is producing goods or services which are clearly meeting local felt needs. In fact, it will be important to develop a process of consultation with local people which involves them in determining just what the needs of the local community are, and how they may best be met. This is the best way to gain identification with and commitment to a new proposal.[33]

Beales suggests that the way out of the dichotomy between full-time workers and peripheral, often exploited, workers is the development of community enterprises and employee ownership. This is a theme that has been picked up several times in this book, in describing economic activity in the Third World and in community activities. At the same time there would still be the need for employment training pledges for those without work. Ralf Dahrendorf's 1989 lecture in Newcastle on the future of the underclass speaks powerfully of the importance of allowing people who have fallen out of the labour market to regain access to these institutions. He notes that the methods may be local, even customized and unorthodox, 'but their most important issue is that of skills'.[34] This is not to ignore the fact that homeworking remains exploitative in some trades (a 1985 survey by the Low Pay Unit records one-third of traditional homeworkers earned 50 pence an hour or less). So alongside community enterprise, and skill training, there will need to be regulation.[35] The question of low pay goes beyond this book, but it remains a serious ethical question.

A final comment on the social aspect of enterprise comes from Frank Field's book *Losing Out*. He describes the growth of poverty in Britain in recent years, and proposes a comprehensive programme to attack this. Nevertheless, he still wishes to extend personal initiatives by funding business ventures from capitalizing National Insurance benefits. He also strongly supports credit unions on a collective basis: 'they give people a sense of having a greater control over their own destiny'.[36] Field is only too aware of the growth of poverty, but he also argues that there must be the devolution of power from central government to collective initiative.

Enterprise as surveyed in the preceding pages has been criticized on many grounds. It may well be that attention paid to the environment, poverty, both national and global, and public morality would result in a very different culture. Nevertheless, the basic desire to take wealth-creation seriously, to express one's own potential and to be creative, remain fundamental tenets of the cultural change of the last decade. What is needed is not to repudiate these changes, which I believe are essentially positive, but to take them into a renewed system of public morality and community enterprise. The challenge, then, to the affluent lifestyle of the West is a real one, but Traidcraft and credit unions do not invalidate the real benefits of delegated responsibility and initiative. Perhaps the environmental issues go much deeper, for Davis's prescriptions for management would imply an enormous change in the way in which industry is organized and in the products it manufactures. At the same time such changes must go on, while public morality is still debated and clear moral guidelines are often difficult to discern. It would be easy for the Churches to lose their nerve, and to retreat back to a hard-and-fast realm of unchallenged values. I believe this would be perhaps the greatest mistake that Churches could make. The social complexity of the growth of self-employment, community enterprise and the devolution of power make it difficult to describe exactly what is happening in contemporary Britain. A dialogue with those who are searching for new values in self-employment may be taxing for the Churches, with their own understanding of morality. Nevertheless, I believe that this is an important element of the mission of the Church, so that it discerns signs of transcendence in the pluralist culture in which we live.[37]

Business ethics

Business involvement in the community has been promoted
by the present government as part of private-sector and
voluntary initiatives. Christie and Fogarty raise the issue as
to whether government has tried to unload on to industry
some of its own responsibilities.[38] The government denies
this, as John Patten, Home Office Minister, said in the House
of Commons on 29 December 1989:

> The government do not regard the charitable world and voluntary
> services as an opportunity for providing a cheap alternative to
> public services. I said earlier that I felt that sometimes charities
> are good at spotting gaps, but there is a world of difference
> between that and their being used for gap-filling.

The government certainly has promoted corporate giving,
both through the encouragement of ministers and through
tax incentives. But it is not simply cash that a company can
give, or even the time of its staff and managers. Business
in the Community supports a wide range of activities: property development for urban regeneration, education/business
partnership, support for the growth of small firms through
enterprise agencies, local purchasing, and involvement with
unemployed young people. It is not surprising that the Policy
Studies Institute report asks what in the end is corporate
giving about? The Policy Studies Institute advocates the
importance of personal, one-to-one contacts and networks,
which can accelerate the culture of community involvement.[39]
The lesson of the United States is important here in building
a concrete culture aware of the local community, and of wider
social responsibility. However, it is still the case that, as in the
case study of Sheffield, there are 'low levels of awareness and
activity among the mass of firms, a lack of skills and marketing
resources in the voluntary sector for dealing with business,
inadequate information flows between business and voluntary
sectors'.[40] Nevertheless, the co-operation between public and
private sectors at the strategic level is now beginning to bring
in the voluntary sector as well. Some of this may involve the
development of local leadership groups, such as Common
Purpose.[41]

Business ethics can develop this idea of partnership inside
a company. Lady Judith Wilcox's lecture, *Excellence and Ethics*,

develops the usefulness of codes and 'mission statements'. Yet she notes that the growing gap between business morality and personal morality is a real one. Can ethical codes, she asks, ever become self-sustaining, 'without a core of basic, religious beliefs to feed and nourish them through the long winter months'.[42] Morality in business then remains a personal matter, whatever the guidelines of corporate communities. This again is a point that has occurred frequently in this chapter. Religious values underpin secular, corporate ones, in terms of bringing future generations into consideration, or of including those who are poor and deprived in the community.

Another way of humanizing relationships is through employee share ownership. Structuring an ethical business will never come through moral crisis management. Perhaps the greatest value in company codes of conduct is actually in creating them, especially where all the staff are involved through training and ethical awareness programmes. Similarly, company audits, whether on social issues or environmental ones, can be of benefit. Non-executive directors can also have an ethical mandate, and the growth of business ethics teaching is important.[43]

Yet a difficulty remains, as Ken Hawkings, the Cambridge industrial chaplain, pointed out to me. 'Most companies ignore signs of stress, and just keep growing. As they explode in size, they have neither the time nor the training to handle it. How do you handle growth?'[44] It is not simply stress that is the problem. Marlene Winfield's study of whistleblowing in British companies reaches severe conclusions: 'failed attempts to raise the issue internally; absence of alternatives or the lack of knowledge of the alternatives; absence of independent advice and support before the whistle was blown; unhappy consequences for all concerned; whistleblower's difficulty in finding another job'.[45]

She suggests that there should be an open door to senior management, with employee participation and ethical contracts negotiated with the workforce and signed by all employees. There should also be ethical training, with the board of directors taking the lead in debating policy, especially through non-executive directors.[46] This will never be an easy issue to address, for it reveals conflict within the company. Paradoxically the virtues of initiative, self-reliance and autonomy that are so much part of the enterprise culture can lead to precisely the tension that Winfield describes so graphically.

Business ethics remains a new area of study in Britain. It is certainly true that the 1980s often seemed to show companies being concerned with growth above all else. Yet there are signs that good management is perceived to include a high ethical framework, especially in Judith Wilcox's lecture to the British Institute of Management. There is a clear reason for the Churches to remain in this area, criticizing companies where there is evidence of malpractice, but more importantly commending the hopeful signs in employee participation and ethical concern.

Notes

1. Interview, 8 February 1990, London.
2. See the lecture by a former banker, Charles Green, *The Christian in Business*, 1990.
3. Routledge 1990.
4. J. Cornford, *A Stake in the Company*, 1990.
5. I. Christie and M. Fogarty, *Companies and Communities*, 1990.
6. G. Mulgan, 'The Buck Stops Here', *Marxism Today*, September 1990, pp. 22–7.
7. *Church Dogmatics*, II/2, p. 641.
8. Mulgan, p. 24.
9. J.D. Godsey, 'Bonhoeffer', in D.F. Ford (ed.), *The Modern Theologians*, vol. I, 1989, p. 63.
10 J. Habgood, 'The Good, the Bad and the Individual', *The Times*, 27 February 1989.
11. Rev. Ken Hawkings, interview, 31 January 1990, Cambridge.
12. R. Evans (marketing director, Traidcraft), 'Business Ethics and Changes in Society', *Journal of Business Ethics* (forthcoming); *Traidcraft: Objectives*, July 1986; R. Adams (founder, Traidcraft), *Who Profits?* 1989; M. Taylor (director, Christian Aid), *Good for the Poor: Christian Ethics and World Development*, 1990.
13. *Adams*, pp. 157–9.
14. Evans.
15. Taylor, p. 85.
16. ibid., p. 85.
17. ibid., pp. 46–63. R. Ridell, *Foreign Aid Reconsidered*, 1987.
18. Macmillan, 1989. Reviewed in *The Independent*, 21 December 1989.
19. Adams, pp. 126–7.
20. J. Davis, *Greening Business: Managing for Sustainable Development*, 1991, and J. Elkington and T. Burke, *The Green Capitalists*, 1989. See also the British

Gas Environmental Issues Series, 1990: D. Pearce, *The New Environmental Policy*; A. Markyanda, *Green Economics*; and J. Elkington, *Community Action: No Thanks, Noah*. Peter Vardy's *Business Morality*, 1989, is an unusual book by a chartered accountant and management consultant who has become a philosopher of religion at London University. He discusses environmental issues on p. 170–8.

21. Centre for Policy Studies, June 1989. See also the discussion by Peter Kellner in *The Independent*, 24 July 1989.

22. Pearce, pp. 4–5.

23. J. Zizioulas, in M. Palmer and E. Breuilly (eds), *Christianity and Ecology*, 1991, quoted in *The Malvern Conference Papers*, section 5, p. 6, 1991.

24. The *Malvern Conference Papers*, section 5, p. 8, quoting *Orthodoxy and the Ecological Crisis*, World Wide Fund for Nature and the Ecumenical Patriarchate of Constantinople, 1990.

25. Davis, p. 103.

26. R. Keat and N. Abercrombie (eds), *Enterprise Culture*, 1991.

27. R. Preston, *Religion and the Persistence of Capitalism*, 1979, p. 72.

28. Keat and Abercrombie (eds), pp. 86–7.

29. J. Habgood, 'Public and Private Morality', in *Confessions of a Conservative Liberal*, 1988, p. 52.

30. P. H. Sedgwick, 'The Enterprise Culture as a New World for the Churches', *Crucible*, July 1990.

31. P. Bachu and, S. Westwood (eds), *Enterprising Women*, 1988, p. 103.

32 *The Independent*, 29 August 1990.

33. C. Beales, *Mainstream and Marginal*, 1990. The research was funded by SPCK as part of this project.

34. R. Dahrendorf, Northumbrian Industrial Mission 1989 Annual Lecture, 'The Future of the Underclass: A European Perspective', *Northern Economic Review*, 1989.

35. See the discussion of homeworking in R. Dawson, *And All that is Unseen: A New Look at Women and Work*, pp. 17–18.

36. F. Field, *Losing Out*, 1989, p. 179. See also Basic Income Research Group, 102 Pepys Road, London SE14 5SG.

37. P. H. Sedgwick, *Mission Impossible? A Theology of the Local Church*, 1990.

38. Christie and Fogarty, p. 61.

39. ibid., p. 134.

40. ibid., p. 103.

41. Business in the Community Report, *First*, 1990. Keynote articles on the relationship between business and the community.

42. British Institute of Management Annual Lecture, 30 October 1990.

43. I am drawing here on the lecture by Professor Jack Mahoney to Expamet International Executives on 5 March 1990. I am grateful to Expamet for the opportunity to attend this day conference.

44. Interview, 31 January 1990. See also O. Nankivell, 'Christian Values in the Market', *Audenshaw Paper 132*, 1991.

45. M. Winfield, *Minding Your Own Business*, Social Audit 1990, p. 41.

46. ibid., p. 48.

7

A Theology of Enterprise

A theology of enterprise is an unusual topic to choose for a concluding chapter, but the choice is deliberate. On the one hand, there is the concern with a theology of wealth-creation. What has been the Churches' attitude to wealth? Can it be reduced to 'the love of money is the root of all evil', or, more succinctly, 'you cannot serve God and Mammon'? On the other hand, there is the need to revise a theology of work. Vocation has been a constant theme of Protestant theology since the Reformation, and this century has seen some important books on a theology of work. However, if the cultural change that this book has described is correct, and there is a permanent shift towards small firms, even if only as a limited part of the economy, then a theology of vocation must be rethought. A theology of enterprise therefore encompasses both a theology of wealth-creation, and of work. The two cannot be seen separately.

Surrounding this debate, of course, has been a much wider one on the values of the market, and the criticism of the New Right. This debate has been a fierce one in the Churches, but it does not help to confuse the two. I have repeatedly been told by businesspeople, academics, teachers and community organizers that the values of enterprise are not synonymous with those of the New Right. Certainly, there are many ethical questions around enterprise, discussed in the previous chapter. Nevertheless, it has become obvious to me that the cultural changes of the last decade will outlast the philosophy of the New Right. With a change in Prime Minister this is already beginning to happen.

Two things follow from this. First, it is wrong for the recent Church of England report on Christianity and contemporary culture, *Good News in Our Time*,[1] to equate the revival of enterprise with the philosophy of Hayek and Nozick, or the views of politicians like Sir Keith Joseph. The report assumes that enterprise culture is the same as 'naked individual competitiveness', and denounces it as a 'moral evil which undermines values of stability, fidelity and other family and community building values'. While helpful on other aspects of our culture in relation to Christianity, the report is simply being perverse here. There certainly has been a challenge by the New Right to the value of our existing culture. However, the surveys of young people described previously show that they are perfectly able to distinguish the desire to run their own business, be independent and self-reliant from the desire to run down the welfare state and adopt a purely competitive philosophy. If *they* are able to do so, why can't a report like *Good News in Our Time* do the same? Setting up a straw man to knock him down proves little. I have myself written articles criticizing the New Right, but it is clear that the views of Hayek, Friedman and others are not now influential in political debate. Equally, the report describes the enterprise culture as being manifested in the Docklands redevelopment in East London. Its criticisms of Docklands as placing affluence against deprivation are very true, but the report entirely ignores the traditional entrepreneurial philosophy of East London.[2]

A second implication follows from the first. How far the market economy should now be assumed to be the most efficient mechanism for creating wealth, and whether its operation should extend into areas of society like health or education, is another controversial subject. Yet the question of enterprise, by which is meant wealth-creation and work, is essentially concerned with the means by which those aims are achieved. It is to do with particulars, such as the working of enterprise in small businesses or schools, and the subtle relationship between how wealth is created and what is created. Nor need wealth simply mean financial wealth, although this will usually be the most obvious meaning. At its simplest, the question is 'Can work ever be enjoyable, a form of play?' This is the topic addressed in this chapter. Therefore this chapter will not be about the market, and the relationship between the working of the economy and deregulation in the economy.[3] The issue of whether the Churches should come to approve of the market is discussed by John Atherton, a member of this project's advisory group, in *Faith in the Nation*.[4] If a theology of enterprise, work and wealth-creation were to include topics in political philosophy, such as the nature of the social market, the subject would become unmanageable.

A theology of the market is concerned with the political philosophy prevalent in society, and whether this should be condemned or criticized in the light of the Christian faith. A theology of enterprise is really a theology of culture: an unwillingness to accept corporate structures and a celebration of the individual human being. Creativity, self-reliance and autonomy all become elements of this rethinking. It is also, of course, a natural area for theology to work in.

Christianity and wealth-creation

The story of Christianity's relationship to wealth is a fascinating narrative. Yet there is no one plot. Rather, there are a series of sub-plots, which interweave within one another. At particular times and places, such as Germany in 1500–50, this interweaving caused such dramatic changes that it *seems* as though there was a break. We call this the Reformation. Yet there are no breaks, and no one story. Under the abstract analysis of the church historian the story dissolves into different strands.

I want to argue that four stories can be told. This is an arbitrary figure, but it appears to cover the main picture. In brief, the story of purity centres around the corruption of spirituality by the pursuit of mammon. It is the story of the camel and the 'eye of the needle', which has recurred across the centuries as a motif. This story is not 'about economics': it is the Church talking to itself, asking itself what it means to be faithful. Secondly, there is the story of wealth. This is the delight in using the riches of God's creation to his praise and glory, and enriching our response to God by the display of beauty and craftsmanship. In a secular age we forget the beauty of the medieval cathedrals, which became centres of artistic excellence. There is also the theme of the enjoyment of riches, as a sign of God's blessing to his people. Thirdly, and in stark contrast, there is the story of poverty. From the prophets of Israel there comes the denunciation of luxury. This is of course the story of purity repeated: the corruption of the soul by the worm of avarice. But there is also the story of what will happen to the poor, and their fate. This in turn is tied up with the belief that 'there can be no rich and honest person': the rich are rich because they exploit the poor. So the story of poverty becomes the story of social justice. There are many implications here, not least the whole story of visions and utopias. Whether this story could be worked out on this earth becomes a central question. Increasingly the people of Israel looked for a transformation of society as well as of the individual. But a transformation so great would go beyond history, and require a new Messiah. Messianism recurs through Christian history, along with the pursuit of the millennium. The story of poverty, then, is a complex one. There is one final twist to it. Historians of Palestine at the time of Jesus speak of the northern region (Galilee, and other surrounding lands) as a burnt-out economy. Overworked soil, too many people and oppressive taxes all led to great despair among the 'humble poor' of Palestine. This raised the question, especially in the wisdom tradition, as to why God allowed the poor to be like this, if they were so devout. It is an economic variant of Job's problem, made more acute by the celebration of riches (with, to be fair, an appreciation of the dangers therein) in wisdom literature. Out of this problem comes a different option of the poor: not social justice, but a belief that the 'humble poor' were especially cherished by God. The belief of the humble poor recurs again, of course, in Wesley's hymns, as a particular sign of the new age in Christ.

A fourth theme is that of vocation. The story of the meaning of work goes back to the accounts in Genesis itself. The debate about vocation, social hierarchy and the religious life goes to the heart of the Reformation controversies, but it is not simply of historical interest. Feminist accounts of women and work are not simply about the injustice of low pay, but are about the vocation that women have in society. There is also the question of the relation of personal worth to paid work. My students at Hull write an essay in the second term of their MA course, drawing on many themes: their own experience of work, arranged visits, sociology, economics and modern theology (on the Christian doctrine of humanity). The title is very simple, yet it is a very hard essay to write. The title runs 'Being a Person, and Having a Job in Britain Today. What is the Connection?'

The question one is left with is, not surprisingly, how the whole story holds together at all. For if there are different sub-plots, there is also the fact that different epochs think in very different ways: the issue of historical relativism. Does the concern for the corrupting effect of wealth in Proverbs, written perhaps by a court theologian in Jerusalem several centuries before Christ, have anything in common with discussions on complex economic policies between a Western European or North American Church's Board for Social Responsibility and civil servants in the last decade? Certainly the world-views are completely different, as are the consequences of their actions.

Perhaps there are two things that hold it all together. First, there is the need for our civilization to make good use of spiritual resources and past heritage in order to find ways of harnessing the enormous power of modern technology and economics for good and not ill. I am especially struck by what Peter Jenkins, a British journalist, calls the end of transformational ideology, or, more simply in his book on Mrs Thatcher, 'the ending of the Socialist Era' (the sub-title). In the West, the last decade has seen the death of the long twentieth-century belief in the march of 'the people'. 'The people' are now a majority (in the West, that is – not, of course, in the underdeveloped world), and in Western Europe an affluent majority. Socialism as a substitute for religion promised the ordering of economic life in such a way that life would be transformed into a new world. This was for two reasons. First, it was argued that all culture was determined by economic reality, as the Marxists argued, so if you changed the economics you would change the culture. Secondly, economic transformation, it was claimed, would end mass poverty and chronic insecurity for millions in modern industrial econo-mies. This vision is a future vision, an economic vision, and involves a total transformation of society. It had two variants, Marxist and socialist, but both involved the end justifying the means. Much, if not all, Conservative philosophy in Western Europe this century was seen as trying to slow down the inevitable march of 'the people'. There was a perversion of it, in National Socialism (Nazism), and an American trans-mutation, which was not socialist but was transformational, as in Roosevelt's New Deal. (For the US transformational ethic, see the films of Frank Capra, especially *It's a Wonderful Life*.) As Peter Jenkins says, this vision is now over. First, there is no belief in any transformational ideologies. Secondly, we know their terrible cost, especially with Marxism in Eastern

Europe. Thirdly, 'the people' are a majority anyway. Finally, there is the real fear of catastrophic environmental damage.

All this leads to three simple questions. First, if it is true that our society (meaning the West) accepted transformational ideologies as a substitute for religion, can we now live our lives with a belief in incrementalism: the step-by-step approach? If so, where is the spiritual dimension of all this: the new understanding of belief, liberty, co-operation? We need to turn back, without nostalgia, to understand what past ideals meant which were not transformational but were enriching, in order to further our current debates. Second, how can we persuade the affluent West to share its wealth-creation with the minority underclass (I use the term loosely, not in a precise, sociological sense) who are likely to be a permanent feature of our society? Even more important, how can we persuade the affluent West to share its wealth with the underdeveloped countries of the South? Where is the good news for the poor, to quote Michael Taylor's 1990 book? Thirdly, how do we provide a moral and spiritual framework to restrain the global destruction of the environment by modern capitalism? What is the interaction of business ethics and spiritual values in the Christian tradition, along with other religious traditions? My first answer to what holds the Christian story together is therefore pragmatic, and none the worse for that. We need to see the story whole, so we can use it in dialogue with contemporary experience to solve the difficult problems of generosity, environmentalism and meaning-of-life that are at the heart of our society's problems today (again, meaning the West). We need to have a tradition because there are no other resources. Transformational ideology is over and, as Peter Jenkins says, confrontational political debates at a general election couched in language of the people or of the nation are as anachronistic as medieval jousting tournaments. It will take time for this point to sink in, but it is irrevocable. There are no big social futures anymore. We only have our contemporary experience to work on, and those who represent past traditions must use them to enrich the present debate. No one else will do it for us. The alternative is, quite simply, no enrichment anyway.

The second reason why the story holds together is that Christians believe it is 'true'. This is a pretentious word as are the terms 'philosophy of history' or 'theology of history', but I do not know of any other that will serve the purpose. Augustine, Aquinas, Calvin, Hegel and such contemporary theologians as Pannenberg and Moltmann all take an overview of what is happening in history. The revelation of Christ has an inner association with the meaning of world history, so that even contemporary history can be read in the light of the purposes of God, as revealed in Christ. There is both an inner unity between social and religious life, and an inner unity between past events and present ones.

There is no doubt that such a view is not an easy one to hold today. First, the cost of transformational ideology includes the holocaust and the Stalinist terror. Such disasters, not surprisingly, make any talk of God's purposes in history seem quite impossible. So vast were they in their consequences, so appalling in their suffering, that it is as if humanity, not God, has taken the controls of history, with results that are only too well known. Secondly, there is a formidable challenge to Christian talk of the meaning of history in the deconstructionist and post-modernist debate in the West. Such people as Derrida, Foucault and Richard Rorty may not be known extensively in British Christianity, but Don Cupitt is, and the power of his writing lies in the fact that he harnesses a very original mind to the extensive work of post-modernists. If all our vision of reality is but a language-game, then it can represent nothing at all. As Foucault said of Augustine, 'there is only the iron hand of necessity shaking the dice box of chance'. An answer to this debate is not easy to give in a few, brief sentences. Nevertheless, it shows very starkly that the unity of the story is not just a pragmatic one for our participation in the modern debate, but is also at the heart of the Christian faith. The truth of Christianity is about the possibility of religious faith at all (beyond the world of immediate, religious experience), and about belief in the interaction of God's relation to the world.

Let me turn to the stories of Christianity and wealth. In summary, before I expound them, I believe that there are four of them. There is the story of the heart which is deceitfully wicked above all things, and never more so in the boardroom when thinking up justifications for personal wealth: the corruption of the soul by power and wealth. Here, as the story will show, is a Christianity deeply suspicious of

the economic world. Secondly, there is that belief which built
most of the churches in this country, and enjoys the fruit of
one's labour. It is put succinctly in the carving on an Anglican
retreat house, once the home of a wealthy Christian industri-
alist, which reads 'God made for us this ease' (in translation
from the Latin). Thirdly, there is the theme of social justice,
and the denunciation of the rich and powerful. There is also
God's love for the poor, as in Mother Teresa of Calcutta,
which is why I have called this story the story of poverty.
Fourthly, there is the meaning of work, and of vocation. The
Anglican collect for St Michael's Day in the Prayer Book takes
up a medieval prayer: 'O God, who has ordered the services
of men and angels in a wonderful order. . . .' The medieval
division of vocation into social hierarchy, and into the work
of monks, nuns and clergy on the one hand and laypeople on
the other (to say nothing of the angels, saints and departed
souls), appears problematical today, at the very least. Yet the
Protestant work ethic, while it may survive in political rhetoric
and have deep and lasting psychological significance for good
or ill, is difficult to defend intellectually as well. The feminist
debate gives the whole issue another, and perhaps crucial,
twist. I have also argued that there is a need to see the story
as a whole, and made a digression into contemporary political
debate in so doing. There are both pragmatic and intellectual
reasons for seeing it all whole, but I do not underestimate the
difficulties of doing this. (John Millbank's book *Theology and
Social Theory*, 1990, is an intellectual defence of Christianity
against deconstructionism; Hugh Montefiore's *Reclaiming the
High Ground: A Christian Response to Secularism*, 1990, is
an attack on secularism as an inadequate response to a
technological society.) All I wish to say is that this is where
much theological energy is now centred. So with this lengthy
introduction, what are the stories of the Christian faith and
economic life?[5]

a) *The story of purity*

The prophetic tradition in ancient Israel was not, it is now
recognized, the exponent of a worked-out social ethic. Nor
was it as separate from the rest of Judaism as might once have
been thought. Instead, the prophets were closely related to the
cultic tradition, especially to the enthronement of Yahweh in

the royal psalms in the Jerusalem Temple. What the pre-exilic and exilic prophets did was to recall and commend the nomadic ideal. The covenant had been made in the desert, and the prophets sought to recall this. They were guardians of the religious tradition, which was threatened by the prosperity of the nation. The relationship of righteousness (*sedaquah*) to justice (*mishpat*) is crucial. Yet it is not only prosperity that can destroy the relationship to God. The story of Naboth's vineyard or Ahab's campaign against the Syrians at Ramoth-gilead (1 Kings 21–22) are stories of a lack of self-denial.

The teaching of Jesus interiorizes the search for purity of heart: delight in riches strangles the seed's growth in the parable of the sower (Mark 4.19); the rich young ruler is told to sell all he has (Mark 10.17); the parable of the rich fool building bigger barns; Dives and Lazarus; the Sermon on the Mount in Matthew 6 on God and money; and above all, the story of the camel and the eye of the needle (Mark 10). The power of the gospel is shown in Zacchaeus giving away much of his wealth. The impurity is not the corruption of the soul by greed (although 1 Timothy 6.10 does say that the love of money is the root of all evils), but the independence that wealth gives from relying on the grace of God alone.

So the story of purity continues. The Rule of St Benedict chapter 33 speaks of personal property as a vice to be totally eradicated. Brother Juniper in *The Little Flowers of St Francis* strips off the silver ringlets hanging from the altar as superfluous distractions: they are to be given to the poor. The Cistercians funded abbeys like Rievaulx in England, far away from civilization. Of course, we know the outcome: the ever-growing wealth of the monasteries. So they in their turn were dissolved, and the apology for the Jesuits in 1661 (Martin Grene) spends much time in rebutting the criticism that they were wealthy. There is a persistent theme in Elizabethan Protestantism on how much co-operation with Elizabeth's policy meant financial wealth for the clergy (see especially the debates with Richard Bancroft). Above all, it is Gerrard Winstanley's version of the rule of the serpent manifested on earth through a professional clergy (the beast with the horn in Daniel); kingly power (the lion); the judiciary (the bear) and the thieving art of buying and selling (the leopard). Christ will bruise the serpent's head of covetousness.

Holy poverty may have been a concern of the revival of

monasticism in England in the nineteenth century. It certainly
was central to the Clapham Sect of wealthy bankers, including
Venn and Wilberforce, that they practised moderation in all
things. The sins of pride and wealth lay heavily on them.
Equally, there are in 1750 William Law's savage pictures of
Christian hypocrisy.

What of the present day? *The Rule of Taize* (1961) gives
one answer: 'the spirit of poverty is to live in the gladness
of today'. Is the call to 'holy worldliness' one answer in
contemporary spirituality? Self-denial through fasting, on
behalf of the Third World, is yet another variant. Perhaps
most of all is the fear of enslavement by the enterprise culture.
As Charles Green has observed in *The Christian in Business*,
the bank balance is the last part of a person's life to be transformed. Certainly the call to Christian discipleship in the City
of London appears to many Christian laypeople (e.g. Andrew
Phillips) to be a hard struggle against covetousness.

b) The story of wealth

A pastoral semi-nomadic people made up mainly of cattle
breeders looked favourably on wealth. This is the age of the
patriarchs, not history in the modern sense, but the aetiologies
of the tribal and family clans. Possessions meant the survival
of the clan, but a wealth of possessions meant feasting among
the camels, showing hospitality and generosity to others. Thus
the patriarchal stories concern such things as birthrights, marriage and intermarriage, and the ways of sheep. The story is
corporate, not communal, and the crucial event is recorded
in Genesis 12.1, where the family group replaces the clan.
There will be blessings on this family if they are faithful to
Yahweh.

Once the Israelites enter Canaan, farming and urbanization
lead to social stratification, wealth-creation (and luxury, which
the story of purity repeatedly attacks) and civilization. The
blessings of the divine relationship are classically expressed in
Deuteronomy on several occasions – see 11: 13–17. Recent
scholarship has stressed how the covenant was related to the
promise of the land. The land could, however, be lost. If
God was disobeyed, the curse meant disaster (Deuteronomy
28.15). This remains a theme across the centuries in the story
of wealth: R.C. Moberly at Oxford in 1900 preached on how

the British Empire was held in stewardship under God.

The celebration of wealth included the possession of the wife by the husband (Exodus 20.17), but there were limits to the concern with property. Unlike Codex Hammurabi (8) or the code of Eshunna (57-70), property violation did not mean death. At worst, stealing a sheep and slaughtering it meant slavery (Exodus 22.1). Burglary at night in other ancient Near Eastern texts meant death. There was the death penalty in the Old Testament, though the Old Testament was probably not a code of criminal law, but the penalty was for offences against the person.

The celebration of wealth continued in the wisdom school, with advice against falling into poverty ('a slack hand causes poverty', Proverbs 10.5), and awareness of the benefits of wealth, including friendship (Proverbs 14.20). Yet there is also the problem of purity of heart. Therefore the Old Testament's celebration of wealth was real, but aware of the dangers.

Jesus made no mention of the material blessings that God might give to his children. Rather, he warned against the dangers of idolatry. Yet in recent years scholars (Wayne Meeks in *The First Urban Christians*) have noticed that Luke 8.3 speaks of women who provided for Jesus and the disciples 'out of all their means'. First Timothy and James do not attack wealth as such, but the wrong use of it. Thus a new use of wealth is found: it is to be shared among the community. Acts 2 and 4 have been much discussed. Certainly Gonzalez and Rowland not only argue that wealth was shared, Gonzalez also argues that as late as 370 Bishop Basil of Caesarea, who was also a leading theologian, gave a practical demonstration of community by sharing his inherited wealth.

Others accepted wealth as useful, but preached on the need to be detached from it internally (Clement of Alexandria, *What Rich Man Will be Saved*?). Riches can produce fellowship and sharing, but they can be a danger. As the Christian Church grew more wealthy, the defence of property became more sophisticated. Property was a human contrivance, not a natural one, argued Aquinas (ST II. II. 66), but was legitimate as it offered certain advantages. This could lead to bishops such as Reginald Pecock in the mid-fifteenth century taking the command to sell all that one has in the same vein as the command to hate one's parents. The Jerusalem church shared at a time of persecution. Clerical endowment leads to

the benefit of the nation, for the wealth of the Church can
be used for the good of all, not for your descendants, as in
the case of lay ownership.

The Reformation (except for radicals like Winstanley) did not
condemn wealth, but it was left to early industrialists to exalt
their freedom to buy and sell as they pleased. The individual
becomes the proprietor of his own person, for which he (or
she) owes nothing to society. The development of a theology
of wealth grew in Victorian Britain, alongside the endowment of churches and chapels by wealthy industrialists. The
doctrine of stewardship developed, although fairly late: the
Wesleyan Methodist Conference did not sanction the offertory
until 1889. But Victorian Britain saw a whole plethora of books
on the right use of wealth: most notably *Gold and the Gospel*
in 1853, which sold widely to wealthy evangelicals.

It has been the same group that has taken up the argument
again recently, especially in the writings of Brian Griffiths.
His influential writings on *Morality and the Market Places*, and
others, attempt a biblical defence of property, and a fusion
of evangelical morality and monetarist capitalism. Equally
striking has been the revival of evangelical Christianity among
congregations that include City bankers. The relation of
wealth-creation to other parts of the Christian economic
story remains controversial.

c) *The story of poverty*

There are three strands to the story of poverty. One is the
theme of social justice, and the denunciation of oppression,
from Micah to Michael Taylor, with Muenzer in the middle.
Secondly, there is the story of why the poor should be poor,
if the poor are the devout: what does Jesus' teaching about
the outcast say about the love of God and poverty? (This
is a major theme in John Riches's fine study, *Jesus and the
Transformation of Judaism*.) Thirdly, there is voluntary poverty,
which is of course not just a Christian theme: it is found in
Hinduism, where the final stage of life is the fourth one (or
asrama), which is the setting aside of wealth and status to
become a wandering recluse (sannyasin) bent upon spiritual
knowledge.

The theme of social justice has developed especially in
liberation theology, and Chris Rowland's *Radical Christianity*

tells the story from the Old Testament to Central and South America well. Amos, Isaiah and Jeremiah denounce the oppression of the poor, the withholding of wages, and explicit corruption. The Levitical Code and the Jubilee Laws tried to mitigate the harshness of the plight of the poor. The Magnificat in Luke (1.53) speaks of sending the rich away, but the New Testament is muted in its social criticism. Again the early fathers are strong on the evil of luxury, but this belongs to the story of purity – exemplified by Jerome looking into a gold chamber-pot, and commenting that pride entered into the most basic of bodily functions.

Indeed Luther condemned the Peasants' Revolt strongly, and Calvin taught social inequality. It is to Muenzer that the real revival of radical Christianity must be traced. He fought in the Peasants' Revolt of 1524–5, and was captured and beheaded. Luther called him 'the Devil of Allstedt', since Muenzer believed that radical reformation could be brought about by military force.

Nevertheless, Muenzer's vision was not taken up again (except by Winstanley) until the Victorian Anglo-Catholic clergy in England did so. The Christian Socialist movement flourished in the 1880s under Headlam, and then revived under Conrad Noel in the period 1918–39. It was especially active in East London, where the movement continues, especially under Kenneth Leech and the Jubilee Group.

Finally, there is the theme of world poverty and injustice, which the Christian aid agencies (CAFOD; Christian Aid, etc.) have developed.There is strong support for this position from the Lutheran theologian Ulrich Duchrow, in Germany, who speaks of the world debt crisis as being like the gas-chambers of the Third World.

A second theme in the story of poverty is that of the fate of the poor. Especially in the wisdom literature there is growing puzzlement as to why the poor should be so oppressed: it occurs also in the Psalms. Partly this is answered by a belief that God would turn the tables on the impious rich (Psalm 72. 15–20), partly by a belief that we are all equal in death anyway. But as the Palestine economy gradually collapsed in Galilee (the evidence is graphically set out in Theissen and Riches), it became harder for the poor peasants to observe religious practices at all if they involved costly sacrifices. Indeed all social norms seemed to be giving way in Galilee, including the growth of crime and roving beggars, not unlike some countries today. Jesus places especial weight on his relationship with these people. He takes images of poverty, social disaster, deprivation and worthlessness, and says 'Blessed are the poor'. There are the ones who can no longer afford to tithe and break the Torah, but who are invited to Jesus' banquets. Co-operation with God in the work of love, forgiveness and peace was what Jesus offered them. Throughout the New Testament (e.g. 1 Corinthians 1.18) there is an emphasis on the low status of the early Christians: 'not many of you were of noble birth'. (See the fine unpublished paper on this passage by Frances Watson of King's College, London, written in 1991.)

The theme of the 'humble poor' occurs again in Wesley's hymn, where they are placed with the blind and lame in praising God. God 'on the side of the poor' has two meanings in Christian social thought: it is a call for social justice, but also a belief that the rich can learn true spirituality from the poor, without any sentimentality (see Austin Smith, *Passion for the Inner City*).

Finally, there is voluntary poverty. From Jesus, who as the Son of Man had nowhere to lay his head, through the pre-Pauline hymn of Philippians 2 laying aside power, the renunciation of riches has been part of the imitation of Christ.

Thus the development of monasticism and voluntary poverty becomes part of the story of purity. From Anthony in Egypt, through St Francis, there has been the call to give up wealth for the sake of poverty. How this voluntary renunciation of wealth relates to the search for social justice is not a question that receives any consistent answer.

d) The story of vocation

There is little in Scripture on vocation: Paul's view was static, where each person remained in the job they held. The call of God to follow Christ was not related to any new consideration of the job (if any) already held. In the Roman Empire certain jobs came to be frowned on for Christians, such as military service, but in general vocation is not of concern to the early Church. There is a stress on the need to work and not to be idle, as in 2

Thessalonians 3.6–12, where those who would not work would not eat.

It is ironically the development of monasticism that was to be most harmful to the Christian doctrine of vocation. The precepts of the Church bound all Christians, but a minority were called to follow the 'counsels of perfection', which were poverty, chastity and obedience.

Luther challenged this directly. The idea of vocation had to be carried out in the world. The service of one's neighbours was part of the royal priesthood of all Christians, and he argued for an understanding of human life as made up of the 'orders of creation'. The three orders of ministry, marriage and civil authority were for Luther grounded in Genesis 1.28, and were the foundation of the general service of our neighbours, which went beyond the daily tasks we were given.[6] These orders formed the realm of creation, and was the place where vocation was worked out.

The impact of the new doctrine of vocation can be seen directly in the edition of the Primer (a devotional book for laypeople in the late Middle Ages) issued again briefly by Edward VI. There are prayers for landlords, merchants and labourers. Others listed are servants, lawyers, gentlemen, maids and children. Once again there is a link between worship and economic life.

Calvinist ethics were more dynamic: the ethic of hard work and thrift, where God might call you into a state of life, as the 1662 Prayer Book Catechism of the Church of England notes. All prosperity depends on the blessing of God (*Institutes of the Christian Religion* 3.7.8). There is a right use of earthly blessings. Above all, there is an insistence on work and frugality, where the Christian responds to his call (predestination) by obedience. It is from this idea that the famous 'Protestant work ethic' came.

Today there are two controversies about vocation in the Christian Churches. One is that there has been a state of 'work in crisis', to quote Roger Clarke's book. Is not a Christian doctrine of vocation about valuing people for what they are, and not what they do: especially if they cannot do it, in an age of mass unemployment? Secondly, there is the growing area of feminist ethics, which stresses the experience of women in our society. Partly this might turn to a concern with poverty and low wages; partly a critique of purity as too much concerned with self-denial; partly a commitment to equality. However, with one or two exceptions (Anne Borrowdale), there is at the moment no fully worked-out feminist theology of vocation. It is, however, clear that 'the Protestant work ethic' has been subject to many reassessments this century.

e) Enterprise and wealth-creation

The danger with a theology of enterprise is that it can simply celebrate those aspects of the history of Christianity that approve of wealth. In the survey given above, this would mean that great attention is given to the biblical and medieval celebration of wealth, and to the Reformation stress on vocation. Little would be said about the biblical concern with poverty, avarice and greed.[7] Far too many discussions simply lapse into quoting biblical texts, without trying to see how they contribute to an overall perspective.[8]

A 1991 Methodist Church report stated:

> This tendency towards a theology of success indicates a serious problem for those who seek a moral basis for market capitalism which comes to terms with biblical values that are clearly not rated highly by modern economics. There is little regard in economics textbooks for service, humility, self-sacrifice and abstinence. There is a failure to recognise the Biblical view of debt and forgiveness, and a reluctance to accept responsibility for poverty in society. There is even less respect for the understanding of communal wealth found in the New Testament.[9]

All this is well said. A theology of enterprise and wealth-creation is concerned with the character of those who create wealth. Creating wealth must not be purely exploitative; this is not simply for moral reasons, but because the character of those who act in such a way becomes debased. Co-operation by the poor in the work of God is for Jesus a form of wealth-creation: it creates a future that has value, and sustains human dignity. It redefines wealth as the transformation of the future into something much more abundant. Relationships are transformed when the future does not become entirely circumscribed. Possibilities are enlarged, and people themselves can become more abundant.

Wealth-creation is the production of material and non-material blessings. Material blessings include the production of goods, as in manufacturing and the creation of services. Financial transactions would be included here. Wealth-creation also includes, however, non-material benefits. This has always been recognized in the patronage of the arts, but I would include such forms of wealth as community life and purpose (as Peter Kellner has pointed out). The Christian celebration of worship, especially in the communion service, takes up both material and non-material elements. All are invited freely to this meal, and this celebration invites us to see that wealth is never to be used for the purpose of domination. There is a shared communal meaning of a social good, which is given meaning by the outpouring of God's self-giving love. Yet the meal does not for one moment deny the validity of wealth and goods, so long as that wealth is seen as coming from the generosity of God. Because the Churches have long been suspicious of capitalism, describing the communion service as a form of wealth-creation may seem offensive to some. Yet this service, and other such forms of worship in non-sacramental communities such as the Quakers, celebrates the abundance of God. 'Whether we shall work for the household of life and experience its joy is our question.'[10]

A theology of wealth-creation and enterprise takes up the ambiguity in the Christian understanding of wealth. It seeks to see wealth as a form of self-expression, either individual or communal, which enables the future to be abundant for those who will inherit it. If that enabling is exploitative, it becomes self-destructive. If it does not become destructive, it enhances the character of those who transform their world. This leads into the final consideration: a theology of creation.

A theology of creation

There is a clear relationship between the nature of society and the nature of God. The Church by its actions, in witness, points to the social nature of the world that God has created. This is a divine ordering of the world, which stems from the presence of God in creation. This ordering allows human beings to re-order themselves. D.W. Hardy has spelt out the profound implications of taking a theological position that views the world as primarily lived in and continually created by God's presence, rather than tracing all social relations back to only the specific redeeming acts of God in Christ.

The most profound implication is that human society is seen as essentially dynamic. Hardy writes that in its true form 'this dynamic [will] generate richer possibilities of social order to meet the contingencies to which human beings are subject, rather than simply . . . maintain the same range of possibilities for social order which were available in simpler situations'.[11]

Thus 'premature stability' or 'the injustice of repressive societies' must be avoided by recovering the historical dynamic of institutions. Social institutions, economic arrangements, personal relationships and culture can all be transformed. The Church may witness to this transformation, but the Church is equally part of it. It does not pronounce God's work outside of society, or speak to society, as though it were not part of it.[12]

The understanding of freedom in such a transformation is directly related to the establishment of an uncoerced society or community, whereby the energies of the individual are placed alongside others. The relationship of our individual freedom to the collective society becomes crucial. Freedom in the enterprise culture is not simply achieved by personal self-assertion, but nor is it to be blunted by appeals to the values of an earlier era. Rather, freedom is to be understood as established through the fostering and nurture of communities that encourage self-worth and creativity. Such communities do not just happen. They require the relaxation of the constraints on the enterprise culture that have been spelled out above.

Yet neither will freedom occur if communities are not fostered. Relaxing the power of government or corporate organizations could lead to either sterile reliving of past confrontations, as often seems to occur in Ireland, or to selfish individualism. A Christian perspective should be carefully developed. First, we must let go of the idea of God's will as infinite force, standing over against human beings. God has been repeatedly seen in the Christian tradition as demanding obedience from outside human life. Instead, the relationship of God to our moral order should be seen as one of God's self-giving, which enables our own self-giving to become possible. There is much in the atheism of the enterprise culture (and of all modern culture) that is a justified protest against the idea of God as pure power and absolute necessity. Such an idea destroys human freedom and responsibility: if God is all-powerful, we may as well become passive recipients of his actions. When the nature of the Church is added to this, the picture becomes dire.

Trevor MacDonald has written:

> The Church, in its secular manifestation, with its structures, hierarchy, committees, and formalized consultative processes, is an institution par excellence. To that extent, as much contemporary evidence demonstrates, it is very difficult, particularly for those integral to its organization, to have an appreciation of sympathy for the enterprise culture.[13]

Therefore any condemnation of the enterprise culture as greedy self-interest writ large is too simple. There are clearly examples of this, and Archbishop Robert Runcie has often pointed out in many interviews on the dangers of a divided society: a pharisaical attitude to the poor; and to an indulgent hedonism.[14] All this is well said, but it is not enough. The picture given above of the enterprise culture is one of change and risk-taking. It is not a development that the Church finds easy to come to terms with. The Church, as an empirical reality, all too easily speaks as a cautious institution.

A theology of freedom is part of the true autonomy given by the Spirit, where freedom is not simply breaking away from overbearing divine power, or rejecting the constricting utterances of a time-bound institution. Instead, while it is true that the world is intelligible in and of itself, which is a claim now irrevocably established by modern culture, there is the possibility that theology may show the full depths and possibilities of modern existence: in this case, the enterprise culture. (At the same time, as with any culture, it can reveal its dangers of individualism and hedonism.)

Freedom is to be understood as part of creativity on the one hand, and human co-operation on the other. The work of the Spirit is to bring into being a community that witnesses to the possibility of authentic human community. Co-operation and service for the sake of others is a hallmark of Christian living. The nature of God's being is one of triunity, of existence in three ways of being, and therefore an existence in relationship. Such a God can give reality to talk of community, and social relationships. Neither the free market seen as 'the play of impersonal and mechanistic forces', nor pure individualism ('a collection of isolated atomic individuals') will be sufficient. Freedom is not the autonomy of the moral agent, but uncoerced living in community alongside others. The understanding of God is that God's grace makes possible both individual transformation and commercial existence. The Church stands or falls by its value in creating a community that can be a witness to human existence.[15]

Creativity is a central part of that existence. Again and again small businesses and innovation reveal the fundamental importance of human creativity. So too does decentralization in the welfare state, whether in housing co-operatives or community businesses. Creativity is not creativity if it is not free. There are obviously limitations on creativity, of material, history, heredity and environment. Nevertheless, to quote the Scottish theologian D.W.D. Shaw: 'Without freedom, novelty cannot be introduced, without freedom, new and different perspectives are impossible, and novelty of vision or interpretation or opportunity as well as shifting of perspectives are included in what is meant by creativity.' Such freedom may well not result in harmony and peace. A creative society, with decentralized welfare arrangements, small mutually supportive groups and innovative entrepreneurs, may often have a high degree of risk.[16]

Such creative freedom does not imply a conscious response to God's creativity. As I have already pointed out, discussing Dan Hardy's writings on the dynamics of creation, the indwelling presence of God in human sociality (all that makes up our social existence) cannot be limited either to what the Church does or says, or to the redemptive acts of God in Christ. Divine creativity is persuasive, appealing to our imagination to seek new and unrealized possibilities of existence. Human freedom is one of the presuppositions of a Christian understanding of God's relationship to the world.

Why not drop all reference to God, then, in talk of freedom and creativity? It is worth quoting Shaw directly here, for he makes his point eloquently:

> God takes the risk, by allowing his creatures a measure of freedom, that the ideal will not be actualized. There is, however, something like an inbuilt directionality which appeals, attracts 'lures', 'persuades', which allows mistakes to be made, even evil (the condition of freedom), but yet is never withdrawn or lets the situation or process get finally out of hand. There is an aesthetic

element to it, the goal being the achievement of beauty, the bringing into harmony of the increasingly complex elements of the cosmos.... The appeal of divine persuasion is not to fear, hope or reward, obedience as such. It is to sensitiveness – both to facts and to the ideal possibility within a whole range of possibilities.

At the same time God through the presence of the Spirit creates in us the authentic humanity that can respond to this persuasive power. Questions of forgiveness, reconciliation and healing press in on us here. Freedom and creativity stand together in an understanding of human society as being a place where dynamic change and transformation is possible. This could be mere rhetoric, but it is crucial that the general principles of freedom and creativity are worked out in concrete examples.

The New Testament presents a picture of St Paul finding the peoples of the world speaking to him of God's actions in Christ. The conviction that each new presentation of the gospel in a new city is itself a constant rediscovering of Christ leads into a new way of looking at the New Testament's record of the missionary journeys of Paul. It is not as though the preaching of Christ was the only significant feature of the early Christian community. The journeys themselves and the encounter with new cultures are also fundamental, for the conviction dawned on the early Christians that the world was not empty but filled with the presence of Christ. 'Travelling the world was for him [St Paul] a constant finding of Christ.'[17] Out of this comes the conviction of the later New Testament epistles that Christ annuls the separation of Jew and Gentile (Ephesians 2.11–17) into one new person; that in Christ all things hold together (Colossians 1.15); that there will be a new heaven and a new earth, where all is made new (Revelation 21.1–5).

There is a close correlation between the travels of the early Christian missionaries and their appreciation of the way in which all societies are rooted in Christ. What is the correlation today? I suggest that as the Churches engage in creating or sustaining new forms of community, this is no more just 'social work' than Paul's journeys were 'travelling'. Travelling led into an appreciation of all societies as rooted in Christ: community endeavours are related to a true Christian understanding of freedom and creativity. As the old forms of state institutions are cut back, and new societies come into being, it is there that the Churches will find an understanding of freedom and creativity.

Freedom, then, is a crucial term for the enterprise culture. The work of the Spirit is a way of speaking of God at work within each Christian, but in a way that respects the freedom and integrity of each believer.[18] Primarily God works by freeing us from false self-images and alienated behaviour, and an enabling of our search for deeper values and possibilities of life. Spirituality and evangelism are also relevant terms, for a proper Christian response to the enterprise culture could enter into dialogue with the search for new creativity and forms of self-expression. Secondly, it is clear that a Christian understanding of freedom must involve reference to forms of community, whereby the relationship between individual and collective can be worked out. This is not easy, and it is a feature at present of many intellectuals, Christian and secular, to point to the collapse of civic society. The problem is that this often results in a false sense of discomfort at a world the intellectual does not enjoy living in. Pursuing this point would be a digression from my main argument, but it is worth quoting from Jeffrey Stout's recent book to illustrate this sense of discomfort:

> We do, however, live in a society where economic forces seem increasingly to produce people who lack the virtues needed to use their freedom well.... What we need to discover ... is the mean between giving approval of the status quo and wistful alienation from it.... Wistful alienation enjoys the comforts of distance from evil. It takes consolation in the moral and epistemic privilege of marginality while denying itself the necessities of engagement and action. Its characteristic tone betokens a failure of generosity, an inability to transcend the limits of its own outrage. Denouncing its age, it implicitly announces its own impotence, escaping despair, if at all, only by gesturing weakly towards the future or the past.[19]

A Christian understanding of freedom must resist the alienation of the disenchanted intellectual. The experience of community is fundamental for a theological appreciation of living together, and interdependence. Thirdly, the nature of God is such that his creation of the world as inherently social means that dynamic change is built into its very existence. There should be an aversion to the confinements of social order, or the moralistic understanding of past historical patterns. The presence of God allows the emergence of new forms and understandings of community. Society is made up neither of fixed institutions or 'orders of creation', nor of individuals, but of ever-changing forms of social life, which constantly press upon institutions and too rigid a compartmentalizing of life into orders of 'work', 'family', 'government', etc.

At this point, however, a caution must be made. There are many passages in Scripture that see work as hard and uncreative. Indeed, Luther's development of the theology of work and vocation is constantly concerned with the issue of serving God in a fallen world. It is a sober vision, where the serpent is cursed, and work is seen as punishment as well as productive labour. Can these passages just be dismissed? A second reason for caution is the sheer sinfulness of many accounts of work, where little regard is given to one's neighbour at all. If work is seen as a form of play, what happens to seriousness and the need for redemption of the world? This is not just a Reformation or Protestant point: many Marxist critiques of capitalism imply equally a fallennness in contemporary culture, which will only be redeemed by a complete abolition of capitalism. Speaking of creativity or work as play in this perspective becomes blasphemous.[20]

Work, then, raises the question of how we can serve God in God's creation, knowing that God will again and again need to redeem what has been made.[21] Work only is of value if it is taken as a summons and invitation to listen to the need for the cosmos to be humanized. No one has put this better than the German theologian Karl Barth:

> The existence of the created world ... is also a summons and an invitation to the active ordering and shaping of things, and therefore to a step into freedom. Man at least exists as this call comes to him and he accepts it.[22]

In response perhaps some biblical exegesis may be of help. In recent decades there has been a high degree of interest in the wisdom tradition, which is found in the Old and New Testament. Such a tradition expressed a belief in the fundamental given-ness of the world, and its moral order. Especially in Job, Proverbs, some of the Psalms and the Apocrypha, this tradition is clearly delineated. It is not an alternative to the prophetic tradition, for the prophets also sought to recall Israel to the demands of the law and a moral way of life. But if prophecy was closely related to worship and the cult finding revelation as the community gathered to enthrone Yahweh as Lord of Creation (the royal Psalms where Yahweh is spoken of as king in the Jerusalem Temple), the vision of wisdom found revelation in the ordering of creation itself. Ultimately the two strands come together: Israel keeps agreement with God (covenant) out of gratitude for the sheer grace of the gift of the promised land (flowing with milk and honey – Deuteronomy 8.8 and 11.14 articulates the ecological sense of blessing) while 'the wise' praise God for the goodness of the created order.

This created order is created by a dynamic God. Within God's own being there is a rich dynamism, so that wisdom rejoices before God always. This is only a personification of the divine attribute of creativity, but it sets out the inner dynamic of the overflowing abundance within God, which means wisdom rejoices in 'the inhabited world', delights in 'the songs of men'. Such a dynamic God has a purpose for the creation, set out in Psalm 8 and Genesis 1, where that purpose is given to Adam. But lest we move too easily to human co-partnership with God, note that the wisdom tradition speaks of the glory of the dynamic creation, where the wild animals range free 'scorning the tumult of the city, deaf to the shouts of the driver' (Job 39.7). God speaks to Job out of the whirlwind, and God overwhelms Job. This is a highly dynamic view of creation.

This creation is the embodiment of moral values, spoken of by the wisdom tradition as light, and not darkness. Such light is continually re-established by God and will not be denied; even if 'I take the wings of the morning, and dwell in the uttermost parts of the sea, even there thy hand shall lead me' (Psalm 139.8–10). Creation of God is for a purpose: God delights in the creation, builds up the moral order in and through creation, and calls humanity to care for this order. Even with evil and human wickedness, 'as long as the earth endures, seedtime and harvest ... will never cease' (Genesis 8.22).

What then is the charge to humanity? 'We go forth to our work, and to our labour until the evening', but, in a nice touch, the morning rush hour meets the rush-home of the lions getting back to their dens before the sun rises. All this is part of God's wisdom, where the Spirit renews the face of the earth: the theme, of course, of the World Council of Churches Assembly at Canberra. Psalm 104 asks God to rejoice in the creation as the psalmist both rejoices in the Lord and prays for the end of wickedness.

The charge to humanity is to respond to the dynamic activity of God, as God orders in a dynamic way the creation: God as the ultimate energy event, pure activity of love and rejoicing in creativity. How do we respond? As the natural creation is affirmed in and for itself, humanity must care for creation in and for itself. Secondly, creation embodies moral values in potentiality. Basic to the wisdom tradition is that moral value (enshrined in the Torah or Law) and the given-ness of creation are both orderings of reality, and both are dynamic. Moral value depends on the lordship of humanity over the creation, while ever respectful to it. As the fruits of the earth and human physical activity interact together, the biological and physical are transformed (without negating the prior state) into the moral and spiritual. Matter and human labour make a house: a house shelters human beings and animals: a house becomes a home for a family: the law is read in the family: the Jewish family praises God and goes back to care for the earth and transform it. It is a spiritual eco-system of wisdom building a house (using feminine attributes) with seven pillars, in which people 'walk in the way of insight' (Proverbs 9.8). Wisdom was there 'before the beginning of the earth' (Proverbs 8.22) as the hills emerged, and at the end, as the wise go to give advice to the rulers and the family tends its crops (Proverbs 11.23-27). It is all one system, moral and natural.

The dynamic activity of God calls, then, for the preservation of creation, and the transformation of creation from the material into the moral and spiritual. Nor is this view simply rational: again and again the wise considered the emotions to be as fundamentally crucial as the mind or the will. The creation of deep emotional bonds enable the bearing from one generation to another of moral obligations and spiritual value. Finally, this history is open-ended: there is the promise of freedom for all creation, the end of suffering and pain, in a narrative of promise and hope. In

Jesus of Nazareth this is spoken of as the coming of the Kingdom of God, which is a symbolic expression of the rule of God over all creation, and its response in penitence and thanksgiving.

I wish to resist the notion that the creation is the source and origin of the sacred. Rather, I wish to place the dimension of the sacred in God, with dynamic order at the heart of God. Such a God in the Judaeo-Christian tradition, and especially wisdom tradition, delights in the creation, and in an equally dynamic moral order. Both the moral order and the ecological balance do not seem in very good shape at the moment. The challenge to Christian theologians is both to affirm their own tradition and enter into worldwide dialogue with other traditions. Equally, moral value must be reaffirmed where there seem to be few living traditions, but only a complex diversity. Out of this moral complexity society has to fashion the means to change public attitudes about the nature of work, and the environment. Perhaps the final point is to emphasize the complexity of the issue, as the wise always worked 'weighing and studying ... with great care' (Ecclesiastes 12.9). This is no academic retreat into learning for its own sake. The wise moved cautiously, since they knew that God watched over the creation, judging every deed, whether good or evil (Ecclesiastes 12.14). It is God's creation that we are given to care for, and we answer for our actions.

We answer for our actions in the market-place of the world, where the power of the free-market often feels overwhelming. 'A rich man's wealth is his strong city, and like a high wall protects him' (Proverbs 18.11). Interestingly, the variant reading on this verse is 'protecting his imagination'. The task of the theologian and ethicist is not to let the market rule our imagination, but to create new understandings of work and enterprise that are sustainable in this fragile world. The definition of a good person by the wise was that there should be 'an inheritance for his children's children' (Proverbs 13.22). So in the last decade of this century we must recognize the moral imperative of long-term caring for creation. For this is part of the wisdom that God grants to his children (Job 28.28). A theology of enterprise, work and wealth-creation will enhance the creativity and freedom of those who work, whether in paid or unpaid

activity, if it recognizes above all the creation we are given
to cherish.

Notes

1. Report of the General Synod Board of Mission, *Good News in Our
   Time*, 1991.
2. ibid., pp. 18–19 and 55–60; P.H. Sedgwick, *Enterprise Culture and the
   New Right*, Association of Radical Methodists (awaiting publication);
   P.H. Sedgwick, 'Freedom, Well-being and the Enterprise Culture',
   Studies in Christian Ethics, vol. 3, no. 1, 1990
3. On deregulation, see Department of Trade and Industry, *The Enterprise
   Initiative*, 1989; *Releasing Enterprise*, Cm 512, 1988; Commission of the
   European Communities, *An Enterprise Policy for the Community*, August
   1989; T. Gorman, *The Enterprise Culture: An A-Z Guide Through the
   Regulatory Maze*, Adam Smith Institute, 1986.
4. J. Atherton, *Faith in the Nation*, 1988. See also his lecture *Christianity
   and the Market in the 1990s*, Industrial Christian Fellowship Annual
   Lecture 1988.
5. *A note on economics*. It is worth noting that the Roman empire never
   achieved a budget, and that all attempts at economic planning, let
   alone taxation, ended in failure. The Roman empire was in terminal
   economic decline long before the Barbarians broke through. Constantine
   saved the Empire for a while at the cost of a vast bureaucracy, centralization and an ever-growing army. The bureaucracy became corrupt
   and, like water leaking from a punctured hose, increasing taxes or printing
   money only made the problem worse. So it is not fair to expect the early
   Church to have anything to say on economics, for the Roman Empire
   had nothing as well. Usury was forbidden by the early Church, but this
   was basically a philosophical argument from Aristotle on the barrenness
   of money.
       Medieval life saw development of capitalism, from the sea-trading
   by agents of the Venetians to Constantinople, across the Atlantic, and
   to Northern Europe. Money from trade went into financing capitalism,
   and money from that went into early manufacturing (see Ozment's *The
   Age of Reform*). Equally, the Black Death and the growth of artillery
   ruined the economic and military usefulness of the nobility. The scene
   was set for the growth of medieval cities with a rising merchant class
   across the whole of Europe. Although the medieval Church condemned
   usury (3rd Lateran Council, 1179), in fact it was practised quite widely.
   So too was the enormous growth of taxation by the Church (alongside
   royal taxation), and various forms of fees for dispensing with canon
   law or purchasing vacant Church offices. The money economy was
   firmly established well before the Reformation.
       What Luther and Calvin did was to legitimate the whole process,
   thus giving rise to Weber's thesis that Protestant piety allowed the
   rise of capitalism (later taken up by R.H. Tawney). Both set limits

on usury, but nevertheless the economic forces were too powerful to be constrained.

It was the age of Enlightenment that developed economic theory. Adam Smith's economic theory presupposed the hidden hand of Providence, and this was taken up by many nineteenth-century writers. The fundamental reconsideration came very late in the day, in the teaching of the papacy (*Rerum Novarum*, 1891) and of Anglican (and other) theologians. Much of this did not wrestle with economic *theory*, but simply addressed the problems of poverty, wealth and vocation already addressed.

It was not until R.H. Tawney that a distinctive approach was made to economic theory which took account of Christian social teaching. A series of Conferences (1924 COPEC, Birmingham; 1937 Oxford) enabled him to influence the Christian Churches, although he came to despair of a Christian condemnation of capitalism. Tawney was a great influence on William Temple, Archbishop of Canterbury during the Second World War, who laid the enduring foundations for a Christian social theory.

This of course brings us to the present day. In the United States, Britain and on the Continent there are now many theologians working on the problem of how there can be moral values built into capitalism: this is sometimes called social market theory. The collapse of socialism ended the possibility of the transformation of capitalism into socialism held by Tawney, Temple, Demant and others. The problem that remains is how social market theory can be reconciled with Christian social ethics.

A final point should be mentioned, which is the growing interest of the Christian Churches in business ethics. Even in a secular society there is still a comparatively large minority of people at work who are Christians, both in the trade unions and management. Part of a reformulation of a Christian idea of vocation is the notion of the responsibility of the business corporation. In such areas as withdrawal from South Africa, the environment, and community involvement, the Churches have sought to influence the business world. For all these sections, see J. Mahoney, 'Wealth in the Judaeo-Christian Tradition', D.W. Hardy and P.H. Sedgwick (eds) *The Weight of Glory. A Vision and Practice for Christian Faith. The Future of Theological Liberalism*, 1991. Also, L. Gonzalez, *Faith and Wealth: A History of Early Christian Ideas on the Origin, Significance and Use of Money*, 1990; and 'The Church and Wealth', *Studies in Church History*, vol. 24, 1987, W. Sheils and D. Wood (eds). In general, on the biblical period, see C. Rowland, *Christian Origins*, 1985, and J. Riches, *Jesus and the Transformation of Judaism*, 1980 (esp. pp. 86–88 on the relationship of economic life to religious practice). There is the 1991 CTPI essay by S.W. Sykes, *On Power, Sex and Money*. For the Reformation debates, see H.A. Obermann, *Masters of the Reformation*, 1981, and S.E. Ozment, *The Age of Reform*, 1980. For the last two centuries, see Ronald Preston's many books: *Religion and the Persistence of Capitalism*, 1979; *Explorations in Theology Vol. 9*, 1981; *Church and Society in the Late Twentieth Century*, 1983; *The Future of Christian Ethics*, 1987. There is also *Religion and the Ambiguities of Capitalism*,

1991. Finally, there is a new reading of Christian history as social protest and living with the poor; see C. Rowland's *Radical Christianity*, 1988.

6. *Dr Martin Luthers Werke* 26, p. 504, 1883.
7. Methodist Church, Division of Social Responsibility, *The Ethics of Wealth-creation*, 1991.
8. Radio 4 Broadcast, 26 July 1991, 8.05 p.m. *Banking and Ethics: The Moral Maze*.
9. Methodist Church, *The Ethics of Wealth-creation*, para. 5.8.
10. M.D. Meeks, *God the Economist*, 1989, p. 183.
11. D.W. Hardy, 'Created and Redeemed Sociality', in D.W. Hardy and C. Gunton (eds), *On Being The Church: Essays on the Christian Community*, 1989, p. 42.
12. ibid., p. 40.
13. Letter to the author, 16 June 1989.
14. 'Myth of Thatcher/Runcie Quarrel', *The Times*, 18 March 1985, and R. Runcie, 8 October 1984, and 4 December 1985, *The Times*.
15. C. Gunton, 'The Gift of Freedom', in *Enlightenment and Alienation*, 1985, pp. 90–107. The preceding paragraphs draw heavily on this chapter.
16. D.W.D. Shaw, 'Creation and Culture', unpublished paper, 1990.
17. Hardy, p. 46.
18. Gunton, p. 103.
19. J. Stout, *Ethics after Babel*, 1990, p. 232.
20. This section owes much to the M. Phil. thesis of A.J. Delves, 'A Theology of Leisure', University of Hull. His work has been pioneering in showing the relationship of theologies of work to theologies of play and leisure.
21. K. Barth, *Church Dogmatics*, 3/4, p. 521.
22. ibid., 4/3, p. 147. See the discussion in J. Macken, *The Autonomy Theme in the Church Dogmatics*, 1990, pp. 75–6, and P. Ballard, *Towards a Contemporary Theology of Work*, 1982.

Conclusion

The story of this project

This book is primarily about attitudes and values. It began with the task of writing a contemporary account of the theology of wealth-creation. It swiftly became apparent that in the language of the 1980s this was mediated through talk of the 'enterprise culture'. While the phrase, the government rhetoric, and the political ideology associated with it have receded with remarkable speed, even during the final completion of this book, nevertheless an underlying permanent cultural change is evident.

It was for this reason that two unusual steps in writing theology were undertaken. One was that instead of writing a book, and then asking people to comment on chapters with a view to revision, a group of predominantly laypeople with considerable expertise were involved from the very beginning. I agree with Ronald Preston when he said at a conference on the relationship of economics and theology:

> If theologians and church leaders are going to produce [pronouncements and edicts], they have to do it with group work behind them.... Good statements come from working with groups of people of relevant but different experience ... and seeing if out of this kind of work, you get some broad judgements as to what are the really significant things going on in the world to which we need to give attention.[1]

Preston's experience of both consensus and conflict echoes the work of the group that met on this project in 1988–91. Group members' backgrounds were diverse: the civil service, British Steel, a small computer firm, a freelance management consultant, the Policy Studies Institute, a theologian, and the secretary of the Church of England's Industrial and Economic Affairs Committee. This book took shape out of the insights generated by this group, although responsibility for the final product is mine alone. The value of this exercise is that there is no pressure on the group either to reach a consensus, or to 'own' the book that resulted from the project. I am very grateful to them for their time and interest.

The second unusual step was to see if there was a way of discovering the permanent changes that might lie beneath the immediate discussion of the 'enterprise culture' in the media and among politicians. This sent me off on some fifty visits, half to small firms and community groups, half to individuals. In addition, Peter Dodd of Newcastle compared the experience of three different regions, which were Tyneside, the Black Country and Southampton, during the decade in question. Finally, Chris Beales visited inner-city groups and businesses in the United States who were working, sometimes with church support, on economic regeneration. Both their reports have been published, and their material used in this book. The visits that I made did not involve a formal questionnaire, but instead a series of lengthy interviews. A strong sense of far-reaching cultural shift emerged from this.

A third way of assessing what was happening was to examine the extensive series of surveys carried out on values and attitudes, both in the press and by such bodies as the Department of Employment Research Department. Only at this point did the shape of the SPCK project on wealth-creation become clear. The extensive literature on small businesses, which is now being carried forward by the Economic and Social Research Council's project on Small Businesses, was helpful, but it was not my main concern. The same would be true of the discussions on community businesses, enterprise in education, and other areas.

It is worth telling the story of this project in this way because without it the engagement with social reality would not have been possible. By this route the conclusions that I reached came close to John Atherton's *Faith in the Nation* or Robert Benne's *The Ethics of Democratic Capitalism*. Atherton concentrated on how participation is possible for rich and poor in the market economy, and gives great attention to social policies. Benne's book is more philosophical, examining the nature of justice in the free-market. This study focuses on values, attitudes and the history of the past decade. The collapse of communism in Eastern Europe paralleled the writing of this book, and in many respects the debate on post-communism (or socialism) simply confirmed many of the conclusions that this project had reached. While the rhetoric of British Conservative politicians in the 1980s will fade, there has definitely been a change in values and attitudes throughout Britain. Any theology of wealth-creation must recognize this fact.

Enterprise and wealth

The ethics of enterprise and self-employment are neither the same as free-market capitalism, nor to be separated from it. Enterprise, as has been often demonstrated in this book, is a wider term than small (or large) businesses. While Schumpeter's analysis of the entrepreneur is fundamental, enterprise goes beyond this. In the approach taken by the Enterprise and Education Unit at Durham University, enterprise uses creativity, problem-solving and decision-making to achieve an objective. The success of this approach is measured both in terms of the objective attained, and the personal development attained.

Wealth creation therefore becomes not a factual term, but an evaluative one. It is of course possible to create wealth in a non-enterprising way. By creating a monopoly and removing competition a company can raise its prices, and make a great deal of money while behaving in a manner that is profoundly non-innovative and reactionary. It can continue like this so long as it can maintain a monopoly. It is a familiar story in industry.

Wealth-creation can also be achieved by the patient accumulation of resources, capital and material, so that eventually a high degree of wealth is produced. This approach has its place, and is perhaps best exemplified in the stewardship of land from one generation to another by traditional classes. It is, however, a profoundly conservative measure. A third approach is both innovative and competitive, with the objective of creating as much financial wealth as possible. Alan Barrell's comment puts this activity in its place. 'We may create wealth, but where is it going? We won't create the basis for a new Industrial Revolution'. It simply recycles financial wealth for the benefit of a few individuals, who then become very rich.

From the perspective of enterprise, wealth-creation must be innovative and competitive, yet create new material wealth.

Some of the firms that I visited were well aware of this necessity, and reinvested heavily. Wealth-creation therefore is different from simply an affirmation of industrial life and its place in our society. Nor is it to be confused with a theology of work, which in past decades has evaluated how the co-operation of each person might together contribute to a greater good. Wealth-creation as enterprise in the economic sphere does not have to be found only in small business. Just as there are some conservative small firms, so equally some larger organizations now concentrate heavily on devolution of responsibilities and the promotion of change. Charles Handy was very helpful on this point. Nevertheless, it is the case that wealth-creation as enterprise will most often be found in the small-firms sector. This sector is the most innovative.

The creation of wealth goes further than the creation of material goods, even if it is important that material wealth is emphasized over purely financial considerations. Wealth-creation, in Peter Kellner's helpful analysis quoted earlier, includes our enrichment through the assets of our society such as education or a better environment. Therefore the question of wealth-creation must take up the issue of wealth, and how it is defined. At this point there can be a convergence between the definition of enterprise and wealth-creation.

Enterprise implies a wider frame of reference than the economic sphere. The section on community groups and educational process shows this clearly. Wealth also can be widened out beyond the economic realm, to include such things as the environment and education. To quote Kellner again, we are enriched 'by things that economic statistics either ignore or fail to measure fully'. The conclusion of this argument is that it is possible to create non-material wealth that is deeply enriching, in a profoundly creative and innovative way. It is enterprise as wealth-creation. This is an articulation of the values and aspirations that are the primary concern of this book. The creation of material wealth is crucial for the economic regeneration of Britain, and there are many examples of this activity given here. The ability to act and implement a strategy in creative and innovative ways also matters a great deal. There is in addition a searching for new forms of self-expression and value that runs through these activities.

How far this change in social and economic life will permeate all aspects of society is difficult to judge. Innovation, creativity and self-realization are not the usual descriptions of British life. It is not surprising that young people and women, who have been most frustrated at their place in society, should be most attracted by the challenge of independence, self-employment, or working in community groups. This did not mean that their values rejected other aspects of our society, such as interdependence and mutual care. These values, embodied in the welfare state, were challenged by some politicians in the last decade, but those I interviewed, and those questioned in Social Attitude surveys, seemed quite capable of being attracted by enterprise, while at the same time having a wider concept of wealth than personal financial enrichment. It is also not surprising that those working in large institutions should also speak of the sheer difficulty of bringing about innovation and devolution. Paxman's book charts precisely those institutions least affected by this cultural change. The judiciary, and the legal profession in general; universities; well-established British companies – all these represent a resistance to change.

The relationship of tradition to social change and the future of public institutions are issues beyond this survey. So too is the vexed question of whether greater social change only excludes further those without wealth and resources although the sections of this book on community groups and ethnic minorities represent some attempt to address this problem. The primary emphasis of this study must be to stress the devolution of management, the greater creativity and innovation that can result, and the relationship of enterprise to wealth. In turn, these social and economic changes embody and create new values and aspirations.

Theology, enterprise and wealth

God's relationality is one that is also characterized by innovation and creativity, bringing forth new patterns of existence and new forms of wealth. Indeed, the very bringing into being and sustaining of the creation is itself the creation of wealth, so that the most fundamental form of wealth-creation is the wealth of all creation, nourished and sustained by God.

It is worth emphasizing this point. I have tried to decentre, or throw off balance, the idea that a theology of work (or wealth) is an affirmation of manufacturing industry. This is true, but I have laid far more stress on the innovation and creativity, which Schumpeter memorably described as 'the perennial gale of continual destruction', present in enterprise. Equally, it is important to decentre the idea of God as the eternal being who is the source of unchanging values. There is truth in this picture of God, but it is only a half-truth. D. W. Hardy puts the position better:

> So the relationality of God is one of energetic involvement and participation, moving toward fuller and fuller relationship.... Seen in such a way, it becomes clear that God is what – from the human point of view – can be called an 'energy event', constituted by a concentration of well-being in a relationship which is inseparable from the extending of this relationship with his people in the world, and from the expression of his well-being in that relationship.[2]

God, then, does not remain within himself. His very being enacts a social world, in which human beings can come to fuller and fuller relationships. That social world is not an abstraction. It is an increasingly complex world, made up of political, economic and religious institutions, individuals and values.

A dynamic, relational God with ever-growing energetic involvement in the world he sustains confers a 'proper form and energy on human relationality'. The dynamics of enterprise and wealth-creation thus mirror the nature of God (enterprise) and his activity (wealth-creation). While this may be far from the accepted picture of God in many congregations, it is I believe not only a truer picture of the Trinity, but also the only means by which faith, worship and action can re-engage with the modern world. If worship is only seen as 'a conventional and undemanding activity whereby Christians continue the beliefs and practices of the past',[3] then divorce between religious faith and economic activity will become unbridgeable.

Having established the nature and activity of God in the world, what consequences follow theologically for enterprise and wealth-creation? First, there are implications for the Churches themselves, in terms of their willingness to change, and to undergo a degree of transformation beyond what has been achieved so far. Once again the question of the place of tradition is paramount. Nevertheless, the idea of 'the Church in the Power of the Spirit', to quote one of Moltmann's titles, remains a guiding principle. While the Church still exemplifies the paradox of being an agent of love and yet is the most reactionary of all institutions, the possibility of reformation remains.

Secondly, there is the question of how far the values of freedom, innovation and community can be seen as able to be reconciled with Christian values. It is remarkable how much suspicion there has been in the Churches about wealth-creation, and even more about free-market capitalism. I have tried to argue that the trinitarian action of God in Christ does allow the possibility of interpreting these changes in ways that are positive, while making strong criticism of the search for unlimited wealth. This unlimited desire is, to reiterate the argument in Chapter 2, a form of pathological behaviour. However, the emphasis should be laid on the positive aspects of this change. In Chapter 7, I have sketched out the outline of a theology of creation, paying particular attention to freedom and creativity. This leads into a consideration of human community, and of the transformation of matter. The wisdom tradition, which speaks powerfully of the delight God has in the creativity of human beings, is a rich source of material at this point.

A third question is raised in this book and that is the issue of business ethics. This in turn leads on to the whole nature of the regulation of the market economy by the state. The collapse of socialism in Eastern Europe has led to greater discussion on this point across the industrialized world, with a vigorous debate on the limits of the free-market economy, and the moral framework that should surround capitalism.[4] Within economic life itself there is the growing area of the moral education of managers, the teaching of business ethics, etc. I have tried to show that an enterprise ethic is not incompatible with concern for the environment or for world poverty, and may indeed be the way forward. Nevertheless, the enormous issues raised in this chapter require fuller treatment elsewhere, which I hope to work on shortly.

The next topic is how the Churches should address those working in economic and social life, which is often far removed from the world of the Church. The concluding part of Chapter 5 considers this issue in some detail, for it is a difficult and important one. It underlies the consideration of the values of the enterprise culture, of business ethics, and the limits of the free market. I have resisted the imperialism of theology on this matter, not from any crisis of confidence, but because only a public philosophy informed by theology can do justice to the subject. A proper dialogue with the secular world is all important. At the same time theology, which can via a public philosophy nourish and sustain values, itself needs to be anchored in the community of praise and worship. The transition needs to be made with some care. Religion in Britain has always been concerned with wider issues than the future of the Churches themselves. A narrow ecclesiastical-centred strategy might produce greater growth in the Churches, but it would abandon those working in the secular world to the resources of their own heart and mind. So the challenge of the previous decade to the Churches remains. If they will, they can (alongside others) create new patterns of creativity, freedom and community.

The final conclusion is not, however, about the Churches. Our society contains both a widening gap between rich and poor, and a new ability to create and plan in innovative ways that could not have been suspected a decade ago. The Churches have concentrated their concern on the problem of poverty, and I share this concern. It will not be easy to sustain a society in which the differences widen ever further. However, there is also the question of what the enterprise culture means for those caught up in it, and for those in public institutions who might wish for less estab-lished patterns of behaviour and more flexibility, devolving responsibility still further. Here the Churches have been very weak, emphasizing the greed of the new culture and ignoring the innovation and freedom that changes have brought. That is why this book both describes this new culture, and commends those who are working it. There are ethical questions that are very complex and serious, but a positive attitude to wealth-creation and enterprise by the Churches would affirm those whose daily lives are now shaped by it. A theology of enterprise is neither political nor adversarial. It is about rediscovering the dynamic of society under the creative energy of God in Christ.

Notes

1. W. Block, G. Brennan and K. Elzinga (eds), *Morality of the Market: Religious and Economic Perspectives. Proceedings of an International Symposium August 9–11 1982, Vancouver, Canada*, 1985, p. 227.
2. D.W. Hardy, *The Foundation of Cognition and Ethics in Worship*, unpublished paper, 1991, pp. 39–41.
3. Hardy, p. 1. See also D.W. Hardy and D. Ford, *Jubilate: Theology in Praise*, 1983, and Hardy's essay on society in D.W. Hardy and P.H. Sedgwick (eds), *The Weight of Glory. A Vision and Practice for Christian Faith. The Future of Theological Liberalism*, 1991.
4. R. Preston, *Religion and the Ambiguities of Capitalism*, 1991. John Atherton also has a forthcoming book on the subject.

Bibliography

Adams, R., *Who Profits?* Lion 1989.

All Are Called: Towards a Theology of the Laity. Report of a working party of the General Synod Board of Education, Church House Publishing 1985.

Alves, C., *Free to Choose? The Voluntary Principle at Work in Education.* National Society 1991.

And All That Is Unseen. see Dawson, R.

Anderson, D. (ed.), *The Kindness that Kills.* SPCK 1984.

Atherton, J., *Faith in the Nation.* SPCK 1988.

Bachu, P., and Westwood, S. (eds), *Enterprising Women.* Routledge 1988.

Ball, M., Gray, F., and McDowell, L., *The Transformation of Britain.* Fontana 1989.

Ballard, P., *Towards a Contemporary Theology of Work.* Collegiate Centre of Theology, University College, Cardiff 1982.

Ballard, P., *In and Out of Work: A Pastoral Perspective.* St Andrew Press 1987.

Barth, K., *Church Dogmatics.* T & T Clark 1965.

Beales, C., *Mainstream and Marginal: Creating Economic Change in Inner City Life.* Board for Social Responsibility, Church of England, Church House Publishing 1990.

Benne, R., *The Ethic of Democratic Capitalism.* Philadelphia, Fortress 1981.

Benne, R., 'Ethics, Economics and the Corporate Life' (*Christian Century,* January 1991.)

Bermant, C., *Point of Arrival: A Study of London's East End.* Eyre Methuen 1975.

Bevan, J., *Barriers to Business Start-Up.* Department of Employment Research Paper no. 71, 1989.

Bevan, J., and Jay, J., *The New Tycoons.* New York, Simon & Schuster, 1989.

Birley, S., 'The Start-Up', in P. Burns and J. Dewhurst (eds), *Small Business and Entrepreneurship.* Macmillan 1989.

Block, W., Brennàn, G., and Elzinga, K., (eds), *Morality of the Market. Religious and Economic Perspectives. Proceedings of an International Symposium August 9–11 1982, Vancouver, Canada.* Canada, Fraser Institute, 1985.

Bolton Report, *Committee of Inquiry on Small Firms.* HMSO 1971.

Borrowdale, A., *A Woman's Work: Changing Christian Attitudes.* SPCK 1989.

Boswell, J., *The Rise and Decline of Small Firms.* Allen & Unwin 1973.

Brinks, M., and Coyne, J., *The Birth of Enterprise.* IEA 1983.

British Council of Churches Community and Race Relations Unit, *Future Investment: The Economic Empowerment of the Black Community. Report of a Visit to the United States.* April 1985.

British Council of Churches Community and Race Relations Unit, *Consultation on the Economic Empowerment of the Black Community.* 2–4 February 1990.

Burns, P., and Dewhurst, J. (eds), *Small Business and Entrepreneurship.* Macmillan 1989.

Business in the Community Report, *First.* 1990.

Carter, S., and Cannon, T., *Female Entrepreneurs.* Department of Employment Research Paper no. 65, 1988.

Casson, M., *The Entrepreneur.* Martin Robertson 1982.

Causer, G., *Inside British Society.* Wheatsheaf 1987.

Centesimus Annus. Encyclical letter of Pope John Paul II, Catholic Truth Society 1991.

Chesshyre, R., *Return of a Native Reporter.* Penguin 1986.

Christie, I., and Fogarty, M., *Companies and Communities.* Policy Studies Institute 1990.

Changing Britain: Social Diversity and Moral Unity. Report by the Board for Social Responsibility, Church House Publishing 1987.

Clarke, R., *Work in Crisis.* St Andrews Press 1982.

Coldstream, P., *Higher Education, Industry and the Journey of Learning.* Hull University Press 1991.

Cornford, J., *A Stake in the Company.* Institute for Public Policy Research 1990.

Cotton, J., *Enterprise/Education/Experience.* Durham University Business School 1990.

Craig Smith, N., *Morality and the Market.* Routledge 1990.

Curran, C., 'A Century of Catholic Social Teaching' (*Theology Today*, July 1991).

Curran, J., and Stanworth, J. (eds), *The Survival of the Small Firm*, vol. 1, Gower Press 1986.

Dahrendorf, R., 'The Future of the Underclass: A European Perspective' (*Northern Economic Review*, 1989).

Davis, J., *Greening Business: Managing for Sustainable Development*. Basil Blackwell 1991.

Dawson, R. *And All that is Unseen: A New Look at Women and Work*. Report by the Board of Social Responsibility, Church House Publishing 1986.

Deming, W.E., *Out of the Crisis*. Cambridge University Press 1984.

Dewhurst, J., 'The Entrepreneur', in P. Burns and J. Dewhurst (eds), *Small Business and Entrepreneurship*. Macmillan 1989.

Dodd, P., *The Influence of Culture upon Enterprise*. Industrial Christian Fellowship Theme Pamphlet no. 44. September 1990.

Elkington, J., *Community Action: No Thanks, Noah*. British Gas Environmental Issues Series 1990.

Elkington, J., and Burke, T. *The Green Capitalists*. Gollancz 1989.

Emmett, D., *The Moral Roots of Democracy*. Tawney Society 1985.

Erlander, L., *Faith in the World of Work. On the Theology of Work as Lived by the French Worker-priests and British Industrial Mission*. Uppsala 1991.

Evangelical Enterprise Works. Evangelical Alliance 1989.

Evans, R., 'Business Ethics and Changes in Society' (*Journal of Business Ethics*, vol. 10, 1991).

Faith in the City. Report of the Archbishop of Canterbury's Commission on Urban Priority Areas, Church House Publishing 1985.

Faith in the City of Birmingham. Paternoster Press 1988.

Field, F., *Losing Out*. Basil Blackwell 1989.

Financial Times, 'Local Management in Schools', 4 June 1990.

Fogarty, M., 'The Churches and the Creation of Wealth' (*The Month*, April 1989).

Ford, D.F. (ed.), *The Modern Theologians*. Basil Blackwell 1989.

Ford, D.F., and Young, F., *Meaning and Truth in 2 Corinthians*. SPCK 1987.

Fullemploy Group (with E. Gretton), *Black Business Development in Nottinghamshire: Report for Nottinghamshire County Council*. 1988.

Fullemploy Group, *Business Development. A Serious Option for the Black Community? The 1989 Consultation*. London 1989.

Fullemploy Group, *Annual Review 1989*.

Galbraith, J.K., *The New Industrial State*. Hamish Hamilton 1967.

Gelinser, O., *The Enterprise Ethic*. IEA 1968.

Gibb, A., *Enterprise Culture*. Durham University Business School Occasional Paper 9047, 1990.

Gibb, A., *Innovative Approaches to Entrepreneurship Education*. DUBS Paper 1990.

Godsey, J., 'Dietrich Bonhoeffer', in D. Ford (ed.), *The Modern Theologians*. Basil Blackwell 1989.

Gonzalez, J.L., *Faith and Wealth: A History of Early Christian Ideas on the Origin, Significance and Use of Money*. New York, Orbis, 1990.

Good News in Our Time. Report of the General Synod Board of Mission, Church House Publishing 1991.

Gould, C., *Rethinking Democracy*. James Clarke 1988.

Green, C., *The Christian in Business*. ICF Pamphlet 1990.

Green, L., *Let's Do Theology*. Mowbray 1990.

Green, L., Todd, N., Allen, M. and Tytler, D., *A Thing Called Aston: An Experiment in Reflective Learning*. Church House Publishing 1987.

Gunton, C., *Enlightenment and Alienation*. Marshall, Morgan & Scott 1985.

Habgood, J., *Confessions of a Conservative Liberal*. SPCK 1988.

Habgood, J., 'The Good, the Bad and the Individual' (*The Times*, 27 February 1989).

Habgood, J., 'Church and Risk', in R. Holloway (ed.), *The Divine Risk*. Darton, Longman and Todd 1990.

Hakim, C., 'Self-Employment in Britain: A Review of Recent Trends and Current Issues' (*Work, Employment and Society*, vol. 2, no. 4, December 1988).

Hancock, G., *Lords of Poverty*. Macmillan 1989.

Handy, C., *The Age of Unreason*. Business Books 1989.

Hardy, D.W., 'The Foundation of Cognition and Ethics in Worship', unpublished paper. Princeton 1991.

Hardy, D.W., and Ford, D., *Jubilate: Theology in Praise*. Darton, Longman and Todd 1983.

Hardy, D.W., and Gunton, C. (eds), *On Being the Church: Essays on the Christian Community*. T & T Clark 1989.

Hardy, D.W., and Sedgwick, P.H. (eds), *The Weight of Glory. A Vision and Practice for Christian Faith. The Future of Theological Liberalism*. T & T Clark 1991.

Harrison, R., *Enterprise Education in Cleveland County*. Durham University Business School 1988.

Hastings, A., *A History of English Christianity 1900–1985*. Collins 1986.

Hastings, A., *Robert Runcie*. Mowbray 1991.

Hauerwas, S., *The Peaceable Kingdom*. SCM Press 1984.

Havel, V., *Living in Truth*. Faber & Faber 1989.

Hewitt, G. (ed.), *Strategist for the Spirit: Leslie Hunter, Bishop of Sheffield, 1939–1962*. Becket 1985.

Hobbs, D., *Doing the Business: Entrepreneurship, The Working Class and Detectives in the East End of London*. Oxford University Press 1988.

Hollenweger, W., 'Ethnic Education' (*Theology*, September 1987).

Holloway, R. (ed.), *The Divine Risk*. Darton, Longman and Todd 1990.

Holmberg, B., *Paul and Power*. Lund, Gleerup 1978.

Iremonger, F.A., *William Temple*. Oxford University Press 1948.

Jenkins, P., *Mrs Thatcher's Revolution*. Jonathan Cape 1987.

Jordan, W., *The Common Good: Citizenship, Morality and Self-Interest*. Basil Blackwell 1989.

Kanter, R.M., *The Change Masters: Corporate Entrepreneurs at Work*. Allen & Unwin 1981.

Kasemann, E., *Jesus Means Freedom*. SCM Press 1979.

Keat, R., and Abercrombie, N. (eds), *Enterprise Culture*. Routledge 1991.

Keeling, M., *The Foundation of Christian Ethics*. T & T Clark 1990.

Kerr, F., 'Cupitt's Dogmas' (*New Blackfriars*, LXII 1981).

Kirby, D.A., *Entrepreneurship Research in the United Kingdom*. DUBS Paper 9059, 1990.

Lawrence, P., *Invitation to Management*. Basil Blackwell 1986.

Leech, K., *Struggle in Babylon*. Sheldon Press 1988.

Leech, K., 'Religion and the Rise of Racism', in D. Ormrod (ed.), *Fellowship, Freedom and Equality*. Christian Socialist Movement 1990.

Leech, K., *The Anglo-Catholic Social Conscience: Two Critical Essays*. Jubilee Co. 1991.

Leighton, P., 'Employment and Self-Employment' (*Employment Gazette*, 91.5, 1983).

Linking-Up: A Report to Sponsors. Manchester 1990.

Living Faith in the City. A Progress Report of the Archbishop of Canterbury's Advisory Group on Urban Priority Areas, General Synod of the Church of England 1990.

Luther, M., *Dr Martin Luthers Werke*. Weimar 1883–.

Macken, J., *The Autonomy Theme in the Church Dogmatics*. Cambridge University Press 1990.

MacIntyre, A., *Secularization and Moral Change*. Oxford University Press 1967.

MacIntyre, A., *After Virtue*. Duckworth 1981.

Mahoney, J., 'Wealth in the Judaeo-Christian Tradition' in D.W. Hardy and P.H. Sedgwick (eds), *The Weight of Glory*. T & T Clark 1991.

Malvern Conference Papers. Hinksey Centre 1991.

Markyanda, A., *Green Economics*. British Gas Environmental Issues Series 1990.

McCann, D.P., and Stackhouse, M., 'A Post-Communist Manifesto' (*Christian Century*, 16 January 1991).

McEvoy, D., and Aldrich, H., 'Survival Rates of Asian and White Retailers' (*International Small Business Journal*, 4.3, Spring 1986).

McEvoy, D., and Jones, T., 'Ethnic Enterprise: The Popular Image', in J. Curran and J. Stanworth (eds), *The Survival of the Small Firm*. Gower Press 1987.

Meeks, M.D., *God the Economist*. Philadelphia, Fortress Press 1989.

Meeks, W., *The First Urban Christians*. Yale University Press 1983.

Millbank, J., *Theology and Social Theory*. Basil Blackwell 1990.

Miller, H., *The Way of Enterprise*. IEA 1963.

Moltmann, J., *The Church in the Power of the Spirit*. SCM Press 1977.

Moltmann, J. *The Trinity and the Kingdom of God*. SCM Press 1981.

Moltmann, J., *On Human Dignity*. SCM Press 1984.

Moltmann, J., *God in Creation*. SCM Press 1985.

Moltmann, J., *Creating a Just Future*. SCM Press 1990.

Montefiore, H., *Reclaiming the High Ground: A Christian Response to Secularism*. Macmillan 1990.

Mulgan, G., 'The Buck Stops Here' (*Marxism Today*, September 1990).

Nankivell, O., 'Christian Values in the Market' (*Audenshaw Paper 132*, 1991).

Not Just for the Poor: Christian Perspectives on the Welfare State. Report by the Social Policy Committee of the Board for Social Responsibility, Church House Publishing 1985.

Obermann, H., *Masters of the Reformation.* Cambridge University Press 1981.

Ozment, S.E., *The Age of Reform 1250–1550.* Yale University Press 1980.

Paxman, J., *Friends in High Places: Who Runs Britain?* Michael Joseph 1990.

Payne, J., 'Young Self-Employed Workers' (*Employment Gazette*, 92.11, 1984).

Pearce, D., '*The New Environmental Policy.* British Gas Environmental Issues Series 1990.

Porter, J., *The Recovery of Virtue: The Relevance of Aquinas for Christian Ethics.* Philadelphia, Westminster, 1991.

Preston, R., *Religion and the Persistence of Capitalism.* SCM Press 1979.

Preston, R., *Explorations in Theology*, vol. 9. SCM Press 1981.

Preston, R., *Church and Society in the Late Twentieth Century.* SCM Press 1983.

Preston, R., *The Future of Christian Ethics.* SCM Press 1987.

Preston, R., *Religion and the Ambiguities of Capitalism.* SCM Press 1991.

Project North-East, *Young Entrepreneurs Report.* 1989.

Rahner, K., *The Shape of the Church to Come.* SCM Press 1974.

Rahner, K., *Foundations of the Christian Faith.* Darton, Longman and Todd 1978.

Riches, J., *Jesus and the Transformation of Judaism.* Darton, Longman and Todd 1980.

Riddell, P., *The Thatcher Decade.* Basil Blackwell 1990.

Ridell, R., *Foreign Aid Reconsidered.* James Curry 1987.

Ridley, N., *Policies Against Pollution.* Centre for Policy Studies, June 1989.

Ritchie, J., *Explaining Enterprise Cultures.* DUBS Paper 8906, 1989.

Ritchie, J., *Concepts of Enterpise and Education.* DUBS Paper 9053, 1990.

Rowland, C., *Christian Origins.* SPCK 1985.

Rowland, C., *Radical Christiantity*. Pluto 1988.

Roy, A., 'The Quiet Millionaires' (*Telegraph Weekend Magazine*, 25 August 1990).

Sahlman, W.H., and Stevenson, H.H., 'The Entrepreneurial Process', in P. Burns and J. Dewhurst (eds), *Small Business and Entrepreneurship*. Macmillan 1989.

Scase, R., and Goffee, R., *The Entrepreneurial Middle Class*. Croom Helm 1982.

Schumpeter, J., *Capitalism, Socialism and Democracy*. New York, Harper & Row, 1943.

Sedgwick, P.H., *Mission Impossible? A Theology of the Local Church*. Collins 1990.

Sedgwick, P.H., 'The Enterprise Culture as a New World for the Churches' (*Crucible*, July 1990).

Sedwick, P.H., 'Freedom, Well-being and the Enterprise Culture' (*Studies in Christian Ethics*, vol. 3, no. 1, 1990).

Sedgwick, P.H., 'A Reply to Richard Evans' (*Journal of Business Ethics*, vol. 10, 1991, pp. 877-91).

Seidl, C. (ed.), *Lectures on Schumpeterian Economics. Centenary Memorial Lectures, Graz 1983*. Berlin 1984.

Shaw, D.W.D, 'Creation and Culture', unpublished paper, Society for the Study of Theology Annual Conference, St Andrews 1990.

Sheils, W., and Wood, D. (ed.), 'The Church and Wealth' (*Studies in Church History*, vol. 24, 1987).

Skidelsky, R. (ed.), *Thatcherism*. Michael Joseph 1988.

Smail, D.J., *Taking Care: An Alternative to Therapy*. J.M. Dent 1987.

Smith, A., *Passion for the Inner City*. Sheed & Ward 1983.

Spreeckley, F., *Developing Community Enterprise*. Community Economy 1989.

Stackhouse, M., *Public Theology and Political Economy*. Grand Rapids, MI, Eerdmans, 1987.

Storey, D., *Entrepreneurship and the New Firm*. Croom Helm 1982.

Storey, D., *Fast Growth Small Businesses*. Department of Employment Research Paper no. 67, 1989.

Storey, D., 'Southern European Partners Lead the Way' (*The Times*, 19 September 1991).

Stout, J., *Ethics After Babel*. James Clarke 1990.

Suggate, A., *William Temple and Social Ethics Today*. T & T Clark 1987.

Sykes, S.W., 'Lutherans and Anglicans on the Catholicity of the Church', unpublished paper for the Anglican/Scandinavian Dialogue, Finland 1986.

Sykes, S.W., 'On Power, Sex and Money', *Vision and Prophecy: The Tasks of Social Theology Today*. Centre for Theology and Public Issues, Edinburgh, Occasional paper no. 23, 1991.

Taylor, M., *Good for the Poor: Christian Ethics and World Development*. Mowbray 1990.

The Ethics of Wealth-Creation. Methodist Church 1991.

The Independent, 'Asian Enterprise in Leicester', 28 December 1989.

Torrey, M., 'Is Money the Sole Arbiter of Worth? (*ICF Quarterly*, 1989).

Torrey, M., *Basic Income*. Basic Income Research Group 1990.

Turner, P., *Sex, Money and Power*. Boston, Cowley, 1985.

Tyers, D., 'Evangelical Helpmeets or Hinderers?' (*City Cries*, no. 19, Summer 1989).

Usher, P., *Putting Something Back*. Glasgow Planning Exchange 1989.

Vardy, P., *Business Morality*. Collins 1989.

Ward, R., 'Ethnic Business and Economic Change: An Overview' (*International Small Business Journal*, 4.3, spring 1986).

Ward, R., and Jenkins, R. (eds), *Ethnic Communities in Business*. Cambridge University Press 1984.

Ward, R., Waldinger, R., and Aldrich, H., *Ethnic Enterprise*. Sage 1990.

Weiss, L., *Creating Capitalism: The State and Small Business Since 1945*. Basil Blackwell 1988.

Werbner, P., 'Business on Trust: Pakistani Enterprise in the Manchester Garment Trade', in R. Ward and R. Jenkins (eds), *Ethnic Communities in Business*. Cambridge University Press 1984.

West, P., 'Cruciform Labour? The Cross in Two Recent Theologies of Work' (*Modern Churchman*, XXVIII, no. 4, 1986).

West, P., 'Divine Creativity and Human Creativity' (*New Blackfriars*, XVIII, 1986).

West, P., 'Karl Barth's Theology of Work' (*Modern Churchman*, XXIX, no. 3, 1987).

Wilcox, J., *Ethics and Excellence*. British Institute of Management Annual Lecture 1990.

Williams, R., 'God and Risk', in R. Holloway (ed.), *The Divine Risk*. Darton, Longman and Todd 1990.

Wilson, P., *Growth Strategies in Minority Enterprise: Case Studies in Corporate Growth of Asian and Afro-Caribbean Business in Britain*. Small Business Research Trust 1987.

Wilson, P., and Stanworth, J., 'Growth and Change in Black Minority Enterprise in Britain' (*International Small Business Journal*, 4.3, spring 1986).

Winfield, M., *Minding Your Own Business*. Social Audit 1990.

Wogaman, J.P., *Economics and Ethics: A Christian Inquiry*, Fortress Press 1986.

World Wide Fund for Nature and the Ecumenical Patriarchate of Constantinople, *Orthodoxy and the Ecological Crisis*. 1990.

Young, H., *One of Us: A Life of Margaret Thatcher*. Macmillan 1989.

Young, Lord, *The Enterprise Years*. Headline 1990.

Appendix

Bibliography on community enterprise

P. Bagshaw, *Quality of Life in Sheffield 2000* 25 February 1990, Conference Report.

On Scotland
Scottish Office: Central Research Unit Papers.
An Evaluation of Community Business in Scotland (Alan McGregor, Andrew McArthur, Veronica Moore), February 1988.
A. McArthur (ed.), *Community Economic Initiatives in Public Sector Housing Estates*, Training and Employment Research Unit, University of Glasgow, 1989.
E. Pilkington, *Reviving Britain's Outer Estates*.
Search 4 (Winter 1990) (features Glasgow).

On Manchester
J. Desmond and A. J. Addy, *Towards a Framework of Evaluation for a Local Community Enterprise Agency*.
William Temple Foundation Ltd, Manchester (n.d.).
Start Up and Community Enterprises, William Temple Foundation Ltd (n.d.).
F. Spreeckley, *Developing Community Enterprise*, Community Economy Ltd, London, 1989.

On Newscastle
A. J. Christie and J. Potts, *Project North East Community Business Report*, February 1990.

On London
Bridge Self Enterprise Project Annual Report, 1988–9, 144 Cambridge Heath Road, Bethnal Green, London.

General

Linking Up: Community Enterprise, Urban Regeneration and the Churches, 12–14 October 1990, Conference report, Manchester.

Interviews on community enterprise

Rev. Derek Seber, Linking Up, Manchester, 21 May 1990.
Rev. David Everett, Linking Up/Church Action with the Unemployed, 4 June 1990, London.
Steve Charters, Director, Bridge Project, Bethnal Green, London, 11 June 1990.
Faisal Mohammed, Somali Project, Bethnal Green, London, 19 June 1990.

Bibliography on enterprise and education

C. Ball, *Towards an Enterprising Culture*, Paris, OECD, 1988.
Segal Quince Wicksteed, *Universities, Enterprise and Local Economic Development*, MSC 1988.
Council for Industry and Higher Education, *Towards a Partnership*, Spring 1987.
Enterprise in Higher Education, Training Agency 1989.
Enterprise/Education Experience, Durham University Business School 1989.

Index

Firms and Organizations Interviewed

Bridge Project 63, 69
British Council of Churches Community and Race Relations Unit (BCC CRRU) 73
British Steel 44, 58
British Steel (Industry) 45, 58–9, 60, 65–6, 69

Council for Industry and Higher Education 45–6, 65, 68

Domino 42–3, 49, 58, 174
Durham University Business School (DUBS) 19, 34, 42–3, 49, 60, 65, 174
Driver and Vehicle Licencing Centre (DVLC) 44–5, 59, 113

Fielden, Marcel 47–8, 59
Fullemploy 70, 74

Hansib Publishing 70–1
Harkers 41–2, 58
Heritage Upholstery 46, 59

Industrial Christian Fellowship 3–4
Industrial Mission Association (IMA) 1–3, 6–7

Korda 42–4, 48, 58, 116

Lincoln Wholefoods 49, 59

Linking-Up 60, 62–3, 69
MICRO-SYS 42–3, 48
Middlesborough Enterprise Centre 46, 59

Nima 43, 48, 58

Plimsoll 49, 59
Property Services Agency (PSA) 59

Rover Group 40, 44–5, 50, 58, 113

Stable Block Design 49, 59

TEC 44–5, 59, 117
TMI 44, 59
Thermica 50, 59, 117

United Engineering (Lincoln) 41, 58

Whale Tankers 40, 58, 116
WM and P 74–5, 79

Other Names

Aston Training Scheme 22
Atherton, J. 56–60, 62, 111, 113, 121–2, 144, 173
Augustine 149
Aquinas 149, 153

Bakshi, G.S. 75
Bancroft, R. 151
Barnett, C. 37

Barrell, A. 43, 174
Barth, K. 108, 165
Basic Income Research Group
130
Beales, C. 2, 6–7, 60, 137, 173
Benedict, St. 151
Benne, R. 105, 117–22, 173
Birley, S. 18, 66
Birch Report (USA) 25
Bloch, E. 105
Body Shop 133–5
Bolton Report (UK) 25
Bonhoeffer, D. 130
Borrowdale, A. 2, 158
British Institute of Management
128, 141
British Rail 23
Business in the Community 54,
128

Casson, M. 42
Calvin, J. 106, 147, 155
Carter, S. and Cannon, T. 94–7
Centre for Black and White
Christian Partnership 21
Changing Britain 104–11,
117–19, 121
Chesshyre, R. 75
Christian Aid 131
Christie, I. 128, 139
Church of England 2–3, 22,
28–9, 33, 60; Board of
Education 66; Board of
Mission 143–4; Board of
Social Responsibility 3, 104;
Industrial Committee, Board
of Social Responsibility 2
Citizens Charter 127
Clarke, R. 2, 6, 157
Clement of Alexandria 153
Coffield, F. 137
Coldstream, P. 45, 65, 68
Cooper, A.C. 18, 36
Craig Smith, N. 127
Cupitt, D. 88, 149

Dahrendorf, R. 137

Davis, J. 127, 135, 138
Demant, U.A. 13
Derrida, J. 149
Dodd, P. 2, 6–7, 28, 61, 173
Duchrow, V. 197

Economic and Social Research
Council 25, 173
Elkington, J. 127
Emmett, D. 104
Employment, Department of 23,
25, 94, 173
Enterprise Allowance Scheme
38, 92–3
Erlander 2, 7
Evangelical Coalition for Urban
Mission 76

Faith in the City 61
Faith in the City of Birmingham
65
Field, F. 127, 138
Fisher, M. 40
Foucault, M. 147, 149
Friedman, M. 144

Galbraith, J.K. 12–13, 16, 120
GEC 18
Gibb, A. 19–20
Goffee, R. and Scase, R. 96
Good News in Our Time 143–4
Green, C. 152
Grene, M. 151
Griffiths, B. 154

Habgood, J. 1–3, 32–3, 122, 130
Hakim, C. 90–1
Halsey, A.H. 122
Hammond, P. 15
Hancock, G. 132
Handy, C. 15, 29, 34, 127
Hardy, D. 51, 53–4, 111–12,
159–63, 177
Harper, M. 17
Harris, R. 25
Hastings, A. 54
Havel, V. 26

Hawkings, K. 140
Hayek, F. von 14, 85, 143–4
Hayman, C. 44, 48, 116
Healey, D. 11
Heelas, P. 136
Hegel, G. 149
Hewitt, G. 2
Hobbs, D. 60–1
Hollenweger, W. 21
Holloway, R. 29
Holmberg, B. 30
Howe, G. 37

ICI 18
ICOREC 127
Institute of Economic Affairs 25
Institute for Public Policy
    Research 128

Jenkins, D. 133
Jenkins, P. 23, 148
Joseph, K. 143
Judaism 27

Kanter, R.M. 15
Kasemann, E. 30
Keeling, M. 64
Kellner, P. 98–101, 159, 175
Kennedy, J.F. 13
Kerr, F. 88

Law, W. 152
Lawrence, P. 42
Lee, G. 67
Leech, K. 2, 77–8, 155
Leighton, P. 90
Low Pay Unit 87, 137
Luther, M. 106, 155, 157, 165

MacDonald, T. 34, 161
MacIntyre, A. 110
Mahoney, J. 120, 122
Marks and Spencer 15, 66
Mayhew, A. 39
McCann, D. 118–19
Methodist Church 158
Millbank, J. 150

Moberly, R.C. 152–3
Moltmann, J. 56, 105–11,
    121–2, 147, 178
Montefiore, H. 150
Muenzer, T. 155
Mulgan, G. 129

National Audit Office 38
National Childbirth Trust 48
National Consumer Council 127
National Westminster Bank 66

Ogunsiji, P. 76

Patten, J. 139
Paxman, J. 53–5
Payne, J. 90
Pearce, D. 127, 134
Phillips, A. 152
Policy Studies Institute 128, 139
Porter, J. 64
Preston, R. 57, 122, 172

Rahner, K. 83–6, 88–9, 103, 117
Ramsey, I. 2–3
Riches, J. 154–5
Riddell, P. 37–8
Ridell, R. 132
Ridley, N. 133
Ritchie, J. 24
Rorty, R. 149
Rowland, C. 153–4
Runcie, R. 54

Schumpeter, J. 9–16, 34, 42,
    120, 174
Shaw, D.W.D. 162
Smail, D. 135–6
Small Business Research Trust
    38
Smith, A. 155
Smith, G. 76–7
Solanke, A. 77
Stackhouse, M. 118
Storey, D. 101–3
Stout, J. 164
Sugar, A. 42

Sykes, S.W. 31, 33

Tawney, R.S. 78
Taylor, M. 132–3, 148, 154
Temple, W. 9, 13
Teresa, Mother 150
Thatcher, M. 8, 37, 98, 147
Torrey, M. 120
Trade and Industry,
    Department of 8, 23, 60
Traidcraft 131–3, 138
Turner, D. 88
Turner, P. 104–11, 117, 121

Virani, N. 75

Watson, F. 156
Wesley, C. 146, 156
West European Network 6
Whitfield, B. 46–9, 117
Wiener, M. 2, 37
Wilberforce, W. 152
Wilcox, J. 139–41
Williams, R. 32–3
Winfield, M. 140
Winstanley, G. 151, 154–5
Wogaman, P. 56–7
World Wide Fund for Nature 127

Young, D. 8, 23–4, 135
Young, H. 23

Zizioulas, J. 134

Subjects

business ethics 139–41, 178

capitalism 10, 118–22, 174
change 9, 29–33, 42, 44, 58, 83,
    99–102, 114, 175–6
children (of entrepreneurs) 97
Church 28–32, 34, 109, 111–13,
    122, 177–9
community 26, 49, 56, 60, 116,
    129, 144, 161, 163, 175; and
    freedom 52; and enterprise
    61–3; and St Paul 163

consumerism 136
co-operatives 71, 83
creation 51, 56, 106–8, 159,
    166–8
creativity 52, 111, 161–3, 179
culture 27, 60, 144

deregulation 37, 40

enterprise: attributes of 16;
    images of 24–7; theology of
    33, 143f, 174–6
entrepreneurship 9–14, 16–19
eschatology (Kingdom of God)
    106, 122
environment 133–5

family 92, 144
freedom 4, 8–9, 48, 52, 68, 74,
    85–6, 90–1, 97, 105, 111, 154,
    159–62, 164 178

grace 56
'green ethic' 43, 48, 126–7

history 148–9, 167

image of God 118
individualism 90, 101, 112, 130
interfaith dialogue 79, 80

laity 3–4, 6
local management of schools 68
low pay 6, 25, 47, 117, 131–2,
    136–8, 145, 154–6

management theory 15
Marxism 105, 107, 119, 129, 136,
    147
middle-range imperatives 57
racial prejudice 75–7
recession 1991 39–40
relationships 53–5, 112–13, 140,
    176–7
responsibility 128–30, 139
salvation 89, 116
small businesses 9, 50, 57,
    95–9, 175
socialism 11–13, 105

training 44–7
transcendence 82–90

transformation 52, 63, 147–8
Trinity 51–2, 161, 177

vocation 50, 108, 146, 156–8
wealth 54–6, 111, 120, 152–4

wealth creation 4, 6, 8–9, 43, 73, 78, 101, 127, 145, 159, 174–6
wisdom tradition 165–7
work 1–6, 8, 15, 106–8, 165
work ethic 2, 72